NOT OUR WAR

Writings against the First World War

Edited by AW Zurbrugg

MERLIN PRESS

Published in 2014 by
The Merlin Press
99b Wallis Road
London
E9 5LN

www.merlinpress.co.uk

ISBN 978-0-85036-614-3

Printed in the UK by Russell Press, Nottingham

CONTENTS

ACKNOWLEDGEMENTS

I would like to thank everyone who has contributed to this book with encouragement, suggestions, ideas and texts. Texts here come from a variety of sources, but I am particularly indebted to Ted Crawford for many of them. Howard Clark gave permission for me to use an extract from Devi Prasad, *War is a crime against humanity*, published by War Resisters' International; Howard died in December 2013, his humanity will be missed.

Timeline of International and National Events

1910

Border war between Mexicans and the USA – continues in fits and start until 1919.

1911

July: *Morocco*: Agadir crisis, French protectorate established; Germany is compensated with territories in Equatorial Africa; British protectorate over Egypt.

September: Italy declares war on Ottoman Turkey and seizes Libya and other territories.

1912

October: Balkans War: Ottoman Turkey versus Bulgaria, Greece, Montenegro and Serbia.

November: Ottoman Turkey defeated. Socialist parties meet in Basel and votes anti-war resolutions. *France*: anti-war demonstration at the Pré-Saint-Gervais, near Paris. CGT union confederation holds conference in Paris and prepares a one day anti-war general strike (held in December).

December: Balkan armistice.

1913

February: Balkan war restarts (ends in May). *Germany*: an extraordinary war tax is voted through by the Reichstag (parliament), with Social-democratic support.

March: *France*: 150,000 protest at Pré-Saint-Gervais, against extension of military service to three years.

June-July: Second Balkan war; Bulgaria loses territories to Greece, Romania and Serbia.

September: *Germany*: Social-democrat congress – defeat of motion condemning military expenditure.

1914

April-December: *USA*: Colorado Coalfield War, the National Guard kills some thirty miners, wives and children in the 'Ludlow massacre'.

June: Assassination of Austrian Crown Prince in Sarajevo. *Italy*: anti-militarist protests escalate in Ancona; 'Red Week'.

July 23: Austria-Hungary sends ultimatum to Serbia. 28-30: Representatives from Socialist parties across Europe meet in Brussels. Austria-Hungary declares war on Serbia. Russia mobilises.

August 1: Germany declares war on Russia, France mobilises. **France:** Jean Jaurès assassinated. 3: Germany declares war on France. 4: Germany invades Belgium, Britain declares war on Germany. French and German Social-democrats vote for war taxes. 26: **France:** Two socialists, Jules Guesde and Marcel Sembat, join government.

September: Lugano anti-war conference of the Swiss Social-democratic Party and the Italian Socialist Party.

November: Ottoman Turkey joins the war as an ally of Germany and Austria-Hungary.

1915

January: *Nyasaland* (Malawi): revolt led by John Chilembwe. *Singapore*: Indian army soldiers mutiny. *China* is presented with '21 Demands' for concessions by Japan.

February: *Mali*: armed revolt against French conscription in Bélédougou.

April-May: International conference of Women for Peace in The Hague.

May: Syndicalists organise international anti-war conference in El Ferrol. *Germany*: Berlin: over a thousand women join protest in front of the Reichstag. Italy declares war on Austria-Hungary.

July: *UK*: Munitions of War Act.

September: Socialists and syndicalists hold anti-war conference in Zimmerwald, (Switzerland).

October: Bulgaria joins war, as an ally of Germany and Austria-Hungary.

November: *UK*: Glasgow women protest against evictions and lead 20,000 strong demonstration against rent rises.

1916

March: Portugal declares war on Germany.

April: Anti-war conference in Kiental, (Switzerland).

May: *Ireland*: Easter rising in Dublin.

June: Internationalist anarchist committee formed in Ravenna. *Germany*: 55,000 metal workers strike in Berlin in support of Karl Liebknecht.

September: *Australia*: Sydney, twelve supporters of the Industrial Workers of the World sentenced to imprisonment under the Treason Felony act.

October: *Austria-Hungary*: Friedrich Adler assassinates Prime Minister Sturgkh.

November: *Algeria*: insurgency against conscription begins in Aurès.

1917

March: *Russia*: Revolution, fall of the Tsar, peasants begin to seize land, workers revolt in cities.

April: USA and Cuba declare war on Germany. *Germany*: 200,000 workers strike in Berlin.

May-June: *France*: Army mutinies. *USA*: Espionage Act sanctions punishment of actions deemed a threat to the war effort.

July: Brazil joins the war in October. *Brazil:* Three day general strike in São Paulo, and Rio de Janeiro (Proletarian Defence Committee formed). **Ireland:** Éamon de Valera, opposing conscription, wins parliamentary election in East Clare.

August: China joins the war. *Italy:* Turin risings, 60 killed. *Spain:* Barcelona general strike, 37 killed. *USA:* IWW labour leader Frank H. Little lynched in Butte, Montana.

September: Anti-war conference in Stockholm. *Australia:* General strike; *France:* Rebel Russian troops at La Courtine are shelled, over 200 killed.

November: Declaration that Britain would support a home for Jewish people in Palestine without prejudice to the rights of existing communities. *Russia:* Second revolution, Lenin heads a government of people's commissars.

1918

January: *Germany:* 400,000 workers strike in Berlin. *Finland:* civil war begins, 20,000 reds die in prison camps and executions.

February: Mutiny in Austro-Hungarian fleet at Cattarro; four rebels are executed and 800 imprisoned.

March-April: Treaty of Brest-Litovsk, between Soviet Russia, Germany and Austria-Hungary. The latter seek to establish their hegemony over the Ukraine and other parts of the former Russian Empire. *Canada:* Riot against conscription in Quebec city. *Ireland:* general strike against conscription.

May: *France:* Strike of 100,000 workers in war industries in Paris; young workers protest against being called up.

June-July: *South Africa:* strike wave around Johannesburg.

August: *Canada:* Murder of miners' leader Albert 'Ginger' Goodwin provokes general strike in British Columbia. *UK:* strike of London Metropolitan police force.

September: Bulgaria asks for an armistice.

October 4: Germany requests armistice. 28: Czechoslovak republic proclaimed. 30: Ottoman Turkey signs armistice. European 'Spanish flue' epidemic, kills millions. *Canada*: the Borden government cracks down on dissidents, banning, criticism of the war, loafing, strikes, the IWW, and much of the socialist and foreign language press.

November 3-9: *Germany*: Kiel Sailors revolt and general strike, protests spread to other ports; Independent Lefts and allies revolt in Munich. Bavarian monarchy abolished. General strike in Berlin. Abdication of the Kaiser. Republic proclaimed. November 11: Armistice on western front. Austria-Hungary breaks up and new states are formed including a Polish republic and a Kingdom of Serbs, Croats and Slovenes (Yugoslavia). *Brazil*: Rio de Janeiro strike for 8 hour day.

Some ten million people have died as a result of the war: 1.8 million Germans, 1.7m in Russia, 1.4m in France, 1.3m in Austria-Hungary; three quarters of a million from Britain and 615,000 Italians. Millions more die from ongoing social disruption, hunger and disease, especially in Africa, Germany and India (estimates of deaths from 'flu in India vary from seven to thirteen million). Over 1m Armenians die in a genocide in Ottoman Turkey. Further wars continue between several successor states in Eastern Europe, and the Balkans.

1919

January: *Germany*: ongoing blockade causes near famine (in Berlin three out of ten babies die of malnutrition); many radicals are assassinated (Kurt Eisner, Leo Jogiches, Gustav Landauer, Karl Liebknecht and Rosa Luxemburg). *Ireland*: Irish parliamentarians declare independence, British troops sent to Ireland, beginning of guerrilla war.

February: Polish forces invade western Russia. *USA*: Five day strike in Seattle.

April: Mutiny in French Black Sea fleet. *India*: famine, Amritsar massacre. *Ireland*: Limerick general strike.

May: Greek army sends 20,000 soldiers to occupy Izmir/ Smyrna. *Canada*: General strike in Winnipeg. *China*: demonstrations in Beijing: protestors demand the return of the Shandong territory and revocation of concessions to Japan.

June: Treaty of Versailles signed. Formation of the League of Nations. Over the summer a series of mutinies occur amongst British forces sent to northern Russia. *Canada*: General strike in Vancouver.

July: *Egypt*: revolt, hundreds killed by British forces.

August: Russian naval base in Kronstadt attacked by British navy. (It was attacked again, in October.)

1920

April: Poland invades Russia.

May: *UK*: London dockers obstruct loading of the *Jolly George* with arms for use against Soviet Russia. (Similar action occurred in France, Germany, Italy and the USA)

August: Ottoman Empire signs the Treaty of Sèvres, but the treaty is overtaken by events; a new state is formed in Turkey, and the Greek army in Anatolia is defeated. The Treaty of Lausanne of 1923 ratifies a peace and an exchange of populations between Greece and Turkey, it also confirms the division of former provinces of the Ottoman Turkey, between Britain, France and new Arab states

1922

June: *Ireland*: Free State formed.

INTRODUCTION

The First World War is often seen as a hapless war, run by senseless generals. Two power blocs emerged. People across the world were caught up by conflict as the cogs of imperial enmeshment moved armed forces and supply lines to confront each other. Like an avalanche, one incident triggered another. One state's army mobilisation set others in motion and war followed in a rhythm determined by railway timetables. Soldiers were sent against machine guns to be slaughtered by the thousand, from one minute to the next.[1]

There were unexpected features in this war: it became a world war, and an industrial war; production and employment expanded over the war years, and deflated when the war ended, throwing many people into long-term unemployment. The war drew in hundreds of thousands of civilians and soldiers in Africa, Asia and the Middle East, peoples who had little or no interest in how, or why, it started. Social relations changed when the men marched away, as women filled the gaps and kept industry turning.

If at first a wave of patriotic emotion, enthusiasm and soldierly romance carried all before it, gradually, that wave began to fall back. 'Khaki fever' – or its equivalent – spread as the press fed stories of atrocities anticipated or fictitious. For one side massacres, stories of barbarity and 'sins against civilization', a catalogue of horrors: women and children being used as shields, Red Cross workers having hands cut off;[2] for the other side Russian savagery, Belgian civilians shooting Germans in the back. Enemies were conjured up endangering the peace of the world. Misinformation – for example revealing telegrams – were planted by press agencies acting on behalf of rival governments. Force had to be met with force.[3] War fever, promoted by a rabid press, raged.[4] On the one hand the state encouraged parts of the press, gave subsidies to the domestic and foreign press, set directions, and planted stories of plots and conspiracies. On the other hand it facilitated the censorship of dissidence and the vilification of protest. In Britain and Ireland the Defence of the Realm Acts of 1914 were used not just to censor military information, but also to ban interviews with labour militants and prevent the reporting of labour disputes. Papers that were deemed subversive or impeding recruitment were suppressed. Others were visited by local police forces, editions were seized and printers warned off. Such action encouraged others to censor themselves. Similar action was taken in other warring states. In the USA, constitutional guarantees were sidelined. The US post office undermined the dissident press, withdrawing the cheaper mailing rates that facilitated its distribution. With the news and the press massaged into conformity it was not easy to understand what was happening. Given huge support from the commercial press for the war, one might have expected the anti-war press – with only a small circulation – would pose little or no danger to warring states. But state action to intimidate and ban critical voices suggests its opposition was feared. Governments also financed friendly supporters such as the American Social Democratic League and, in Britain, a National Socialist Party and a Workers' League. Such bodies were accused of acting as proxies for their respective governments.

It is difficult to know just how much support there was for this war. Because opposition could be found in many places need not imply that it was overwhelming. Likewise, absence of overt opposition does not necessarily mean that there was support for the war. Wherever visible opposition was repressed it made sense to remain invisible. A study by Jeanette Keith concluded that what Americans actually felt about the war in 1918 could not be known. People were constrained and threatened if they failed to offer public support for the war: they might have a visit from US authorities, face prison or death at the hands of vigilantes.[5] Overt opposition from African-Americans would have been suicidal.[6]

Where there was support from marginalised sectors for the war, such support might be motivated, in part or in whole, by the hope that concessions would be given; some were fighting for their own particular agenda, and saw support for the war as a means for making progress.

This anthology presents opinions from people who openly expressed their opposition: men and women, liberals, radicals and pacifists, anarchists, socialists, soldiers and non-combatants. A hundred years on from 1914 such thinking is often ignored.[7] On occasion 'Britain' is still presented as fighting a defensive war for survival against a 'Germany'[8] bent on fighting a war of conquest and aggression.[9] Such writing seeks to rehabilitate the war and works to promote a discourse about it as a struggle between 'nations'. Konni Zilliacus, who had over fifteen years' experience observing international diplomacy, wrote that this was a war of imperial interests, and Britain fought to preserve its Empire.[10] There was a 'vast gulf' between the motivations of the rulers and the ruled, with the latter believing they were fighting for human rights, and the rights of small nations like Belgium.

These texts present dissident voices: people who challenged the policy and authority of the powers that were. Dissidents and socialists sought not only to represent the agenda of subaltern classes and groups, but also to ask critical questions: Why things happened as they did? They wanted to reflect on how things might have been prevented and sought to spark further protest. Some of these voices came to oppose the war after reflecting on experience, others opposed it on principle, before a shot was fired; they may have been few in number, but gradually their influence rose.

What is presented here is a work of selection: selected opinions and small, often very small, extracts from larger documents. And a small book cannot present the range of material that exists even amongst opponents of war. It is not a complete appraisal of all the questions addressed, nor is it the last word on the subject, but it seeks, at least, to raise some key questions.

After a short timeline which may help situate the sequence of events, the book comes in four parts. How did people react to the war? Some short sentences painting brief images come first. A second chapter presents texts from those who campaigned against militarism and tried to prevent war. The third chapter considers claims that this was a war for civilization, or for the freedom of small nations. A fourth and last chapter responds to questions such as: Should this war have been fought? How could it have been prevented?

I WEPT …

Crazy? – Angelica Balabanoff, Italian Socialist
'Adler and Jules Guesde looked at me as if they thought I were crazy.'

29 July 1914. Socialist parties from across Europe had come to a meeting of the Bureau of the Second International in Brussels. Representatives from each country had their turn before Angelica Balabanoff, the representative of the Italian Socialist party, had a chance to speak, calling for a general strike. The executive called for the intensification of anti-war demonstrations but nothing more. Victor Adler was a leader of the Austrian Social-democrats;[11] Jules Guesde was a key figure in the French Socialist party; both supported their governments in the war; Guesde becoming a government minister. Angelica Balabanoff along with many Italian socialists opposed the war. See also final section pages 129-30 for the Bureau resolution passed at that meeting. From *My Life as a Rebel*, London: Hamish Hamilton, 1938, p. 133.

Duty – Jean Jaurès, French Socialist
'Socialists everywhere are aware of their duty. The vigorous demonstrations of German socialists are a magnificent reply to those who denounce their pretended inertia.'

29 July. Berlin: many anti-war demonstrations were organised by the Social-democratic party, denouncing war-mongers. Some street gatherings were broken up by mounted police armed with sabres. Across Germany 750,000 people take part in anti-war protests.[12] Jean Jaurès represented French Socialists at the Socialists' meeting in Brussels and tried to encourage resistance to the war. He was assassinated on the following day. From *L'Humanité*, 30 July 1914.

Feeling Bad – Hugo Eberlein, German Social-democrat

'I walked that night with Rosa Luxemburg from the *Vorwärts* building on the Lindenstrasse, towards the Sudende. We felt very bad. War had come and the proletariat had not budged. … from the platform we hear only empty phrases… on our way home Rosa said: "we should expect the worst".'

3 August 1914. Berlin: the leaders of the Social-democratic Party had changed sides; they had abandoned opposition to war and had moved on, rallying to the support of the German state. SDP representatives in the Reichstag (parliament) voted for war credits. Rosa Luxemburg and friends are inconsolable. *Vorwärts* was the newspaper of the German Social-democratic Party (SDP). From: http://raumgegenzement.blogsport. de/2009/10/26/hugo-eberlein-erinnerungen-an-rosa-luxemburg-bei-kriegsausbruch-1914/

Did my eyes deceive me?
– Julius Braunthal, Austrian Social-democrat

'Throughout all the years, since I had entered the movement, I had respected the declarations of the Party as the expression of a well-considered Socialist policy…'

5 August 1914. Julius Braunthal was conscripted against his will into the Austro-Hungarian army. He saw a copy of *Arbeiter-Zeitung*, (the Workers' Newspaper of Vienna). Hitherto it had defended a socialist policy and written of the holy cause of the international working class. Now it talked of the 'holy cause of the German people'. He could not understand this change, or the news that the German Social-democrats had voted war credits. From Julius Braunthal, *In Search of the Millennium*, London: Victor Gollancz, 1945, p. 138. Later in that book the author writes that it was a disgrace to socialism, to support the war; warring 'socialists' had, in Plato's words, 'a lie in the soul'; imperialism could not be conquered through the victory of one side over another. Every nation had to conquer imperialism in its own country. (p. 177.)

Where was the world of solidarity?
– Alexander Shlyapnikov, Russian Social-democrat

'We were stupefied by what we learnt. Telegrams, press articles said that the leaders of German Social-democracy were justifying the war, were voting war-credits. Our first thought was that this was false news and that they wanted to work on Russian Social-democratic opinion to bring it into line. Soon we had the means of verification... However monstrous the fact was, we nevertheless had to face up to it. Workers assailed us with questions. We were asked what was the meaning of the behaviour of these German socialists whom we had been used to considering as models; where then was international solidarity? For us the news that the German army – with so many organised workers – was devastating Belgium and that Belgian soldiers were defending their country whilst singing the *'Internationale'* was particularly distressing.'

August 1914. Most Labour and Social-democrat parliamentary parties voted taxes to support the war effort of their respective states; or abstained. Only the Serbian party and a few members of the British Labour party voted against supporting their governments. From: *On the Eve of 1917*, London: Allison & Busby, pp. 16-17. Our translation from: http://www2. cddc.vt.edu/marxists/francais/chliapnikov/works/1920/00/05.htm

Passion
– Fenner Brockway, British Socialist

'I covered the whole front page with a manifesto in black type. Both at the top and bottom were the slogans: "Down with the War!" The contents were a simple working-class appeal: "Workers of Great Britain, you have no quarrel with the workers of Europe. They have no quarrel with you. The quarrel is between the *ruling* classes of Europe. Don't make this quarrel yours ..."'

6 August 1914. Brockway edited *Labour Leader,* the newspaper of the Independent Labour Party. Years later, looking back at that day's edition he wrote: 'I can still feel something of the passion with which it was prepared.' Brockway passed much of the war in prison; like some 800 members of the ILP he was tried for his opposition to conscription. Another Labour Party leader, Ramsay McDonald condemned the government but said it would have his support if Britain was in danger. From: *Inside the Left*: Nottingham: Spokesman, pp. 44-5. First published 1942.

I hate them – Louis Lecoin, French Anarchist & Pacifist

'It was as if, in August 1914, a shadow had fallen on the faith I had in human beings. The leaders of the CGT who had been my teachers now caused me only revulsion.'

August 1914. The French General Labour Confederation (CGT) had agreed to call a general strike to stop the war, but when it broke out that policy was not implemented. Lecoin was imprisoned repeatedly for anti-military activities. From *Le Cours d'une Vie*, Paris: Louis Lecoin, 1965, p. 70.

I Wept – Sylvia Pankhurst, British Suffragette & Socialist

'When first I read in the press that Mrs. Pankhurst and Christabel were returning to England for a recruiting campaign I wept. To me this seemed a tragic betrayal of the great movement to bring the mother-half of the race into the councils of the nations.'

September 1914. Sylvia stuck to her principles. The Pankhurst family had been leading suffragettes and critics of militarism. Facing imprisonment for unlawful suffragette activities Mrs Pankhurst had fled to France in July. She returned to London and called off all suffragette campaigns. She and her eldest daughter, Christabel, chose to support the war effort. Her prison sentence was suspended and suffragette prisoners were released. The *Suffragette* newspaper became *Britannia.* Many French suffragists took a similar line and supported the war effort. So too did an organization of German gays, the Scientific Humanitarian Committee, inspired by Magnus Hirschfeld.

Patriotism – Ernst Toller, German Socialist

'The words "Germany", "Fatherland", "War" had had a magic power ...'

1914. Ernst Toller began the war as an enthusiastic German soldier, intoxicated with patriotic feelings. From: *Eine Jugend in Deutschland, / I was a German*, New York: Paragon House, 1991, p. 119. Similar feelings erupted in Britain. Guy Chapman, a Royal Fusiliers junior officer wrote of 'intoxication': *Passionate Prodigality*, London: MacGibbon & Kee, 1965, p. 226.

A good bed – Bill Brinson

'There's two ways of looking at that. There may have been some who were going to chop the Kaiser's heads off, and willing to do it, and that sort of thing. But there were also a lot of them who wanted a good bed and food and clothes.'

Interview, quoted in Julia Bush, *Behind the Lines: East London Labour*, London: Merlin Press, 1984, p. 38.

Not my War – Augustin Souchy, German Anarchist

'The war for Emperor and fatherland was not my war.'

August 1914. Souchy campaigned in Sweden against the war. From: Augustin Souchy, *Beware! Anarchist! A Life for Freedom: An Autobiography*, Chicago: Charles Kerr, 1992, p. 9.[13]

I received a hammer blow
– Pierre Monatte, French Syndicalist & Socialist

'Had socialism been killed? Had the war swept away class consciousness (esprit), our hopes for workers' liberation in all countries?'

1914. Monatte was seeking a way out from despair. Things had melted around him, chauvinism had exploded. It was difficult to believe that yesterday's ideas had fallen into miserable ruin. Many syndicalists and anarchists, and most socialists, were derailed. So great was the wave of patriotism that engulfed France that hope for a general strike to stop the war evaporated. From *La lutte syndicale*, Paris: Bibliothèque socialiste, 1963. Quoted from: http://www.pelloutier.net/glossaire/detail.php?id=4

I Denounce – Kate Richards O'Hare, American Socialist

'I denounce the present policy of the governing class of the United States; I declare that the blood of the European continent stains their souls…'

March 1915. O'Hare wrote that the war was to decide which group of capitalists should rule world markets, she was imprisoned for dissent and obstructing conscription. From: *The National Rip-Saw*, XII. http://womhist.alexanderstreet.com/kro/intro.htm

Our meetings were dispersed
– Fred Bower, British Syndicalist & Socialist

'It was: believe what Bottomley, and Lloyd George, and the *Daily Mail* say, or be damned! It is not too hard to be a parrot, and repeat what your masters and pastors tell you …'

Early in the war. Those who tried to speak out against the war were roughly handled. Horatio Bottomley was the editor of *John Bull*, and helped recruitment campaigns. From: Fred Bower, *Rolling Stonemason: An Autobiography*, London: Jonathan Cape, 1936, p. 225.

We can't speak – Romain Rolland, French Pacifist

'The tragedy of our situation is that we are only a handful of free spirits, we are separated from the larger number of our army, from our people who are imprisoned and buried alive in the depth of the trenches. We should be able to speak to them, but we cannot … a dictatorial regime bears down on us all over Europe.'

May 1915. From a letter to a French feminist/pacifist, Jeanne Halbwachs; cited in Annette Becker, 'L'exil intérieur des pacifistes intégraux, 1914-1918', In: *Matériaux pour l'histoire de notre temps*. 2002, No. 67. pp. 28-35.

Me, a Soldier? – Bruno Misèfari, Italian Anarchist

'Could it ever be possible that I should become a soldier? How could I possibly become part of that monstrous military organism? What is the function of a soldier? To kill ... I should be the man who says: Better to be killed than to kill. Better to disobey one's country... better to disobey war and slavery and obey peace and freedom.'

25 June 1915. Italy had joined the war on the side of Britain, France and Russia in May 1915. Bruno Misèfari took refuge in Switzerland. From: Furio Sbarnemi & Bruno Misefari, *Diario di un disertore*, Florence: La nuova Italia, 1973, pp. 22-4.

A Refusal to carry out Field Punishment
– An Anonymous German Miner

'I looked at him for a long time and did not deign him worthy of an answer. He then turned to the "criminal" who told him that I could not get myself to do the job as we were old comrades and friends. Besides, I did not want to fetter a man who was exhausted and dead tired. "So you won't do it?" he thundered at me, and when again he received no reply – for I was resolved not to speak another word to the fellow – he hissed, "That b---- is a red to the marrow!" I shall never in my life forget the look of thankfulness that Lohmer gave me; it rewarded me for the unpleasantness I had in consequence of my refusal. Of course others did what I refused to do; I got two weeks' confinement. Naturally I was proud at having been a man for once at least. As a comrade I had remained faithful to my mate. Yet I had gained a point. They never ordered me again to perform such duty...'

1915? *New Yorker Volkszeitung*, republished as *German Deserter's War Experience*, New York: B. W. Huebsch, 1927. On another occasion soldiers killed their officers.

A sharper mind – Ernst Toller

'It was more by accident than necessity that I had sided with the ranks of striking workers. What drew me towards them was their struggle against the war; only now did I become a socialist. My mind grew sharper – grasping society's social structure, the circumstances of the war, the terrible lies of the judiciary and the law, which allowed the masses to go hungry whilst a few were allowed to enrich themselves – the relations between labour and capital and the meaning of the historical development of the working class.'

1916. Toller was wounded after thirteen months at the front. Back in Germany he began to realise that he had been duped. After being invalided out of the army he joined anti-war protests and was then imprisoned. He joined an anti-war youth organisation. It was suppressed and German members were conscripted. From: *Eine Jugend in Deutschland, / I was a German*, New York: Paragon House, 1991, p. 119. A Heidelberg Professor, Friedrich Wilhem Förster, was able to evade Germany censorship by being published in Switzerland. He inspired a pacifist current. Toller took part in the creation of the Bavarian Council republic in 1919.

Abuse – Edmund Dene Morel, British Pacifist

'I have been one of the best-abused men in the British Isles. Not even my friend and colleague, Mr J. Ramsay MacDonald, has had to endure such malignant misrepresentation. No dishonour too profound, no motive too base, has been attributed to me.'

May 1916. Edmund Morel was one of the chief movers in the British Union for Democratic Control. The UDC campaigned for open diplomacy and a fair, negotiated peace. Morel wrote that agreements between Britain and France over division of imperial interests across the world had cemented a secret alliance and this alliance had been a principle factor in engendering the war. Such views were offensive to the *Daily Express* which accused him of working for the enemy. Censorship intimidated dissident campaigns and publications. In Britain a National Council for Civil Liberties was set up to help defend activists. In 1917 Morel was sentenced to six months prison for sending an anti-war pamphlet to Romain Rolland in Switzerland. From: Personal forward to *Truth and the War*, London, National Labour Press, 1916; https://archive.org/details/truthwar01more See also dspace.wbpublibnet.gov.in:8080/jspui/bitstream/10689/.../3/ Preface.pdf

Already Forgiven
– Lilly Connolly and a member of the execution squad who had killed Lilly's husband, James

'I am a miner. My father was a miner, and my grandfather was a miner – they were both very busy in the trade union. How can I go back home? They would know about James Connolly even if I didn't. I haven't been home on leave. I can't go home. I'd let something slip, and they'd know I'd killed James Connolly. Oh, why was I chosen to kill a man like that?'

Lilly Connolly replied: 'James Connolly has already forgiven you. He realised you were being forced, he realised you were only a working-class boy.'

Connolly was executed, after the 1916 Easter rising, by British forces commanded by General John Maxwell. Some day later his widow Lilly answered the door of her Dublin home. Standing there was a young-looking and distraught soldier. He was Welsh and had served in the firing squad that had killed her husband. Since that day, he had learnt a little bit about the man he had shot. This was their conversation. From: James Connolly Graveside Oration 2012, Robert Griffiths, General Secretary of the Communist Party of Britain; http://www.irishdemocrat.co.uk/features/james-connolly-oration-2012/

Protest in Munich – Erich Mühsam, German Anarchist
'Suddenly, we heard wild screams and the clamouring of women. Everyone started to run. The policemen had pulled their sabres and rode across the square, swinging

in all directions. You could hear the wounded cry out and anonymous yells of disgust fill the evening air: "Pfui! Pigs! Prussian slaves! You call yourselves heroes!? Attacking women and children – very courageous! Pfui! Pfui!" … We will never know how many were arrested and wounded, nor to what extent. We will only hear rumours. However, I am certain that this episode was only a beginning.'

18 June 1916. The blockade of Germany had a sharp effect and food became scarce. Protesters demanded bread; confronting soldiers and the police, they said: the French wouldn't attack wives and children like you do. Some of the soldiers were none too happy. Some shrugged and said: 'But we have to…' Pfui equates to 'Shame on you' Mühsam was a member of the Socialist Federation. He was murdered by Nazis in the Oranienburg concentration camp in 1934. From: Erich Mühsam, (Ed. Gabriel Kuhn), *Liberating Society from the State and Other Writings: A Political Reader*, Oakland: PM Press and London: Merlin Press, 2011, p. 110.

Fed up with the war
– Karla Pfeiferová, Czech Social-democrat

'"How long will the war slaughter last, when children will stop this terrible starvation?" This was a question moving the minds of all of us. But our anger was increasing even further, when bells were taken away from churches, and priests gave them a holy blessing. There were no more iron fences; brass door-handles were replaced and the awareness that church bells should be turned into murdering bullets, so that the bloody war could be prolonged, outraged religious people, and the churches were half empty. Nobody believed the news in the papers anymore, not even the Social-democratic press, which, like the bourgeois press, was arguing that it was necessary to continue fighting …'

1916. Karla Pfeiferová was working as a weaver in the Mauthner's textile factory in Šumburk. (An area in the Austro-Hungarian Empire now part of the Czech Republic). Workers had little or no food, but round the back of shops rich folk could be seen collecting supplies. The sons of rich folk didn't have to join up because they had key jobs. From Red Flag http://www.autistici.org/tridnivalka/down-with-tyrants-and-traitors-all-contribution-to-the-communist-critique-of-the-proletarian-movement-in-the-czech-lands-of-the-austro-hungarian-monarchy-1914-1918/2/

No Hargreaves, no work!
– Brother Jack Parsons, British Trade-unionist

'It was the first time we could say that in Sheffield solidarity showed itself. It was fought on principle – the principle that a skilled man should not be taken into the army. For the first time we forced the employers of Sheffield to such an extent that it was either Hargreaves coming back or no munitions from Sheffield. It was the first real victory we were able to pull off.'

November 1916. Leonard Hargreaves, a member of the Amalgamated Society of Engineers (ASE) at Vickers in Sheffield, was forcibly conscripted into the army. A massive strike forced the government to have him released. From: Bill Moore, 'Sheffield Shop Stewards 1916-1918', *Our History*, London: CPGB, 1960.

Adieu – Soldier's Song

'Goodbye my life, goodbye my love,
goodbye to women all,
We're at our end, and no escape,
yes now we're good and done,
On this plateau, up on Craonne,
we're going to lose our skin,
Condemned are we, yes one and all,
we're out for sacrifice!'

Summer 1917. A recent offensive had brought over 125,000 casualties. French soldiers refused to carry out further attacks. Tens of thousands of soldiers mutinied. Estimates of the number who mutinied vary – from 60 to 90,000. *Adieu la vie, adieu l'amour, Adieu toutes les femmes. C'est bien fini, c'est pour toujours, De cette guerre infâme. C'est à Craonne, sur le plateau, Qu'on doit laisser sa peau, Car nous sommes tous condamnés, C'est nous les sacrifiés!*

Four Rebel Soldiers Speak

1.   'The Russians were a hundred years behind, now they are a hundred years ahead of the rest of humanity.'

2.   'Give us passes for leave, or we'll kill the colonel, either permits or revolution.'

3.   'Let's sing the Internationale, like brothers – anarchists and revolutionaries.'

4.   'As has been proved by 33 months of war, to go on with an unequal struggle – with armaments inferior to that of the German and with commanders who aren't up to the job – is madness.'

May-June, 1917. A variety of motivations and hopes lay behind the mutinies in the French army. Many soldiers wanted passes to go on leave; some sang the 'Internationale', a few had red flags. Quoted in André Loez, *14-18. Les refus de la Guerre: Une histoire de mutins*, Paris: Gallimard, 2010, pp. 151, 349, 350, 390. See www.crid1418.org/doc/mutins

Beware! – Emma Goldman, Russian-American Anarchist

'The same is bound to take place in America should the dogs of war be let loose here. Already the poisonous seed has been planted.'

March 1917; Goldman saw militarism and reaction as rampant in Europe; conscription and censorship had destroyed every vestige of liberty. People were being whipped into blind obedience and slavery. From: 'The Promoters of War Mania', *Mother Earth*.

Whose war is this? Not mine
– John Reed, American Socialist

'I know that hundreds of thousands of American workingmen employed by our great financial 'patriots' are not paid a living wage. I have seen poor men sent to jail for long terms without trial, and even without any charge. Peaceful strikers, and their wives and children, have been shot to death, burned to death, by private detectives and militiamen. The rich have steadily become richer, and the cost of living higher, and the workers proportionally poorer. These toilers don't want war – not even civil war. But the speculators, the employers, the plutocracy – they want it, just as they did in Germany and in England; and with lies and sophistries they will whip up our blood until we are savage – and then we'll fight and die for them.'

April 1917. American journalist John Reed had seen war first hand in Europe and Mexico. From: *The Masses*, ww.marxists.org/archive/reed/1917/masses02.htm

Not me!

'Don't send me in the army, George,
I'm in the ASE
Take all the bloody labourers,
But for God's sake don't take me!
You want me for a soldier?
Well that can never be…
A man of my ability,
And in the ASE…'

A shop stewards' movement developed in Britain in the course of the war. In Sheffield it developed within the Amalgamated Society of Engineers (ASE) and fostered the protection of skilled workers such as Leonard Hargreaves. A massive engineers strike broke out in May 1917 when conscription threatened skilled labour. 20,000 workers came to a mass meeting. The shop stewards' movement began to develop a wider agenda. Committees brought in representation of all shop workers – skilled and unskilled, men and women. Stewards were responsible to those who elected them, rather than to officials in trade union organisations. Strikers organised a group of motor-cyclists to keep in touch with workers in their region. They also attended demonstrations armed with thick sticks. Radicals hoped that through the shop stewards' movement a wider labour revolt was beckoning. From: J.T.Murphy, 'The Workers' Committee', http://www.marxists.org/archive/murphy-jt/1917/xx/workers_committee.htm)

Fed up

'I have to tell you that all combatants are fed up with their existence. There are many deserters. Ten in my company have fled – for fear of having to attack. I think we shall be doing things like the Russians, no one wants to go on. It's true, it isn't worth a life, to have one's skin shot up, to win a trench or two, to win nothing.'

Letter reported on 30 May 1917, picked up by French Army intelligence. Quoted in G. Pedroncini, 1917, *Les mutineries de l'armée française*, Paris: Archives Julliard-Gallimard, 1968; cited in Robert Frank, *Histoire 1e: L, ES, S,* Paris: Belin. 1994, pp. 98-99. 20,000 Frenchmen were condemned for desertion in 1917.

Slaves – Joe Naylor, Canadian Socialist

'Here we have patriotism's most convincing object lesson and expression…While we are fighting for democracy and the liberty of small nations the slaves of the Canadian Collieries Ltd are not allowed to organize for the purpose of in any manner bettering their conditions…'

1 June 1917. A campaign against conscription attracted widespread support in Western Canada. From: *British Columbia Federationist*.

Honour – Emma Goldman

'We are always ready to receive our friends the police, I retorted, but we are careful not to take chances with the names and addresses of those who cannot afford the honour of an arrest.'

June 1917. The USA joined the war in April 1917. The police demanded the membership list of the No-Conscription League. Goldman was imprisoned for two years and then deported. From *Living my Life*, Volume 2, New York: Dover, 1970, p. 611.

Shame – Wilf McCartney, British Anarchist & Syndicalist

'Harmless German shopkeepers had their shops wrecked, their goods thrown into the street, their homes ruined, and endured personal injury, all in the cause of smashing Prussian militarism. For the first time in my life I was ashamed of my class.'

1917. Prince Albert of Saxe-Coburg, the husband of Queen Victoria, had given his name to the British royal family. In July of 1917 anti-German feeling led King George V to change the family name to Windsor. In London and elsewhere German shops were ransacked. From: 'Dare to be a Daniel!' First published as *The French Cooks' Syndicate* in 1945. http://libcom.org/history/dare-be-daniel-wilf-mccartney Enemy aliens were interned in parts of the British Empire and in the US. Such chauvinism found other targets and the British government gave 'Friendly aliens' – including Jews and Russians – a choice of being conscripted or repatriated, neither option being desirable for many. Alien dissidents – whatever their origin or legal status – were often deported, or threatened with deportation. See: Julia Bush, *Behind the Lines: East London Labour*, London: Merlin Press, 1984, pp. 174ff.

Alone – Herbert Runham-Brown, British Pacifist

'One night I sat alone in my prison cell. Men had been killing each other for three years, and for two years I had sat in this same little cell, looking out on the small cabbage

patch which covered the space between my window and
the great wall which surrounded the prison. My thoughts
went back to the first night when the door had clanged
behind me. I was not alone now as I was then. That first
night, with all the faith and courage I could muster, I had
tried to believe that I was not alone. I tried to think of all
the men and women who had folded their arms with a
determination that not one act of theirs should help to
carry on that war. It was not without some success that
spirit joined spirit that night, but oh! How I longed for
the human touch, just the sound of a comrade's voice, or
a grip of the hand!'

1917. Herbert Runham-Brown had joined the No Conscription Fellowship
in 1915. He was released on medical grounds in November 1918, after two
and a half year's imprisonment. He had refused to do any substitute work
in place of joining the British army, and was court-martialled three times.
He was also tried under the Defence of the Realm Act for circulating a
letter from a conscientious objector, G. H. Stuart Beavis, in which Beavis
stated he had been threatened with the death penalty. When he was first in
prison, Herbert Runham-Brown thought he was alone. Later there were
3,000 men like him in prisons around the Britain. When the War Resisters'
International was founded he became its first secretary. From Devi Prasad,
War is a crime against humanity: The Story of War Resisters' International,
London: War Resisters' International, 2005, p. 90. Many pacifists and
members of the Independent Labour Party refused conscription. At least
eighty died as a result of harsh conditions in prison.

Comrades – Louise Bryant, American Socialist

'T'avarishi! I come from the place where men are digging
their graves and calling them trenches! We are forgotten
out there in the snow and the cold. We are forgotten
while you sit here and discuss politics! I tell you the army
can't fight much longer! Something's got to be done!
Something's got to be done! The officers won't work with
the soldiers' committees and the soldiers are starving and

the Allies won't have a conference. I tell you something's got to be done, or the soldiers are going home! ... Over and over and over like the beat of the surf came the cry of all starving Russia: Peace, land and bread!'

Autumn 1917. Russia: a tired, emaciated little soldier had mounted the rostrum – covered with mud from head to foot and with old blood stains. He blinked in the alarming light. It was the first speech he had ever made. He began with a shrill hysterical shout ... From: *Six Red Months in Russia*, New York: George H. Doran, 1918.

One Solid Month of Liberty – John Reed

'In America the month just past has been the blackest month for freemen our generation has known. With a sort of hideous apathy the country has acquiesced in a regime of juridical tyranny, bureaucratic suppression and industrial barbarism, which followed inevitably the first fine careless rapture of militarism.'

September 1917. John Reed was appalled by two recent atrocities: a race riot in East Saint Louis where thirty men and women were butchered and the Negro town burnt; and the deportation at gunpoint of a hundred striking miners from Bisbee, Arizona. He saw much of organised labour lying supine. The leader of the American Federation of Labor, Samuel Gompers, was consorting with labour's bitterest enemies. In the light of such things a 'war for civilization' was empty talk. From *The Masses*, Vol IX, No. 11.

Protest – Louis Lecoin

'I firmly believe that men may refuse to assassinate others and should do so. This war, brewed world capitalism, is the worst of transgressions, I protest against it by not responding to [army] orders to report for service. In not obeying military injunctions, in refusing to join up I am acting in conformity with my anarchist ideals.'

December 1917. Declaration to the military governor of Paris. He had been imprisoned for anti-militarist activities and was only released in 1916. The statements above resulted in a new period of imprisonment which lasted until November 1920. News of this sentence was censored.

Brotherhood – John Maclean, British Socialist

'I appeal exclusively to them [working people] because they and they only can bring about the time when the whole world will be in one brotherhood, on a sound economic foundation. That, and that alone, can be the means of bringing about a reorganisation of society. That can only be obtained when the people of the world get the world, and retain the world.'

May 1918. From a speech at his trial for sedition. He was imprisoned for five years, but in the face of a lively defence campaign the government had him released in December 1918.

And Me? – Bruno Misèfari

'I am still not dead – through taking part without arms – in all this human fury. That's my karma and that's how things are. Two anarchists shot. The same for twelve soldiers for lagging behind, I am still alive.'

October 1918; …and our 'great' leaders can advance over the bodies of fallen soldiers! From: Furio Sbarnemi & Bruno Misèfari, *Diario di un disertore*, Florence: La nuova Italia, 1973, p. 143.

A New Day – Kiel Mutineers

'Comrades, in the history of Germany, yesterday will remain memorable. For the first time political power is in our hands. There will be no return to the past.'

5 November 1918.

What is our task?
– David Lloyd George, British Prime Minister

'To make Britain a fit country for heroes to live in.'

24 November 1918. A speech in Wolverhampton.

Volunteer to fight in Russia?
– Andrew Rothstein, Russian-British Socialist

'I said that we had all enlisted for the duration of the war. Well, that war's over. How would you like it if the Russian army came here and started telling us who we should be governed by?'

December 1918. Rothstein became a member of the British Communist Party.

What is being done? – Former soldier

'I beg to suggest that it is such things as these that cause the spread of Bolshevism. I should be glad if one of your numerous readers would advise me what to do; also whether I can be forcibly ejected. I should also like to know what the Prime Minister is doing towards redeeming his promises of making this land of ours a place fit for heroes to live in.'

16 August 1919. A soldier asks for help – nine months after his return from being a prisoner of war – being threatened with eviction from the two rooms he rents in West Ham (London). *Stratford Examiner*, quoted in Julia Bush, *Behind the Lines: East London Labour*, London: Merlin Press, 1984, pp. 204-5.

Notes

1   For example, Robert Graves tells of a conversation before an attack
     in August 1915 painting a picture of incompetence: plans were
     not secret, soldiers were not properly fed, a commanding general
     could not read a map, nor did he know where his troops were. He
     also relates consequences, e.g. one platoon being mown down by a
     machine-gun: *Goodbye to All That*, Harmondsworth, Penguin, 1977,
     pp. 125; 131.

2   In the *Daily Mail*: J. Lee Thompson, *Politicians, the Press &
     Propaganda: Lord Northcliffe & the Great War, 1914-1919*, Kent State
     University Press, 1999, p. 37.

3   Much as George W. Bush would conjure up an 'axis of evil' in 2002.

4   George Seldes documents pressures at work and the truth or lack of
     it in the mainstream press e.g. in: *You Can't Print That*, New York:
     Payson & Clarke, 1929, pp. 11ff.

5   Jeanette Keith, *Rich Man's War, Poor Man's Fight: Race, Class, and
     Power in the Rural South during the First World War*, Chapel Hill:
     University of North Carolina Press, 2004, p. 200.

6   Ibid, p. 84.

7   *History Today* has had an article arguing that 'Britain was right to
     fight Imperial Germany in 1914'; it criticised British government
     plans for commemorating the outbreak of the First World War
     because they failed to challenge the dominant popular view that the
     'war was futile and the deaths meaningless'. Professor Gary Sheffield,
     'The Great War was a just war', *History Today* (London), August
     2013, p. 6.

8   Edward Carpenter criticised the use of these labels in: *The Healing
     of Nations and the hidden sources of their strife*, New York: Charles
     Scribner's Sons, 1915, p. 10.

9   German diplomats cited the danger of a French invasion of Germany
     through Belgium as a reason for their own invasion of Belgium.

10   Konni Zilliacus, *Between 2 Wars*, Harmondsworth: Penguin, 1039, p.
     50. (Zilliacus worked for the League of Nations from 1920 to 1939.)

11   Father of Friedrich Adler, who assassinated Count Sturgkh, the
     leader of the Austrian imperial government, in 1916.

12   Demonstrations took place in many cities and towns in the week
     before war is declared. Jeffrey Verhey, *The Spirit of 1914: Militarism,
     Myth, and Mobilization in Germany*, Cambridge University Press,
     2003, p. 55.

13   Souchy was later deported from Sweden because of his anti-militarist propaganda work. He circulated a leaflet pointing out that German firms made weapons used by the Russian and the Serbian armies. German workers and peasants were being killed by weapons made in Germany! And huge profits were going to arms manufacturers such as the Krupp combine. Augustin Souchy, *Beware! Anarchist! A Life for Freedom: An Autobiography*, Chicago: Charles Kerr, 1992, p. p. 12 see also http://www.anarchismus.at/anarchistische-klassiker/augustin-souchy/7674-augustin-souchy-warum-antimilitaristisches-flugblatt-1915)

AGAINST MILITARISM

Nothing was ever anything so gallant, so smart, so brilliant, and so well organised as the two armies. Hell itself never had such harmony as was made by its trumpets, fifes, oboes, drums, and cannons. First cannons knocked down some six thousand men on each side; then muskets swept away nine or ten thousand ruffians who infested the surface of this best of worlds. Also the bayonet was a 'sufficient reason' for the death of several thousand. The lot might add up to thirty thousand souls. Candide, trembling like a philosopher, hid himself as best he could during this heroic butchery. Finally, while the two kings had Te Deum sung, each in his own camp, Candide resolved to try to make sense of these effects and causes.

From: *Candide*, by Voltaire, (first published in 1759).

For Voltaire militarism was an abomination. He lampooned pomp and ceremony, gore and glamour, splendid uniforms and military bands, all hallowed by the church. A hundred and fifty years after he wrote these lines militarism was still a vibrant and sanctified part of a macho official culture. In the USA and in the British Empire elite schools[1] and universities were associated with armed forces' cadets and officers commanded social prestige.

In peace time the armed forces drew on voluntary recruitment, albeit that the lack of work may have driven some to join up. Forcible recruitment was common in the overseas imperial territories. In continental Europe conscription was the norm. If working people thought of war as a waste or a misfortune, few had experienced it first-hand. Workers on strike suffered the unkind attentions of armed forces; otherwise their experience was limited to periods of military service. Some rebels found ways to avoid conscription and rejected nationalism and there was a widespread view that workers had no country. Radicals pledged their allegiance not to a nation state, but rather to the country of 'life and liberty'. Pacifists rejected war on principle. All sorts of socialists, anarchists and syndicalists opposed militarism as a symptom of class rule.

In Western Europe the most vigorous opposition to militarism, going beyond the passing of anti-war resolutions, came from libertarians and syndicalists. Anti-militarism was at its strongest and most resolute in the French labour confederation – the CGT. It organised campaigns to influence and retain the loyalty of young workers liable for conscription. In Germany, where they were few and far between, anarchists and syndicalists tried to spread anti-military propaganda whilst mainstream leaders of the Social-democratic party took a softly-softly approach, limiting their campaigning to complaints about the harsh, arbitrary and abusive discipline suffered by recruits.

Many socialists followed Marx and Engels in seeing Russian Imperialism (Tsarism) as the epitome of conservative reaction. In this perspective it was legitimate to support a war of national defence – for progress – against reaction. Some French radicals campaigned against war – but many others looked towards a popular nationalism, the idea of a nation in arms, as in the 1790s. But times changed and the content within one or other nation, and between classes and peoples, earlier and later, also changed. When 'France' became an ally of 'Russia', was it appropriate for the workers and peoples in the German Empire to see a war as a matter of self-defence against Russian autocracy? Self-defence slipped easily into taking sides with one or other of the military alliances. Who was to decide which countries, nations and states were progressive? Should 'civilized' Europeans use force against the 'uncivilized'? Should progressive 'democratic' France be defended against an 'undemocratic' German Empire? Should working people refuse to support either side in a war between two imperial coalitions? Who was to decide if a particular war was a case of self-defence, who would arbitrate? Should the left act unilaterally? In the absence of immediate and clear decision-making by unions or parties, it would be for governments to make these decisions over the heads of working people. It was easy to pass resolutions condemning war and militarism, but, where they wanted to implement such decisions, it was much more difficult for Socialists and syndicalists to work out how to act to prevent or obstruct war.

An international anti-war conference with 555 delegates from Socialist Parties was convened in Basel, Switzerland in November 1912. It passed resolutions to impede war.[2] Weeks later, 600,000 French workers responded to a call from the CGT[3] and supported a one day strike to protest against preparations for war. In the following year more protests erupted in France when military service was extended from two to three years. For students and for syndicalist anti-capitalist youth, opposition to militarism was a key campaign. 150,000 demonstrators supported an anti-war protest at Pré-Saint-Gervais, near Paris in May 1913. In May and June, 1913, mutinies broke out in several army units – soldiers demonstrated and sang 'The Internationale'. Some recruits were punished with weeks of imprisonment, others

– 'ring-leaders' – were sent to punishment battalions. The government also ordered searches of the offices of the labour press, and of all sorts of union organisations throughout France. The CGT was accused of harbouring an anti-French, treasonous conspiracy and there was talk of it being banned. In July some twenty CGT activists were charged with possession of anti-militarist literature. A defence campaign was started in the CGT's journal *La Bataille syndicaliste*. There were calls for another general strike on 24 September, but the national CGT developed cold feet and decided against it.[4] When war broke out, in 1914, thousands of Frenchmen evaded the call-up.[5]

In Italy radicals and subversives made their presence felt through propaganda and agitation. On one famous occasion, as Italian troops were being sent from Bologna to Libya in 1911, an anarchist, Augusto Masetti, opened fire on his colonel crying: 'Down with war! long live anarchy!' 20,000 anarchists, republicans, socialists and syndicalists supported anti-militarist campaigns. In June 1914 an anti-militarist day was held in Ancona, calling for the liberation of soldiers who had opposed the war against Libya. Speeches were made by Nenni for the Republicans, by the syndicalist Pelizza, and by Malatesta for the anarchists. Forces of order intervened and three young men were killed. A week of riots, occupations and strikes followed. In Spain too libertarians fought against overseas colonial adventures in North Africa.

In Britain, Keir Hardie once reported on the activities of the Parliamentary Labour Party:

Questions of foreign affairs, education, the welfare of subject races, militarism (that sinister foe of progress) … have been dealt with by members of the party speaking for their colleagues … these things, however, have been merely incidental to the *real* work of the Party.[6]

In this view opposing militarism was no great priority. Even amongst radicals there was a curious mixture of ideas – one of the extracts below ends with 'Britain for the British,[7] and the world for the workers!' a mixture which to a modern eye may look somewhat doubtful. There were a few resolute dissidents who campaigned vigorously. A Glaswegian socialist, Henry McShane, volunteered for the army, hoping to subvert fellow soldiers, when war broke out. He soon concluded that the volunteers he found in the British army were not ready to listen to anti-war propaganda and that he should have waited until conscription had been introduced.[8] Two and a half million men volunteered for the British forces, between the start of the war and March 1916. As casualties mounted more men were needed. Conscription was introduced in January 1916 under the Military Service Act. Opposition to it came from Quakers and other Christians and pacifists, as well as socialists and radicals. Public speaking against conscription was prohibited and speakers were fined or imprisoned.

Conscription was commonplace in most of Europe from the start of the war. Some defaulters fled to neutral countries: the Netherlands, Spain, Sweden and Switzerland. The draft met with opposition in the USA. It became clear that it was falling more heavily on working people. Three million draftees sought to have their call up deferred. Some Southerners saw it as a Yankee war and retreated to swamps and forests. Remote and unpopulated areas served as places of refuge. Recent immigrants had a hard time in the American army – especially those unable to understand orders in the English language.

In Canada compulsory enlistment was forced through in 1917 against the feelings of French-Canadians in particular; to avoid it some Canadians took refuge across the American border. In the British Honduras colony many Spanish speakers, fearing conscription, also voted with their feet and crossed the border into Mexico. In Australia Irish Catholics were part of a coalition that successfully opposed conscription. Referenda proposing the introduction of compulsory overseas military service were defeated in 1916 and again in 1917. In South Africa conscription for foreign service was not imposed out of fear of opposition from Afrikaner nationalists. Recognising the dangers of acerbating tension in Ireland the United Kingdom government delayed and postponed conscription there, although Ireland was at that time a part of the UK. In the rest of the UK conscription was introduced in 1916, and gradually extended in severity and applied to all men between the ages of 18 and 51. In India over a million men were recruited, without state compulsion.

Avoiding conscription was not easy. Some who refused to fight were allowed to work as labourers, stretcher-bearers and health orderlies. Police forces sought out defaulters. Some recruits were helped to reach neutral countries by regular escape routes. In Britain dockworkers secretly helped provide defaulters with false papers (Britons were made into 'Irishmen' as conscription was not applied in Ireland), or were given berths as merchant-seamen allowing them to take refuge in overseas ports. However, the need to avoid publicity was underlined in 1915, when in the midst of a conscription crisis Irishmen attempting to sail on the *Saxonia* from Liverpool to America were met with a jeering mob.[9]

Millions died in the fighting and millions more lost their lives behind the front-line. Soldiers condemned generals for their incompetent management of the war but had no power to force them to account. Generals, however, held powers of life and death over soldiers and they could condemn subordinates to death. Official figures[10] suggest that the number of executions was (approximately):[11]

British and Imperial forces:	330
French army:	600[12]
German army:	48
Italian army:	750

For every man executed there were nine more whose death sentence was commuted. Official figures also omit undisclosed 'unofficial' and summary executions.[13] These were, most likely, much greater than the numbers officially declared.

Many official executions were public ceremonies, carried out to deter others from refusing to obey orders. The units of the condemned men provided the firing squad and witnessed punishment. Those to be shot had their army badges removed and had targets pinned to their chest. Such public spectacles were designed to warn and intimidate. If units were held responsible for some setback, and made examples of, the choice of victims targeted for retribution and punishment was often arbitrary – sometimes the youngest unmarried men were shot. On at least one occasion a member of the French CGT union federation (Félix Baudy) was chosen because of his union membership. Such victims were chosen for being in the wrong place at the wrong time.

There were many mutinies and riots over the course of the war. The biggest were the French army mutinies in the summer of 1917. A recent offensive had been a dismal failure, over the course of a few days 30,000 had been killed, bringing the overall number of Frenchmen killed towards the million mark. Generals were seen as incompetents and butchers. Some 40,000 infantrymen refused to go 'over the top', or to return to the front line. The mutineers had mixed motivations: some soldiers sought to establish that they had rights and that their protests were legitimate, some wanted leave, others had a radical political agenda. French officers sentenced thousands to punishment and condemned 554 to death, but 'only' carried out some 49 executions.

The Russian revolution of February 1917 set an example and raised hopes that the war would soon come to an end. Rebellious Russian troops were interned and later one army camp was shelled to force mutineers to surrender.[14] The Russian example also impacted on the German army in France. Troops transferred from Russia brought rebellious thinking with them. Ultimately the war ended when soldiers refused to go on fighting.[15] The armed forces of Russia, Austria-Hungary and Germany began to break up. Many soldiers voted with their feet and went home.

Amongst British and Imperial forces mutinies became more frequent after the armistice. Soldiers resented bad conditions. There were protests and mutinies in: Biggin Hill, Calais, Deolali, Étaples, Folkestone, Kantara, Kinmel,[16] Poona, Shoreham, Southampton, Taranto[17] and Victoria (British Columbia).[18] Many conscripts had had enough. The slow pace of demobilisation was widely resented. Soldiers were angered by disparities of treatment and compensation – soldiers of the British West Indies Regiment were denied a wage rise of sixpence given to white troops. In 1920 one blind Canadian soldier asked: 'I had my pension fixed at $600, I want to know how it is that the eyes of a Brigadier-General in Canada are worth $2700, while my eyes are only worth $600.' Soldiers had news of labour unrest. Doubts over their loyalty constrained the British government which might have used them against workers.[19] Attempts to extend conscripts' service and to use them for campaigns in India, Russia and elsewhere came up against protests. (Hands-off Russia campaigns were formed and dockers refused to load ships with weapons destined for counter-revolutionaries.) Although militants were scarce, red flags were being raised. Feelings were changing; soldiers had a new determination to assert their rights.

The texts in this section document dissidents' and socialists' attempts to oppose militarism.

To render war impossible
– International Workingmen's Congress

'The International Workingmen's Congress recommends to all its sections, to the members of working men's societies in particular and to the working classes in general, to cease work if war is declared in their country. The Congress counts upon the spirit of solidarity which inspires working men of all countries, and entertains the hope that in such an emergency the means of supporting peoples against their governments will not be found wanting.'

1868, Brussels Congress of the First International.

Anti-militarism – Domela Nieuwenhuis, Dutch Socialist

'When I proposed a strike against militarism to the Brussels congress [of the Second International] in 1891, there was much opposition and the proposal was declared to be utopian and fantastic. So much for the progress of socialism over twenty years![20] Unfortunately there was retrograde progress. When workers of various countries refuse to present themselves [for war] what will governments do with mobilisation? The example of some would draw out a greater number to follow them. If there were thousands, could they all be imprisoned? It would become impossible. Some might be shot – to give an example of discipline – but aren't there sufficient forces available to reply to such an atrocity? And [in consequence] would not an armed insurrection be provoked? If there was a systemic refusal to obey, the strongest of governments would be unable to force socialists into fratricidal action. I prefer civil war, to a war between nations …'

1901. Domela Nieuwenhuis asked: how wars can be prevented? He called for work to encourage fraternisation between armed forces. He noted that the supply of mules from New Orleans for the Boer war had been obstructed. He called on conscripts to refuse conscription in peace time, and for strikes in the event of war. From: *Le militarisme et l'attitude des anarchistes et socialistes révolutionnaires devant la guerre*, Paris: Temps nouveaux No.17, 1901, pp. 28.[21]

New Handbook for Soldiers
– Georges Yvetot, French Syndicalist and Anarchist

'... They say that the homeland (*Patrie*) is the country of our birth, where we live, where we work, where we take a part in communal life. We should love our country. But would we cease to love her, if we seek happiness by coming to an understanding with those who live elsewhere, on the other side of rivers and seas? Do we cease to love her, because we dare to love those who live around her – in other countries, where language, custom or climate is different? ...

That word – *Patrie* – is the motto for every infamy, every cruelty, ever corruption, every deceit. On account of that word we are locked up [conscripted] for three years, [we are] made into slaves, or perhaps into assassins, or [we] become victims of brutal non-commissioned officers. Taxes crush us, for *la Patrie*; our money is extorted for *la Patrie*; and its army – for twelve or fourteen hours, day after day – we have to do as we are told, labouring like a beast for a starvation wage. ...

No! Militarism is a means of enslavement. The barracks make us into obedient machines... What is the legacy of the barracks: moral cowardice, a pattern of [fear and] trembling and subservience. When they leave the forces men show up having become traitors to the working class: as scabs or policemen. And the army has another role as the nation's gendarme. In strikes, when workers, are driven out of work by the avarice of the employer and rightly think that their place is on the streets, it is soldiers who are sent in with the fixed bayonets and loaded rifles; it is they who gallop and charge down the streets. And it is not just with the rifle that the army runs to assist capital. When strikes occur the soldier may even take the place of the worker. The national army, the army formed from people's youth, serves the bosses and lines up against the people. The army with all its capacity to murder, is loaned out to the bosses....

Hypocritical statesmen say that the army guarantees the right to work. A lie. The army ensures the success of the exploiter over the exploited. The soldier is also used, [indeed] is primarily used, for the social war while he waits to serve in some foreign war. The wealthy and the statesman, if they are in fear of losing their money or power, never shrink from using force. The evidence of this truth is red with blood, in our history, as in the history of every other country. Whenever the sons of the people press for a little more freedom, and a little extra comfort, it is the gun that answers them. Leave aside the great massacres – like those of 1830, 1848 or 1871, when proletarians fell by the thousands to the bullets of the 'defenders of order' – not a year goes by without workers being massacred somewhere or other. Every time workers try to strike to secure a few meagre benefits, some minor improvement in their circumstances, troops are sent in. Every move brings the striker up against the soldier. We are proletarians, which is to say that in the present we are the ones who bear the full burden and all the misery of society. The primary underpinning of today's society is the army. And to cap it all, it draws its recruits from among the most wretched, from the victims most afflicted by the power of capitalism. On the day that the better part of the workers, those who are conscious, choose to demand their share of the wealth of society, which they produce, cannon, guns and bayonets will be sent against

To Arms!

Capitalists, Parsons, Politicians, Landlords, Newspaper Editors and Other Stay-At-Home Patriots.

your country needs
YOU
in the trenches!!

WORKERS

Follow your Masters

WHY I AM A
CONSCIENTIOUS
OBJECTOR

Being Answers to the Tribunal Catechism

By WALTER AYLES
A. FENNER BROCKWAY
A. BARRATT BROWN
CLEMENT BUNDOCK
J.H. HUDSON, K.O. MEN-
NELL & HUBERT PEET

Price Twopence

NO-CONSCRIPTION FELLOWSHIP
5 YORK BUILDINGS

CONFÉDERATION GÉNÉRALE DU TRAVAIL

GUERRE à la GUERRE!

TRAVAILLEURS

La Guerre déclarée!

OR, LE PEUPLE NE VEUT PAS LA GUERRE!
... QUELLE VEUT LA
PAIX A QUI PRIX!...

TRAVAILLEURS

Nous voulons la Paix! Refusons-nous à faire la
Guerre! LE COMITÉ CONFÉDÉRAL.

AUSTRALIAN LABOR PARTY
Anti-Conscription Campaign Committee.

" VOTE
NO
MUM

they'll
take
DAD
next "

VOTE
☒ NO

Authorised by
B. Mulvogue,
Trades Hall Hall.

them. Workers' sons and brothers will become murderers – unless they can find the courage to refuse to open fire – to refuse to take part in a massacre. All the bombast beneath the Flag and all grand speeches of *Patrie* end up with this. If we admire this insane chauvinism we are merely justifying and consolidating an invincible power that is turned against us by exploiters and the state...

... as soon as he puts on his uniform, the man of the people despite himself, betrays his own. The proletarian soldier is the 'man of the people' set up to defend the rich and powerful, armed and equipped against his brothers... The army is not merely an academy of crime, it is a school of vice, a school of treachery, of laziness, hypocrisy and cowardice....

Advice to Conscripts – Young men full of vigour and health, you who are about to be snatched away from your work, your hopes, your loved ones; young men about to don the uniform of honour (that is how it is described that uniform of slavery and crime) for a three year stretch; young men, think about what you should do! Be brave! If you think you may be unable to endure vexations, insults, idiocies, punishment and all of the turpitude that await you in the barracks: *Desert!* Better that than serving as a plaything for the alcoholic torturers and irate fools who might be looking after you in the military prisons. If you think that there is no chance of spreading the propaganda of revolt in barracks; if you think that the risks involved in making such propaganda is too great; if you think that there is no way that you could serve out your three years without carrying out a propaganda that you reckon unproductive and harmful for yourself: *Desert!* Your unions, your federations, your trades' councils will do everything possible to bring you moral and financial support. For their sake you will find a fraternal welcome abroad – and in the process you will learn that the *Patrie* is everywhere where there are people in struggle: thinking, suffering, working, hoping and revolting against the injustices of society. …

Advice to Serving Soldiers … Your conscience as a worker forbids you to fire upon other workers. If they should send you in against strikers: *Don't shoot*! If they want to turn you into a killing machine: *Revolt!* And finally, let them tremble, those who dare arm you against your brethren, for you have only one enemy: the one who exploits, oppresses, commands and deceives you! And if they insist on your being murderous – with the arms they have given you – *don't kill your brother!*'

The *New Handbook for Soldiers (Nouveau Manuel du Soldat)*, first published in 1902, was written for the French General Labour Confederation (CGT). Successive editions of 10 to 15,000 were distributed throughout France as part of a campaign against militarism. At one point 100,000 copies were sold in two years. It warned parents of the poisonous potential of children hearing glorious tales of war, growing up playing with toy soldiers. The effects of the CGT's anti-militarist campaigns cannot be precisely known, but in the years before the First World War thousands of men refused to join up. Extracts are quoted in A.J. Brossat & J.Y.Potel, *Antimilitarisme et Révolution*, Volume 1, Paris: UGE, 1976, pp. 144ff.; and in *The New Soldier's Handbook,* http://www.katesharpleylibrary.net/66t21j

The question has been asked
– Gustave Hervé, French Anti-militarist

'If the Socialist Party puts the conquest of electoral and parliamentary public power above all else, if it is, despite its revolutionary declarations, only a party of reform, a party of slow and quiet evolution […] then it should say that it is patriotic. But, on the contrary, if the Socialist Party is truly a party of revolution which does not sacrifice either its ideals, or the future, to momentary shabby electoral preoccupations, then it will respond resolutely that it is anti-patriotic. Whilst waiting for the entire international congress to get up to speed with this, the next congress of the Socialist Party, the French Section of the Workers' International, should be warned that it has to respond to this grave question of tactics and principles. The question has been asked. [...]

For us there are only two countries in the world: that of the privileged and that of the disinherited, or rather that of the conservatives and that of the rebels, whatever language they may speak, or whatever the land may be which chanced to give them birth. Our compatriots are not the capitalists here, who would have us massacred if they could, just as they massacred our fathers in the Commune. Our compatriots are the conscious proletarians, the socialists, the revolutionaries of the whole world, who wage everywhere the same battle as ourselves for the establishment of a better society. And in full agreement with them we only await the opportunity in this Europe, where the railways, the telegraph, cheap newspapers, and the same capitalist system have suppressed distance and rendered uniform the conditions of life, to found that free European federation, prelude to the great human federation, in which the countries of today will be absorbed, just as the ancient provinces became absorbed in the France, England, and Germany as we now know them.'

1905. Gustave Hervé argued that being exploited in Germany was pretty much the same as being exploited in France. As for wars, even if one side had declared war, it might well be the other that had provoked it; very often 'defensive war' was a nonsense. He was imprisoned for campaigning against militarism. At this time his viewed the tricolour as the flag of those who had killed the Paris Commune and the workers' flag as the red flag. However, in 1914, he supported the war and he subsequently embraced fascism. From: (1) *Leur Patrie*, Paris: Bibliographie sociale, 1905; and http://archive.org/stream/leurpatrie00herv/leurpatrie00herv_djvu.txt (2) Defence speech, published by the Industrial Workers of the World, *Patriotism and the Worker*, Chicago: IWW, 1912.

Tax the rich! – German Social-democrats

'The masses have hitherto borne the greater part of these burden. Our representatives in the Reichstag[22] will reiterate our old demand – for burdens to be imposed on those who can bear them most easily, and whose professed patriotism induces them constantly to vote fresh additional estimates for unproductive projects and armaments, while keeping a close fist on their own spoils. We demand the introduction of an Imperial progressive income tax on all incomes over £250 …'

January 1907; Social-democratic Party election address. The party wanted the rich to pay more tax.[23] From: R.C. Ensor, Ed., *Modern Socialism as set forth by Socialists in their Speeches, Writings and Programmes*, London: Harper, 1910, pp. 373-4. A further extract, reflecting party thinking colonial policy and imperialism is quoted below on page

A Soldier's Handbook
– Arnold Roller et al, Austrian and German Anarchists

'Do Germans kill Blacks in their African colonies because the German homeland is in danger? It is matter of plunder, of plunder pure and simple …

If we were to accept that Germany had real political freedoms, such as [might exist in] France or Switzerland; would such political freedoms really be so valuable then, that proletarians – by hundreds of thousands – should sacrifice their lives? A smaller, milder dose of oppression and persecution is, in truth, not to be bought or maintained at the price of a hundred-thousand proletarian corpses…
When the officer returns from war in one piece he then awaits rewards, promotion, a better pension; if he comes back wounded he has a medal, a full pension and a trouble-free life. If he is killed his family is richly looked after by the state. But when you, a soldier are wounded in conflict or return crippled or unfit for work, you are forced to go

a-begging or your wife and children will starve in misery, because no state will look after you. And if death claims you in battle your wife and children will soon follow you there, because they will be left to starve undisturbed.

To be free, one must have the capacity to be able to enjoy life and this is what proletarians do not have, not even in Switzerland, in the classic country of freedom.

Your enemy is not the other side of the frontier! Your enemy is your master! Your enemy is anyone who would set themselves up as a master over you, who pushes you down and makes you beg...

They will tell you what a great honour and duty it is to defend the King, to give your life for the King who gives you the order to shoot your mother and father.

But, really, think about it – why – what does the King give you? When he needs it he takes everything from you: your freedom, your blood and your life. He sends you off to fight, when he personally wants to fight something which has nothing to do with you – and if in the end you are crippled and in need, then there will be no King to look after you, and you can starve and rot.

You are to defend the "Fatherland" against both the "outsider" and against the "internal" enemy, and you are to preserve order and law. You should defend the Law! But all laws only protect the rich.[24] .... "Don't answer: I am not responsible... I have to obey!" – haven't you a mind of your own, to think and decide for yourself? You are responsible for things. It is feeble cowardice to shelter behind the will and the order of someone else.'

February 1907. German anarchists published this text drawing inspiration from the French 'Manuel du Soldat'. Hundreds of young workers, it warned, were being driven to commit suicide by army life. Recruits remained slaves, even when their term was done; they were enrolled in the army reserve, constrained to attend further weeks of training. Their jobs might be lost whilst they were back in the army. Recruits had a way out, they should avoid the call-up, or desert; they would find support and solidarity abroad. Soldiers should refuse to attack strikers, and refuse to be cannon fodder. The first edition of the Handbook was printed in London. In an attempt to disguise it, this and subsequent editions, were printed with Imperial icons on the cover and purported to be printed by 'A Patriotic Publisher'. From: Arnold Roller (Siegfried Nacht) *Soldaten Brevier*, in Ulrich Bröckling, Ed, *Nieder mit der Disziplin! Hoch die Rebellion – Anarchistische Soldatenagitation im Deutschen Kaiserreich*, Berlin: Harald Kater Verlag, 1988, and http://www.anarchismus.at/texte-antimilitarismus/7307-anarchistische-soldatenagitation-soldaten-brevier

What has been done?
– Karl Liebknecht, German Social-democrat

'The attempt to develop special anti-militarist propaganda in Germany has been resisted by influential leaders of the movement, who say that there is no Social-democratic party in the whole world which fights militarism as hard as German Social-democracy. There is much truth in this. Ever since the German Reich has existed ruthless and tireless criticism has been levelled by the German Social-democrats in parliament and in the press against militarism, the whole of its content and its harmful effects. It has collected material to indict militarism, enough to build a gigantic funeral pyre, and has waged the struggle against militarism as part of its general agitation with great energy and tenacity. In this respect our party needs neither defence nor praise. Its deeds speak for themselves. Nevertheless, there is more to be done.

The final goals of the anarchist and Social-democratic forms of anti-militarism, if we are satisfied with a slogan, are the same: the abolition of militarism, abroad as well as at home. But Social-democracy, in accordance with its conception of the essence of militarism, regards the complete abolition of militarism alone as impossible:[25] militarism can only fall together with capitalism, the last class system of society. Capitalism of course is not something fixed, but a constantly evolving system which can be influenced and weakened to a considerable degree by contrary tendencies contained within it, and above all by proletarian tendencies. In the same way militarism, the manifestation of capitalism, is not incapable of being weakened, as is shown by the different forms it takes in different countries. Its connection with capitalism can also be loosened.

Social-democratic anti-militarism, on the other hand, is based on the class struggle, and is therefore directed in principle exclusively to those classes which are necessarily enemies of militarism in that struggle – though of course it is happy to see the bourgeois splinters which fall in its direction in the course of disintegration. It educates in order to persuade, but the subject which it teaches is not that of categorical imperatives, of humanitarian positions, of ethical postulates of freedom and justice, but that of the class struggle and of the interests of the proletariat in this struggle, of the role of militarism in the class struggle and the role which the proletariat plays and must play in the same struggle. It deduces the task of the proletariat in the struggle against militarism from the interests of the proletariat in the class struggle.

... The agitation must never directly or indirectly incite military disobedience. It will have attained its goal if it shows up the essence of militarism and its role in the class struggle, if it raises indignation and disgust in response to its exposure of the real character of militarism, its function as an enemy of the people.'

From *Militarism and Anti-Militarism*, 1907. Liebknecht was on the left of the party and was one of the few who campaigned against militarism. In October 1907 he was sentenced to eighteen months imprisonment, for treason on account of these writings: neither the caution with which he expressed his views, nor millions of Social-democratic votes availed him any protection. In December 1914 he was the first socialist Reichstag (parliamentary) deputy to refuse to vote credits for the war; he was called up, and spent much of the war in prison. He was murdered by proto-fascists in 1919. See: http://www.marxists.org/archive/liebknecht-k

Subversion in the Russian Imperial Army
– Yemelyan Yaroslavsky, Russian Social-democrat

'Sunday: Organised an advanced meeting, four soldiers came, two of them social-revolutionaries; also organised a basic meeting, spoke about the party's programme.

Monday: Organised amongst the first company an advanced meeting of three soldiers. There are good future prospects to come. Given very severe surveillance at the moment it is not possible to organise activities in the circles. Also two comrades have begun propaganda in the barracks. All of us seek to draw in five or six persons. Literature is in demand; more serious – one group wants *Political Economy*, another *Darwin*. Karl Marx's *Capital* given to the most conscious.'

An extract from a report by an activist of the Russian Social-democratic party on subversion in the army. In 1906 a party organization in Lithuania had resolved to carry on systematic propaganda and to organise a party organisation to prepare the way for insurrection. The mass insurrections and revolutionary movements that shook Russia in 1905 were accompanied by the development of a subversive press that circulated in large numbers. From A.J. Brossat & J.Y.Potel, *Antimilitarisme et Révolution*, Volume 1, Paris: UGE, 1976, pp. 185, 188-9.

Against War – International Congress of Socialist parties

'The congress is convinced that, under the pressure of the proletariat, by a serious use of arbitration in place of the miserable measures of the governments, the benefit of disarmament can be secured to all nations, making it possible to employ the enormous expenditures of money and energy, which are swallowed up by military armaments and wars, for cultural purposes. If a war threatens to break out, it is the duty of the working classes and their parliamentary representatives in the countries involved, supported by the coordinating activity of the International Socialist Bureau, to exert every effort in order to prevent the outbreak of war by the means they consider most effective, which naturally vary according to the sharpening of the class struggle and the sharpening of the general political situation. If, nevertheless, war should break out, it is their duty to intervene in favour of its speedy termination and with all their powers to use the economic and political crisis created by the war to rouse the masses and thereby to hasten the downfall of capitalist class rule.'

18–24 August 1907. A Social-democrat International Bureau facilitated regular contacts between European parties. Meetings could elaborate policies – but did not organise campaigns. German socialists faced the prospect of prison if they campaigned overtly against their army; they thought there was too much talk about militarism in France. This text was adopted at the International Socialist Congress in Stuttgart where German Social-democrats opposed a commitment to an anti-war general strike.

The Hypocrisy of Ambitious Politicians
– Pierre Ramus, Austrian Anarchist and Pacifist

'We ask: what is its meaning, what influence does German Social-democracy have in parliament, where does it make manifest its anti-militarism? Where, in all the wide world, is it expressed – this Social-democratic anti-militarism?

Social-democracy is developing in its parliamentary activity a perfectly conservative element of militarism, everyone who reads and understands the speeches of Bebel[26] (Noske says nothing different to him) – and his international colleagues has to take account of that. They combat the 'abuses' of militarism, whilst it is, in itself, a unique danger... Let us summarise: Social-democratic anti-militarism is the hypocrisy of ambitious politicians, for them, making a reality of it, means not the abolition of militarism but rather a change in its forms and functions ...'

26–31 August 1907; speech at the International Anarchist Congress, Amsterdam. Rudolf Grossmann, a.k.a Ramus was arrested in 1914 on charges of espionage and treason and spent much of the war in prison or under house arrest. August Bebel was a veteran German Social-democrat leader; Gustav Noske was on the right of the SDP.

By Every Means
– International Anarchist Congress

'We engage our comrades, and all those who aspire to freedom generally, to struggle as circumstances and temperament allows, by every means: by individual revolt, by individual and collective refusal of [military] service, by passive and active disobedience and by military non-compliance; and by the root and branch destruction of instruments of domination. We express the hope that the people of all countries affected by a declaration of war will respond with insurrection, proclaiming our belief that anarchists will set the example.'

26–31 August 1907; International Anarchist Congress, Amsterdam.

A Defensive War?
– Karl Kautsky, German Social-democrat (as reported by Jean Jaurès)

'One day the German government might show German proletarians that they had been attacked, on its side the French government might show the same thing to French proletarians, and we would have a war in which German proletarians and French proletarians would follow their governments with the same enthusiasm, reciprocally killing and slaughtering each other. It is against this that we need to be forewarned, and we will be forearmed against this danger if we adopt not that criteria, but the criteria of proletarian interest.'

28 September 1907; *L'Humanité.*

Superficial anti-militarism – Domela Niewenhuis

'Social-democrats do not want to grab militarism by the root, they only want a people's army... they want to change form but not essence. What Social-democrats call anti-militarism is in reality army reform... and the radical bourgeoisie wants this too.'

1908. From: 'Sozialdemokratischer und anarchistischer Antimilitarismus' *Die freie Generation*, Volume 2, Number 16, 1908, p. 230, cited in Gernot Jochheim: *Antimilitaristische Aktionstheorie, Soziale Revolution, und Soziale Verteidigung*, Frankfurt am Main; Haag und Herrchen, 1977, p. 130; see http://www.anarchismus.at/texte-antimilitarismus/334-idk-was-ist-eigentlich-anti-militarismus At a socialist congress in Brussels in 1891 Karl Liebknecht had replied to Domela Nieuwenhuis's call for a general strike saying this was a utopian policy and that those who advocated it would be shot before they had a chance to act.[27]

Infamous fratricide – Italian Socialist youth

'Across the centuries the bourgeois concept of 'homeland' has been nothing but the official justification of every instance of infamy and crime. [....Congress calls for:] Towards the family, an intensification of anti-militarist and anti-patriotic propaganda, so that their sons – particularly future conscripts – are educated not in hate but in love; a son of the people who fires on the people is an infamous fratricide.'

September 1910. Florence, Youth congress of the Italian Socialist Party. From : Amadeo Bordiga, *Histoire de la gauche communiste*, Volume 1, 1912 – 1919, Saguenay, Québec, 2005, chapter 12. www.matierevolution. org/IMG/doc/hist_gc_1.doc

A New Army – Jean Jaurès, French Socialist

'The first point, therefore, of army reform is the diplomatic point; no war must be declared unless arbitration has first been offered; thus alone can you get that national conviction of self-defence which will make the family-man as eager a fighter as the first-line youngster. Under these circumstances, our strategy must be as predominantly defensive as our diplomacy. With this conviction of an entirely just cause, and with men trained from boyhood upwards in all the most scientific possibilities of defensive warfare on a great scale, we can better utilize the million reservists who, by our present system, are separated by so unnecessary a gulf from the younger men. We must organize recruiting and mobilization on as close a territorial system as possible, so as to call out our reservists at the shortest possible notice. We can confront the invader with these vast masses of men, falling back where necessary upon carefully prepared positions in the rear and again fresh positions behind those. Thus the enemy, always and everywhere, will have to lose heavily in attacking prepared positions, while his own communications are extending, and our main forces are massing behind to seize the first opportunity of striking back heavily. In face of a nation with self-control enough to adopt this resolute and calculated defensive, any predatory policy of adventure would run enormous risks.'

The author was a leader of the French Socialists. He wanted the army reformed and socialised. He presented a proposition for a new army law on 10 November 1910. It called for a popular army with officers promoted by competitive examination (therefore including members of the working class). Some soldiers might keep arms at home,[28] barrack-life would be reduced and reformed. Georges Yvetot criticised this approach. Libertarian radicals looked for more resolute action to oppose militarism.[29] http://marxists.org/archive/jaures/1907/military-service Also http://gallica.bnf.fr/ark:/12148/bpt6k81579h

Is it true that Socialists intend to do away with the army and navy? – Robert Tressell, Irish Socialist

'Yes; it is true. Socialists believe in international brotherhood and peace. Nearly all wars are caused by profit-seeking capitalists, seeking new fields for commercial exploitation, and by aristocrats who make it the means of glorifying themselves in the eyes of the deluded common people. You must remember that socialism is not only a national, but an international movement and when it is realized, there will be no possibility of war, and we shall no longer need to maintain an army and navy, or to waste a lot of labour building warships or manufacturing arms and ammunition. All those people who are now employed will then be at liberty to assist in the great work of producing the benefits of civilization; creating wealth and knowledge and happiness for themselves and others – socialism means peace on earth and goodwill to all mankind. But in the meantime we know that the people of other nations are not yet all socialists; we do not forget that in foreign countries – just the same as in Britain – there are large numbers of profit-seeking capitalists, who are so destitute of humanity, that if they thought it could be done successfully and with profit to themselves they would not scruple to come here to murder and to rob. We do not forget that in foreign countries – the same as here – there are plenty of so-called 'Christian' bishops and priests always ready to give their benediction to any such murderous projects, and to blasphemously pray to the Supreme Being to help his children to slay each other like wild beasts. And knowing and remembering all this, we realize that until we have done away with capitalism, aristocracy and anti-Christian clericalism, it is our duty to be prepared to defend our homes and our native land. And therefore we are in favour of maintaining national defensive forces in the highest possible state of efficiency. But that does not mean that we are in favour of the present system of organizing those forces. We do not believe in conscription, and we do not believe that the nation should continue to maintain a professional standing army to be used at home for the purpose of butchering men and women of the working classes in the interests of a handful of capitalists, as has been done at Featherstone and Belfast; or to be used abroad to murder and rob the people of other nations. Socialists advocate the establishment of a National Citizen Army, for defensive purposes only. We believe that every able bodied man should be compelled to belong to this force and to undergo a course of military training, but without making him into a professional soldier, or taking him away from civil life, depriving him of the rights of citizenship or making him subject to military 'law' which is only another name for tyranny and despotism. This Citizen Army could be organized on somewhat similar lines to the present Territorial Force, with certain differences. For instance, we do not believe – as our present rulers do – that wealth and aristocratic influence are the two most essential qualifications for an efficient officer; we believe that all ranks should be attainable by any man, no matter how poor, who is capable of passing the necessary examinations, and that there should be no expense attached to those positions which the government grant, or the pay, is not sufficient to cover. The officers could be appointed in any one of several ways: they might be elected by the men they would have to command, the only qualification required being that they had passed their examinations, or they might be appointed according to merit – the candidate obtaining the highest number of marks at the examinations to have the first call on any vacant post, and so on in order of merit. We believe in the total abolition of courts martial, any offence against discipline should be punishable by the ordinary civil law – no member of the Citizen Army being deprived of the rights of a citizen.'

1910 (First published 1914). From: Robert Tressell, (alias Robert Noonan), *The Ragged Trousered Philanthropists*, London: Lawrence & Wishart, 2002, pp. 538-40.

When war threatens, Strike!
– An interview with Gustav Landauer, German Anarchist

'Does the Worker have an interest here?
Looting is something that goes with conquest, the business of exploiters, because they do not want to work. Workers in one state will wish only that their comrades in other states should be spared this experience, ... work and peace come side by side ... when workers strike war becomes impossible....
So you mean that a mass strike should erupt not just when war breaks out, but before? Certainly...'

December 1911; extract from a pamphlet for the anti-militarist campaign of the Socialist Federation – libertarian socialists who had broken away from the German Social-democratic Party – 100,000 copies were seized by the police. Landauer was murdered by proto-fascists in Munich in May 1919.
http://www.anarchismus.at/texte-antimilitarismus/335-gustav-landauer-die-abschaffung-des-krieges-durch-die-selbstbestimmung-des-volkes

Don't Shoot!
– Fred Bower, British Syndicalist and Socialist

'Men! Comrades! Brothers! You are in the army. So are we. You in the army of destruction. We in the industrial, or army of construction. We work at mine, mill, forge, factory, or dock, producing and transporting all the goods, clothing, and stuffs, which make it possible for people to live. You are working men's sons. When we go on strike to better our lot, which is the lot also of your fathers, mothers, brothers, and sisters, you are called upon by your officers to murder us. Don't do it! You know how it happens. Always has happened. We stand out as long as we can. Then one of our (and your) irresponsible brothers, goaded by the sight and thought of his and his loved ones' misery and hunger, commits a crime on property. Immediately you are ordered to murder us, as you did at Mitchelstown, at Featherstone, at Belfast. Don't you know that when you are out of the colours, and become a "civvy" again, that you, like us, may be on strike, and you, like us, [will] be liable to be murdered by other soldiers. Boys, don't do it! "Thou shalt not kill", says the book. Don't forget that! It does not say, "unless you have a uniform on." No! Murder is murder, whether committed in the heat of anger on one who has wronged a loved one, or by pipe-clayed tommies with a rifle.

Boys, don't do it! Act the man! Act the brother! Act the human being! Property can be replaced! Human life, never! The idle rich class, who own and order you about, own and order us about also. They and their friends own the land and means of life of Britain. You don't! We don't! When we kick, they order you to murder us. When you kick, you get court-martialled and cells. Your fight is our fight. Instead of fighting against each other, we should be fighting with each other. Out of our loins, our lives, our homes, you came. Don't disgrace your parents, your class, by being the willing tools any longer of the master class. You, like us, are of the slave class. When we rise, you rise; when we fall, even by your bullets, ye fall also. England with its fertile valleys and dells, its mineral resources, its sea harvests, is the heritage of ages to us. You no doubt joined the army out of poverty. We work long hours for small wages at hard work, because of our poverty. And both your poverty and ours arises from the fact that Britain with its resources belongs to only a few people. These few, owning Britain, own our jobs. Owning our jobs, they own our very lives. Comrades, have we called in vain? Think things out and refuse any longer to murder your kindred. Help us to win back Britain for the British, and the world for the workers!'

August 1911. This 'Open Letter to British Soldiers' was printed as a leaflet to incite soldiers to refuse orders to break strikes. It was reprinted in the Syndicalist and Socialist press. Several activists and editors were imprisoned for inciting mutiny. Fred Bower wrote an autobiography *Rolling Stonemason*, forthcoming from The Merlin Press.

Strike Against War
– French General Workers' Confederation (CGT)

'Recalling the key elements of these decisions: "Workers should respond without delay with a revolutionary general strike to a declaration of war."

So to prepare for the application of these decisions:

1. A circular letter should be sent by the CGT to each syndicate [union] inviting them, immediately, to prepare members to apply at an opportune moment these decisions

2. Each Federation [of unions] should immediately undertake a search for the best means of accomplishing a general strike in its profession and within its industry

3. Each Bourse du Travail [Trades' Council] each body

[Union] of syndicates, and each isolated syndicate should have within it a General Strike sub-committee – unless the General Committee of that organisation has already taken that task in hand.

The mission of these sub-committees (without derogating the duties of all organisations) should be to intensify anti-militarist and antipatriotic propaganda.

Such propaganda should be directed to peasants, workers, employees and women …'

October 1911, resolution from an extraordinary CGT conference. There had been a mass demonstration of 60,000 in the 19th arrondissement of Paris over the previous weekend. Support for anti-militarist campaigning was somewhat patchy both in France and further afield. The CGT was a member of a trade union international and campaigned there for the general strike as a response to war. Such militancy was opposed by the German Free trade unions – allies of the Social-democratic Party. A general strike was something that the leaders of the German trade union movement refused to contemplate. Karl Legien, secretary of the trade union international, argued that a general strike would be general madness. From: *Le Prolétariat contre la Guerre et les Trois Ans*, CGT Paris: Maison des Fédérations, n.d. 1914?

Against the Italian Tyrant
– Errico Malatesta, Italian Anarchist

'For Italy's honour we hope that the Italian people will come to their senses and will be able to impose on government a withdrawal from Africa; or if not, we hope that the Arabs win and throw them out.'

Italy went to war against Ottoman Turkey in September 1911, seizing Libya and islands in the Aegean. There were protests throughout Italy and hundreds were arrested. From: 'La guerra e gli anarchici', *La Guerra Tripolina;* April 1912.

Defaulters Today, Rebels Tomorrow,
Deserters in the future
– French Anarchist Communist Federation

'The state disposes of everything without consulting us –
our liberties, our very lives – it demands that we should go
off for an apprenticeship with weapons of murder and live
in barracks for two years. Serving whom? Our country –
we don't have one! We weren't even 'electors'. How could
we approve the law of conscription? ... We do not believe
that it is through going passively to barracks that we attain
that end – we want the abolition of militarism, all armies
should disappear. On the contrary, against this attack on
our freedom and with all the energy that we can muster,
we protest! We refuse to give in, we refuse to obey ...'

October 1912; conscripts' group of the Fédération communiste-anarchiste.
A few months earlier an article in *La Vie Ouvrière*, declared: 'We believe
that the head of a band of Apaches, who kills ten bourgeois every year is
less criminal than a general, who coldly and methodically organises the
massacre of millions of men.' 20 May 1912; *La Vie Ouvrière*, No. 64.

Le Sou du Soldat
– French General Labour Confederation (CGT)

'The fact of a worker being forced, for two years, to abandon
workshop, office, field or factory should not in any way
justify the abandoning of his sympathies and affiliations.
Having entered a syndicate to defend his interests and
to improve his life the union [syndicat] has the duty of
proving to him, throughout his two year's absence, the
principle of the spirit of solidarity which inspires it, and
its hope to see him return to it as soon as he is freed from
the barracks. Transported into a new arena, transformed
into a repressive auxiliary of exploitation and capital, the
first priority of this comrade is that he should preserve,
through regular contacts, a clear sense of his duty towards

his exploited comrades, and his elevated conscience should be the most real of obstacles to [playing] the retrograde and brutal role which is expected of him by the exploiting class. Wage earners should remain united and overcome all the hazards of life. As for the army and homeland – no belief, no prejudice – [nothing] should impede fraternal cohesion – not for a moment should anything diminish the burning hope that one day their class should be liberated from capitalist servitude.'

1912(?) The CGT raised funds to support recruits. From: *Le Prolétariat contre la Guerre et les Trois Ans*, CGT Paris: Maison des Fédérations, 1914?

Thesis Three[30] – Robert Grimm, Swiss Social-democrat

'The party protests against the use of soldiers in strikes. As this has in fact occurred on many occasions in recent years, it demands necessary guarantees against the repetition of such abuses. It will organise opposition – by all means at its disposal – against a new military dispensation, so long as such guarantees are lacking. Until these are obtained, if soldiers are ordered to raise arms and attack striking workers, *it will advise them to refuse to obey*. Should need arise, the Social-democratic party will do what it can to alleviate the financial consequences of such acts for isolated defaulting [conscripts] and their families. To this end it will liaise with unions. In the opinion of the party, the best guarantee against troops being used against strikers is provided if the Swiss people having ongoing and systematic information about the modern workers' movement, the destination of armies, the strengthening of unions and political organisations and thus of the political weight of the proletariat in society and in the state. ... Like democracy itself, the militia has become, as a function of capitalist development, an excellent tool in the hands of reactionaries. [...]

It may be possible for a resolute Social-democratic policy to struggle against modern tendencies of military development, to prevent the perfectly abusive use of militias in the interest of capitalists. In that case the phrase – "The introduction of a militia would augment the weight of the forces in politics and the importance that they acquire for all international action would further increase" – may be correct. But one can in no way deduce for Social-democracy that the militia system can represent a universal panacea[31] in the matter of the military. ...'

1912. Social-democrats looked to the Swiss army, with each man having a rifle at home, as a model and contrasted it to the Prussian army officered by landlords. Grimm contended that there was little democracy in the Swiss army. It was quite impossible for a citizen without means to become an officer. To do so required years of expensive military education. The Swiss army was used to break strikes and kill workers, he listed ten occasions between 1869 and 1907. Grimm helped organise the Zimmerwald and Kiental conferences. He was a member of the Olten committee that organised a Swiss general strike and was sentenced to six months imprisonment in 1919. From: A.J. Brossat & J.Y.Potel, *Antimilitarisme et Révolution*, Volume 1, Paris: UGE, 1976, pp. 225-233.

A Good Soldier – North London Herald League

'A good soldier is a blind, heartless machine. At the word of command he will put a bullet in the brain of the bravest and noblest man who [has] ever lived. He respects neither the grey hair of age, nor the weakness of childhood. He is unmoved by tears, by prayers or by argument. He is indifferent to human thought or human feelings. *Don't be a soldier – be a man.*'

1913? Leaflet.

Patriotism and Militarism
– Earl Ford & William Z. Foster, American Socialists
& Industrial Unionists

'The socialist is necessarily a patriot and a militarist. According to his theory, for the workers of a given country to emancipate themselves, they must control their government. Naturally, for this government to have any power, it is necessary that it enjoy political independence. Hence the socialist considers each nation justified in warring on other nations to secure or maintain this independence.[32] The international Socialist Party stands committed to this patriotic policy. This, of course, involves militarism, and socialists the world over are militarists. August Bebel, the German Socialist leader, in his book, *Nicht Stehendes Heer, sondern Volkswehr*[33] urged that, in order to the better defend Germany, every able-bodied male should be a soldier from earliest boyhood to old age. He says school and work boys should be drilled during their spare time, Sundays, evenings, etc. Jaurès, the noted French socialist leader, advocates that the sons of labour union officials be placed in command of the companies of boy soldiers he would organize to defend France. The militarism of various other socialist leaders, such as Ramsay McDonald of England, and Pablo Iglesias of Spain, is notorious.

The syndicalist is a radical anti-patriot. He is a true internationalist, knowing no country. He opposes patriotism because it creates feelings of nationalism among the workers of the various countries and prevents co-operation between them, and also, because of the militarism it inevitably breeds. He views all forms of militarism with a deadly hatred, because he knows from bitter experience that the chief function of modern armies is to break strikes, and that wars of any kind are fatal to the labour movement. He depends solely on his labour unions for protection from foreign and domestic foes alike and proposes to put an end to war between the nations by having the workers in the belligerent countries go on a general strike and thus make it impossible to conduct wars.

This syndicalist method of combating war is looked upon with violent disfavour by the socialists, who consider war a political question and, therefore, no concern of the labour unions. A few years ago, during a Morocco crisis, the CGT[34] sent a delegate to the Socialist labour unions of Germany to organize an anti-war demonstration to propagate the plan of meeting a declaration of war by an international general strike. He was referred to the Socialist Party as having jurisdiction, and thus action on the matter was avoided. At the international Socialist convention, in Copenhagen, 1910, the German Socialist Party delegates successfully opposed a similar proposition on the grounds that the labour unions alone had authority to declare a general strike. Thus the socialist politicians, on one occasion, referred the question to the Socialist Party, and on the other to the labour unions, and in both cases avoided taking action on this momentous question. This is a fair example of socialist perfidy when the interests of the working class conflict with those of the Socialist Party.'

1913. From: Earl C. Ford & William Z Foster, *Syndicalism*, Chicago: W Z Foster, 1913, pp. 29-30. At the time W Z Foster advocated a strategy of radicalising the American Federation of Labour trade unions. After 1918 he became a leader of the Communist Party of the USA. Foster's picture is somewhat black and white – he does not recognise that there were varied forms of socialism and syndicalism.

War in Paterson – John Reed, American Socialist

'There's war in Paterson. But it's a curious kind of war. All the violence is the work of one side – the mill owners. Their servants, the police, club unresisting men and women and ride down law-abiding crowds on horseback. Their paid mercenaries, the armed detectives, shoot and kill innocent people. Their newspapers, the *Paterson Press* and the *Paterson Call*, publish incendiary and crime-inciting appeals to mob-violence against the strike leaders. Their tool, Recorder Carroll, deals out heavy sentences to peaceful pickets that the police-net gathers up. They control absolutely the police, the press, the courts.'

June 1913, New Jersey. Silk workers had gone on strike in February. Thousands joined the Industrial Workers of the World, demanding better conditions and an eight hour day. On 29th March the *Paterson Press* called for new cemeteries – 'the first graves to be filled with Haywood and his crowd.' (Bill Haywood was a popular IWW leader.) Owners hired thugs. Strikers and others were shot and a bystander, Valentino Modestino, was killed. There were 1,850 arrests. The strikers were defeated and returned to work in July. From: *The Masses*, www.marxists.org/archive/reed/1913/masses06.htm

For the Citizen Army
– James Connolly, Irish Socialist and Industrial Unionist

'The Irish Citizen Army was founded during the great Dublin lock-out of 1913-14, for the purpose of protecting the working class, and of preserving its right of public meeting and free association. The streets of Dublin had been covered by the bodies of helpless men, women, boys and girls brutally batoned by the uniformed bullies of the British government. Three men had been killed, and one young Irish girl murdered by a scab, and nothing was done to bring the assassins to justice. So since justice did not exist for us, since the law instead of protecting the rights of the workers was an open enemy, and since the armed forces of the crown were unreservedly at the disposal of the enemies of labour, it was resolved to create our own army to secure our rights, to protect our members, and to be a guarantee of our own free progress. The Irish Citizen Army was the first publicly organised armed citizen force south of the Boyne. Its constitution pledged and still pledges its members to work for an Irish Republic, and for the emancipation of labour. It has ever been foremost in all national work, and whilst never neglecting its own special function has always been at the disposal of the forces of Irish nationality for the ends common to all. Its influence and presence has kept the peace at all labour meetings since its foundation, and the knowledge of its existence and of the spirit of its members has contributed to prevent the employers and the government from proceeding to extremes against the fighting unions. It has in a true and real sense added many shillings per week to the pay of the union members, since it and it alone has prevented the government doing in Dublin what it has done in Barry, namely, send soldiers in to do dockers' work during a strike. Nationally it has done much more.

… An armed organisation of the Irish working class is a phenomenon in Ireland. Hitherto the workers of Ireland have fought as parts of the armies led by their masters, never as members of an army officered, trained, and inspired by men of their own class. Now, with arms in their hands, they propose to steer their own course, to carve their own future. Neither home rule, nor the lack of home rule,[35] will make them lay down their arms. However it may be for others, for us of the Citizen Army there is but one ideal – an Ireland ruled, and owned, by Irish men and women, sovereign and independent from the centre to the sea, and flying its own flag outward over all the oceans. We cannot be swerved from our course by honeyed words, lulled into

carelessness by freedom to parade and strut in uniforms,
nor betrayed by high-sounding phrases. The Irish Citizen
Army will only co-operate in a forward movement. The
moment that forward movement ceases it reserves to
itself the right to step out of the alignment, and advance
by itself if needs be, in an effort to plant the banner of
freedom one reach further towards its goal.'

August 1913; the Dublin lockout and transport strike was a high point in
struggles involving recently formed mass unions on both sides of the Irish
Sea. The Irish Transport workers failed to achieve their objectives and
returned to work in January 1914. From *Workers' Republic*, 30 October
1915. http://www.marxists.org/archive/connolly/1915/10/forca.htm The
Irish Citizen Army, formed to protect the labour movement, may be
contrasted with the Swiss 'Citizen' Army, often used to break strikes.

Should we accept war?
– Rosa Luxemburg, German Social-democrat

'If they expect us to murder our French or other foreign
brothers, then let us tell them, no, under no circumstances!'

25 September 1913; speech in Flechenheim. Luxemburg was sentenced to
a year's imprisonment. In the following year she was also prosecuted for
remarking on the frequent suicides of recruits. In her defence, witnesses
were called who testified that recruits suffered violence – slaps, beatings
or worse – on a daily basis. Embarrassed by such testimony the case was
adjourned to deter further revelations being made.

Onward, Christian Soldiers
– Industrial Workers of the World (USA)

'Onward, Christian Soldiers, march into the war,
Slay your Christian brothers as you've done before.
Plutocratic masters, bid you face the foe,
Men who never harmed you, men you do not know.

Raise the Christian war-whoop, you who love the Lord,
Hearken to your masters, buckle on the sword;
Bombshells, bullets, grapeshot, shower on the foe,
Heed your Christian chaplain, into battle go.

Heed not dying groans from those whom you have slain,
Heed not pleas for mercy, nor the shrieks of pain;
Plunge the sword and dagger through your brothers'
heart,
Never shirk your duty, always do your part.'

December 1913. From: *Voice of the People* (USA).

Red Week – Errico Malatesta

'These events have proved that the mass of people hate
the present order; that the workers are disposed to make
use of all opportunities to overthrow the government;
and that when the fight is directed against the common
enemy – that is to say the government and the bourgeoisie
– all are brothers, though the names of socialist, anarchist,
syndicalist or republican may seem to divide them.'

7 June 1914. Revolt had spread into districts in the vicinity and lasted for
some ten days. From: 'The General Strike and the Insurrection in Italy',
Freedom, July 1914.

Struggling against the Abuse of Soldiers
– Paul Levi, German Social-democrat

'In working to stop the mistreatment of soldiers we are
on the attack against the nerve system (*Lebensnerv*) of the
state. As blind obedience ceases, so too will militarism
and with it the whole state, like a pack of cards. ... The
struggle against the abuse of soldiers is in reality only a
part of our comprehensive struggle for freedom.'

13 July 1914; Frankfurt am Main. Paul Levi acted as Rosa Luxemburg's defence lawyer. From: Paul Levi, *Luxemburg-Prozess und Soldatenmisshandlungen: Rede gehalten am 13. Juli 1914*, Frankfurt (Main): Buchhandlung Volksstimme, 1914. http://library.fes.de/pdf-files/ bibliothek/bestand/a-32266-levi.pdf Levi was conscripted but obtained a medical discharge. He spent three years in Switzerland and supported the new left that emerged in 1918; he died in 1929.

Conference of French General Labour Confederation (CGT)

'Drawing on the strength of CGT Congress resolutions, conference notes that it is the duty of every conscious wage-earner to fight with all passion the extension of militarism – which is contrary to the development of civilization and of the liberation of the working class.'

13 – 15 July 1914. From *Le Prolétariat contre la Guerre et les Trois Ans*, CGT Paris: Maison des Fédérations, 1914?

Mere Cant – John Maclean, British Socialist

'It is mere cant to talk of German militarism when Britain has led the world in the navy business.'

26 September 1914. From: *Forward* (Glasgow).

Above the Battle – Romain Rolland, French Pacifist

'As for the representatives of the Prince of Peace – priests, pastors, bishops – they go into battle by the thousand, rifle in hand, carrying out God's command: *Thou shalt not kill*, and *Love one another*.'

22 September 1914. This text 'Au-dessus de la mêlée' was published in the *Journal de Genève* and caused a sensation in France. Rolland – a Frenchman later awarded a Nobel Prize for literature – noted that the press was envenomed by a minority vitally interested in engendering hate. He highlighted the failure of Christianity and Socialism, both were

promoting nationalism. 20,000 French priests were marching with the colours. Each nation has its own national God. The full text, in copyright in much of Europe as we go to press, is available in French on http://fr.wikisource.org/wiki/Au-dessus_de_la_m%C3%AAl%C3%A9e/Au-dessus_de_la_m%C3%AAl%C3%A9e An English language edition: *Above the Battle*, London: Allen & Unwin, 1916; can be found on http://www.gutenberg.org/ebooks/32779

The War and our immediate Tasks
– Alexandra Kollontai, Russian Social-democrat

'The war has shown us that the workers' party made a great mistake in underestimating the danger of militarism and offering too weak a resistance to its influence. The principled position of the Social-democratic parties on the question of how the workers are to behave in case of war was too ill-defined, too imprecise. The resolutions adopted by the International worked to the benefit of nationalist trends. Now, however, when German Social-democracy has allowed itself to be fooled by the Prussian Junker state and is pursuing a mistaken tactic in support of war, it has become clear that it will be the duty of the future International to state its position on this issue clearly and precisely and to determine upon a firm, clearly defined revolutionary tactic as regards the threat of war. There can be no doubt that, as soon as this dreadful war is over, all the workers' parties will have the task of mounting a campaign against militarism.'

November 1914; from http://www.marxistsfr.org/archive/kollonta/1914/wartime.htm Kollontai became a Bolshevik in the course of the war, and was a Commissar in the new state created after the October 1917 revolution.

War on War
– War on War League, Cape Town
(Wilfred Henry Harrison)

'It is today *not* murder, it is war! So let us give it the necessary analysis and for the moment cast aside sentiment. Picture the "hero" glorified and awarded the Victoria or Iron Cross in the mêlée that brought him his fame. The reports of the pistol, the clash of the sword, the dying moans of those whom he has slain, and over whom he stands a maddened and excited victor bespattered in human blood. The heads of mothers' sons and children's fathers lie at his feet, their blood and brains besmear the ground, while in a dark garret today these mothers and children mourn with bitter tears their loss that has been his fame. These and other gruesome deeds are demanded of you who respond to the ironical call of "your country needs you!" Truly it does! In your country there is always unemployment, high rents and dear goods, there is always bad housing and starvation there is squalor and filth in home and factory, there is poverty and starvation. So *your* country needs you! And yet in your country there are factories filled with goods eaten with moth and decay, and there are palaces and mansions in which a superfluity of luxury abounds.

Yes! *your* country needs *you*. Are you prepared to fight for your country and help to bring wealth, happiness and peace with *all* people.'

The War on War League attracted thousands of people to meetings. Harrison was jailed for disseminating this leaflet.
Wilfred Harrison, *Memoirs of a Socialist in South Africa 1903–47*, Cape Town: Stewart Printing, 1947?

Anti-War ballad
– Alfred Bryan, Canadian/American songwriter

'I didn't raise my boy to be a soldier,
I brought him up to be my pride and joy.
Who dares to place a musket on his shoulder,
To shoot some other mother's darling boy?'

1915; an American song that became popular in Britain, the Caribbean and Australia.

British Militarism – Bruce Glasier, British Socialist

'[I]s it not an ominous circumstance that in order to destroy German militarism in Germany we should be adopting something closely akin to German militarism at home? For observe, it is not in external appearance only that our country is becoming Prussianised in this way. …

Militarism is not the outcome of the "will-to-power" notions of a few or many army leaders, nor, as I have said, is it peculiar to the army profession. It is a system of thought and feeling which grows out of class traditions and interests. It is always there, latent or active. "Prussianism", as I think Mr. Norman Angell puts it, "is not a geographical expression, but a state of mind." And though the sentiments I have quoted may not be always entertained by army men, they are sentiments nevertheless which express, I believe, the inherent spirit of what we term the military "caste" and the ruling classes.'

From: J. Bruce Glasier, *Militarism*, London: Independent Labour Party, 1915, pp. 2, 29.

Militarism – James Connolly

'Every day gives fresh proof of the gravity of the danger facing the workers of this country from the ever-increasing power of the military. In Belfast the military have been employed to do ordinary labouring work at salvaging in the docks. One of the docks was the scene of a great fire, and members of the Irish Transport and General Workers' Union were afterwards employed to do the salvage work in sorting out the burnt goods and rescuing any material that could be saved. As these men naturally held out for proper wages they were informed one day last week that they would have to go, and next morning they found the military in their place. The soldiers did not want the job. They had not enlisted to scab upon their brother workers, but they found out that what they fancied they had enlisted for, and what they were really used for were two different things. Would it be a fair question to ask if such military interference with labour does not do more to discourage recruiting than all the anti-militarist speeches we could deliver? In Barrow, in Glasgow, on the Tyne, in short in every great industrial centre, the same tale is being told. All trade union rights are assailed, all trade union liberties are denied, the working class is everywhere menaced by an unscrupulous master class in alliance with a military power in the hands of men who have grown up in hatred of democracy, and with a contempt for the class from which the private soldiers are drawn. More than ever it is necessary for labour to spring to arms in defence of its birth-right.'

21 August 1915. A quarter of a million Irishmen volunteered to serve in British forces. James Connolly would have said they had made a wrong choice. From: *Workers' Republic*, http://www.marxists.org/archive/connolly/1915/08/militarism.htm

Inhumanity – Olive Schreiner, South African Radical

'The militarism, the spirit of hate and inhumanity which affects all people who have lived through a war, are much worse than the fighting and dying.'

January 1915. From 'Olive Schreiner to Edward Carpenter, lines 15-16, National English Literary Museum, Grahamstown, Olive Schreiner Letters Project transcription'. Copyright transcription: © Olive Schreiner Letters Project.

Woman must have every country!
– Charles K. Ogden & Mary Sargant Florence,
British Radicals

'Militarism has been their curse for centuries; its ideals have ever stood in the way of women's rights. ... It must always produce an androcentric society, a society where the moral and social position of women is that of an essentially servile and subordinate section of the community.'

April 1915. Some feminists looked to women to oppose militarism, and to obstruct armament and conscription; for the future they hoped to see an international community pledged to work for co-operation and understanding. From: C. K. Ogden & Mary Sargant Florence, *Militarism versus Feminism, An Enquiry and a Policy*, London: Allen & Unwin, 1915, p.3,   64;   http://digital.library.upenn.edu/women/florence/feminism/feminism.html

French State Censorship – Jean Grave, French Libertarian

'The public has been treated as an infant in France, or as an idiot incapable of managing its own affairs. Censorship – supposed to have been directed only towards whatever concerned military operations, inasmuch as it might furnish information for the enemy – has been extended to every field of thought. It is not only forbidden to research into how the war might have been avoided, but there is also a prohibition in place against discussion of opinions as to what the details of any future peace should be.'

October 1915. An earlier iteration of this article was censored, even though Grave sided with Kropotkin calling for support for the war. From: *La Libre Fédération*, 'La censure et la guerre'.

Down with Conscription! – Liberty Press, Oxford

'Resist Prussianism! Men and Women Workers! – The government are conspiring to rob you of what little freedom you have left. The Defence of the Realm Act deprived you of freedom of speech, and the Munitions Act deprived you of the legal right to get better wages or even to leave your employer for a better job. Your brothers, your husbands, your sweethearts, have shed their blood, as they supposed, to protect our liberties and crush Prussian militarism. Your rulers are now trying to crush you with British militarism.

In South Wales, on the Clyde, and in many other places discontent is rampant among your fellow workers, but the government will not allow the press to give you the facts. Now they are demanding conscription, so as to put the chains more firmly on your necks. They do not want conscription so much to end the war as to make workshop slaves of you by putting you under military control. This will rob you of your last remnant of freedom. To prevent this you must act at once. Be fearless in opposing it, you will not stand alone, as the great mass of workers are ready to resist.

Down with conscription! Married or single, attested or unattested! If the compulsory service bill becomes law, down tools.'

1915, Anti-conscription leaflet.

Christmas

'On Christmas morning one of the Germans came out of a trench and held up his hands. Then lots of us did the same, and we met half-way, and for the rest of the day we fraternized, exchanging cigars, cigarettes, and souvenirs. The Germans also gave us sausages, and we gave them some of our food. The Scotsmen then started the bagpipes, and we had a rare old jollification, which included football, in which the Germans took part. The Germans said they were tired of the war, and wished it was over. Next day we got an order that all communication and friendly intercourse must cease.'

Christmas 1915. Quoted in: Edward Carpenter, *The Healing of Nations and the hidden sources of their strife,* New York: Charles Scribner's Sons, 1915, pp. 262-5. Some soldiers were surprised to find that the other side was also fighting for peace and civilization! 'Among those who took part in this memorable meeting was Herbie Bell, a lifelong socialist from Wallsend. He describes how both British and German soldiers said they were heartily sick of the war and realised it was not being fought in their interests but on behalf of the rich.' Raymond Challinor, *The Origins of British Bolshevism,* London: Croom Helm, p. 142. It was not uncommon on quiet sectors of the front for both sides to agree to 'live and let live'. Adam Hochschild, *To End All Wars,* London: Pan Macmillan, 2012, p. 172.

What is to be done? – Alexandra Kollontai

'The war had not yet ended, indeed its end was still not in sight, but the number of cripples was multiplying: the armless, the legless, the blind, the deaf, the mutilated... They had set off for the bloody world slaughter-house young, strong, healthy. Their life still lay ahead of them. Only a few months, weeks, even days later, they were brought back to the infirmaries half dead, crippled ... "Heroes," say those who started a European war, who sent one people out against another, the worker from one country out against his fellow worker from another. At least now they have won an award! They will be able to walk around wearing their medals! People will respect them! However, in real life things are different. The "hero" comes home to his native village or town, and when he arrives he cannot believe his eyes: in place of "respect" and joy he finds waiting for him fresh sufferings and disillusionment. His village has been reduced to poverty and starvation. The menfolk were dragged off to war, the livestock requisitioned … Taxes must be paid, and there is no one to do the work. The women have been run off their feet. They are haggard and starved, worn out with weeping. Cripple-heroes wander about the village, some with one medal, some with two. And the only "respect" the hero gets is to hear his own family reproach him as a parasite who eats the bread of others. And the bread is rationed!

The "hero" who returns to the town fares no better. He is met with "respect", his mother weeps from both grief and joy: her darling son is still alive, her ageing mother's eyes have beheld him once again. His wife smiles … For a day or two they will fuss around him. And then …

Since when do working people have the time, the leisure, to look after an invalid? Each has his own affairs, his own worries. Moreover, times are difficult. Not a day passes but the cost of living rises.'

1916. Alexandra Kollontai wrote that on both sides people had been deceived, on both sides the main enemy was in the rear – guns should be turned on the real, common enemy. 'If we want peace, we have to put those who started the war on trial. Let everyone struggle in his own country against our oppressors, let's clear the country of the true enemies of people: tsars, kings, emperors…' From: 'Who needs War?' an anti-war pamphlet published in German and Russian, in huge numbers.

http://www.marxists.org/archive/kollonta/1915/whoneeds.htm   See also: Cathy Porter, *Alexandra Kollontai: A Biography*, Pontypool: Merlin Press, 2013, p. 209.

Official Report on Wilhelm Wechner,
a German syndicalist

'In front of the assembled company he declared to his captain, that he would not do this; he had had already said to him, that he would not allow himself to be trained as a killer of men, and he would rather prefer that he should be arrested. He was then led back to his barracks by the corporals and shortly after, without permission, he left his unit and after six days was arrested in Schweinfurt. In the course of investigations he was asked what his reply to the charges was, he again replied he had another world-view to other people, he was an anarchist, he did not recognise compulsion, [but] only freedom ....'

1916. Quoted in Helge Döhring, *Syndikalismus in Deutschland 1914-1918*, Lich (Hessen), 2013, p. 133.

Truth and the War – Edmund Dene Morel, British Pacifist

'For years they had shared a common conviction that Europe's statesmen were drifting to a catastrophe which, if it eventuated, would overwhelm mankind. In their several ways they had endeavoured to rouse public opinion to the terrible gravity of the situation; and they had failed. The monster of militarism had mastered the diplomats whose tortuous evolutions and medieval proceedings had done so much to create it. The peoples – dominated by fear and panic, neither informed nor consulted – had been whirled, after a few short weeks of confused and secret negotiations between their rulers, into a maelstrom of passions and mutual slaughter.'

1916. By 1917 the UDC had 10,000 individual members and some half a million affiliated members.[36]

Repeal the Act – No-Conscription Fellowship

'*Fellow citizens*: Conscription is now law in this country of free traditions. Our hard-won liberties have been violated. Conscription means the desecration of principles that we have long held dear; it involves the subordination of civil liberties to military dictation; it imperils the freedom of individual conscience and establishes in our midst that militarism which menaces all social graces and divides the peoples of all nations.

We re-affirm our determined resistance to all that is established by the Act.

We cannot assist in warfare. War, which to us is wrong. War, which the peoples do not seek, will only be made impossible when men, who so believe, remain steadfast to their convictions. Conscience, it is true, has been recognised in the Act, but it has been placed at the mercy of tribunals. We are prepared to answer for our faith before any tribunal, but we cannot accept any exemption that would compel those who hate war to kill by proxy or set them to tasks which would help in the furtherance of war.

We strongly condemn the monstrous assumption by parliament that a man is deemed to be bound by an oath that he has never taken and forced under an authority he will never acknowledge to perform acts which outrage his deepest convictions. It is true that the present act applies only to a small section of the community, but a great tradition has been sacrificed. Already there is a clamour for an extension of the act. Admit the principle, and who can stay the march of militarism?

Repeal the Act. That is your only safeguard.

If this be not done, militarism will fasten its iron grip upon our national life and institutions. There will be imposed upon us the very system which statesmen affirm that they set out to overthrow.

What shall it profit the nation if it shall win the war and lose its own soul?'

May 1916; the signatories were Clifford Allen, Edward Grubb, A Fenner Brockway, W J Chamberlain, W H Ayles, Morgan Jones, A Barratt Brown, John Fletcher, C H Norman and Rev. Leyton Richards. Officers of the No-Conscription Fellowship were charged under the Defence of the

Realm Act for conduct 'likely to prejudice the recruiting and discipline of His Majesty's forces'. They were all fined £100 – or faced 61 days imprisonment; some who refused to pay and were sent to prison. This text was later republished by the *Manchester Guardian*. The state announced that those who were refused the status of conscientious objectors would be deemed to have been conscripted anyway. It was believed that anyone who disobeyed orders in France could be shot. In the USA members of the southern Churches of Christ and Mennonites, as well as Quakers, resisted conscription.

Thrilled – Arthur Horner, Welsh Socialist

'As a small nationality ourselves, we had watched with sympathy the Irish people's fight for independence long before the Great War broke out. When war came we were told the fighting in France was for the rights of small nations . . . So it is easy to understand how we, who had seen the viciousness of the coal-owners, regarded what was happening in Ireland as the real struggle for the rights of small nations in a war-torn world. We were thrilled by the Easter Rising in 1916 and saddened by its defeat.'

Horner volunteered to work for the Irish Citizen Army in Dublin. He was sentenced to six months imprisonment when he returned to Britain, and South Wales miners campaigned for his release. In later life he joined the Communist Party and became a leader of the National Union of Mineworkers. See Nina Fishman: *Arthur Horner: A Political biography*, Volume 1: 1894-1944, London: Lawrence and Wishart, 2010.

Condemning War
– Industrial Workers of the World, USA

'We, the industrial workers of the world, in convention assembled, hereby reaffirm our adherence to the principles of industrial unionism, and re-dedicate ourselves to the unflinching prosecution of the struggle for the abolition of wage slavery, and the realization of our ideals in industrial democracy. With the European war for conquest and exploitation raging and destroying the lives, class consciousness, and unity of the workers, and the ever-growing agitation for military preparedness clouding the main issues, and delaying the realization of our ultimate aim with patriotic, and, therefore, capitalistic aspirations, we openly declare ourselves determined opponents of all nationalistic sectionalism or patriotism, and the militarism preached and supported by our one enemy, the capitalist class. We condemn all wars, and, for the prevention of such, we proclaim the anti-militarist propaganda in time of peace, thus promoting class solidarity among the workers of the entire world, and, in time of war, the general strike in all industries. We extend assurances of both moral and material support to all the workers who suffer at the hands of the capitalist class for their adhesion to the principles, and call on all workers to unite themselves with us, that the reign of the exploiters may cease and this earth be made fair through the establishment of industrial democracy.'

November 1916. From: IWW, Official Proceedings of the 1916 Convention, p. 138.

On the slogan of disarmament
– V.I. Lenin, Russian Social-democrat

'An oppressed class which does not strive to learn to use arms, to acquire arms, only deserves to be treated like slaves. We cannot, unless we have become bourgeois pacifists or opportunists, forget that we are living in a class society from which there is no way out, nor can there be, save through the class struggle and the overthrow of the power of the ruling class. In every class society, whether based on slavery, serfdom, or, as at present, on wage-labour, the oppressor class is always armed. Not only

the modern standing army, but even the modern militia
– and even in the most democratic bourgeois republics,
Switzerland, for instance – represent the bourgeoisie
armed against the proletariat. That is such an elementary
truth that it is hardly necessary to dwell upon it. Suffice it
to recall that in all capitalist countries without exception
troops (including the republican-democratic militia) are
used against strikers. A bourgeoisie armed against the
proletariat is one of the biggest, fundamental and cardinal
facts of modern capitalist society.

And in face of this fact, revolutionary Social-
democrats are urged to "demand" "disarmament"! That
is tantamount to complete abandonment of the class-
struggle point of view, to renunciation of all thought of
revolution. Our slogan must be: arming of the proletariat
to defeat, expropriate and disarm the bourgeoisie. These
are the only tactics possible for a revolutionary class, tactics
that follow logically from, and are dictated by, the whole
objective development of capitalist militarism. Only after
the proletariat has disarmed the bourgeoisie will it be able,
without betraying its world-historic mission, to consign
all armaments to the scrap-heap. And the proletariat
will undoubtedly do this, but only when this condition
has been fulfilled, certainly not before. If the present war
arouses among the reactionary Christian socialists, among
the whimpering petty bourgeoisie, only horror and fright,
only aversion to all use of arms, to bloodshed, death, etc.,
then we must say: capitalist society is and has always been
horror without end. And if this most reactionary of all
wars is now preparing for that society an end in horror, we
have no reason to fall into despair. But the disarmament
"demand", or more correctly, the dream of disarmament,
is, objectively, nothing but an expression of despair at a
time when, as everyone can see, the bourgeoisie itself is
paving the way for the only legitimate and revolutionary

war – civil war against the imperialist bourgeoisie. A lifeless theory, some might say, but we would remind them of two world-historical facts: the role of the trusts and the employment of women in industry, on the one hand, and the Paris Commune of 1871 and the December 1905 uprising in Russia, on the other.

The bourgeoisie makes it its business to promote trusts, drive women and children into the factories, subject them to corruption and suffering, condemns them to extreme poverty. We do not "demand" such development, we do not "support" it. We fight it. But how do we fight? We explain that trusts and the employment of women in industry are progressive. We do not want a return to the handicraft system, pre-monopoly capitalism, domestic drudgery for women. Forward through the trusts, etc., and beyond them to socialism! That argument takes account of objective development and, with the necessary changes, applies also to the present militarisation of the population. Today the imperialist bourgeoisie militarises the youth as well as the adults; tomorrow it may begin militarising the women. Our attitude should be: All the better! Full speed ahead! For the faster we move, the nearer shall we be to the armed uprising against capitalism. How can Social-democrats give way to fear of the militarisation of the youth, etc., if they have not forgotten the example of the Paris Commune? This is not a "lifeless theory" or a dream. It is a fact. And it would be a sorry state of affairs indeed if, all the economic and political facts notwithstanding, Social-democrats began to doubt that the imperialist era and imperialist wars must inevitably bring about a repetition of such facts. A certain bourgeois observer of the Paris Commune, writing to an English newspaper in May 1871, said: "If the French nation consisted entirely of women, what a terrible nation it would be!" Women and teenage children fought in the Paris Commune side by side with the men. It will be no different in the coming battles for the overthrow of the bourgeoisie. Proletarian women will not look on passively as poorly armed or unarmed workers are shot down by the well-armed forces of the bourgeoisie. They will take to arms, as they did in 1871, and from the cowed nations of today – or more correctly, from the present-day labour movement, disorganised more by the opportunists than by the governments – there will undoubtedly arise, sooner or later, but with absolute certainty, an international league of the "terrible nations" of the revolutionary proletariat.

The whole of social life is now being militarised. Imperialism is a fierce struggle of the great powers for the division and re-division of the world. It is therefore bound to lead to further militarisation in all countries, even in neutral and small ones.

How will proletarian women oppose this? Only by cursing all war and everything military, only by demanding disarmament? The women of an oppressed and really revolutionary class will never accept that shameful role. They will say to their sons:

You will soon be grown up. You will be given a gun. Take it and learn the military art properly. The proletarians need this knowledge not to shoot your brothers, the workers of other countries, as is being done in the present war, and as the traitors to socialism are telling you to do. They need it to fight the bourgeoisie of their own country, to put an end to exploitation, poverty and war, and not by pious wishes, but by defeating and disarming the bourgeoisie.

If we are to shun such propaganda, precisely such propaganda, in connection with the present war, then we had better stop using fine words about international revolutionary Social-democracy, the socialist revolution and war against war. The disarmament advocates object to the "armed nation" clause in the programme also because it more easily leads, they allege, to concessions to opportunism. The cardinal point, namely, the relation of disarmament to the class struggle and to the social revolution, we have examined above. We shall now examine the relation between the disarmament demand and opportunism. One of the chief reasons why it is unacceptable is precisely that, together with the illusions it creates, it inevitably weakens and devitalises our struggle against opportunism.

Undoubtedly, this struggle is the main, immediate question now confronting the International. Struggle against imperialism that is not closely linked with the struggle against opportunism is either an empty phrase or a fraud. One of the main defects of Zimmerwald and Kiental – one of the main reasons why these embryos of the Third International may possibly end in a fiasco – is that the question of fighting opportunism was not even raised openly, let alone solved in the sense of proclaiming the need to break with the opportunists. Opportunism has triumphed – temporarily – in the European labour movement. Its two main shades are apparent in all the big countries: first, the avowed, cynical, and therefore less dangerous social-imperialism of Messrs. Plekhanov, Scheidemann, Legien, Albert Thomas and Sembat, Vandervelde, Hyndman, Henderson, et al.; second, the concealed, Kautskyite opportunism: Kautsky[37]-Haase and the Social-democratic labour group in Germany; Longuet, Pressemane, Mayéras et al., in France; Ramsay MacDonald and the other leaders of the Independent Labour Party in England; Martov, Chkheidze, et al., in Russia; Treves and the other so-called Left reformists in Italy. Avowed opportunism is openly and directly opposed to revolution and to incipient revolutionary movements and outbursts. It is in direct alliance with the governments, varied as the forms of this alliance may be – from accepting ministerial posts to participation in the war industries committees. The masked opportunists, the Kautskyites, are much more harmful and dangerous to the labour movement, because they hide their advocacy of alliance with the former under a cloak of plausible, pseudo-"Marxist" catchwords and pacifist slogans. The fight against both these forms of prevailing opportunism must be conducted in all fields of proletarian politics: parliament, the trade unions, strikes, the armed forces, etc.

What is the main distinguishing feature of both these forms of prevailing opportunism? It is that the concrete question of the connection between the present war and revolution, and the other concrete questions of revolution, are hushed up, concealed, or treated with an eye to police prohibitions. And this despite the fact that before the war the connection between this impending war and the proletarian revolution was emphasised innumerable times, both unofficially, and officially in the Basel Manifesto.[38] The main defect of the disarmament demand is its evasion of all the concrete questions of revolution. Or do the advocates of disarmament stand for an altogether new kind of revolution, unarmed revolution?

To proceed. We are by no means opposed to the fight for reforms. And we do not wish to ignore the sad possibility – if the worst comes to the worst – of mankind going through a second imperialist war, if revolution does not come out of the present war, in spite of the numerous out bursts of mass unrest and mass discontent and in spite of our efforts. We favour a programme of reforms directed also against the opportunists. They would be only too glad if we left the struggle for reforms entirely to them and sought escape from sad reality in a nebulous "disarmament" fantasy. "Disarmament" means simply running away from unpleasant reality, not fighting it.

Incidentally, certain Lefts fail to give a sufficiently

concrete answer on the defence of the fatherland issue, and that is a major defect of their attitude. Theoretically, it is much more correct, and in practice immeasurably more important, to say that in the present imperialist war defence of the fatherland is a bourgeois-reactionary deception, than to take a "general" stand against defence of the fatherland under "all" circumstances. That is wrong and, besides, does not "strike" at the opportunists, those direct enemies of the workers in the labour parties. In working out a concrete and practically necessary answer on the question of a militia we should say: we are not in favour of a bourgeois militia; we are in favour only of a proletarian militia. Therefore, "not a penny, not a man", not only for a standing army, but even for a bourgeois militia, even in countries like the United States, or Switzerland, Norway, etc. The more so that in the freest republican countries (e. g., Switzerland) we see that the militia is being increasingly Prussianised, and prostituted by being used against strikers. We can demand popular election of officers, abolition of all military law, equal rights for foreign and native-born workers (a point particularly important for those imperialist states which, like Switzerland, are more and more blatantly exploiting larger numbers of foreign workers, while denying them all rights). Further, we can demand the right of every hundred, say, inhabitants of a given country to form voluntary military-training associations, with free election of instructors paid by the state, etc. Only under these conditions could the proletariat acquire military training for itself and not for its slave-owners; and the need for such training is imperatively dictated by the interests of the proletariat. The Russian revolution showed that every success of the revolutionary movement, even a partial success like the seizure of a certain city, a certain factory town, or winning over a certain section of the army, inevitably compels the victorious proletariat to carry out just such a programme.

Lastly, it stands to reason that opportunism can never be defeated by mere programmes; it can only be defeated by deeds. The greatest, and fatal, error of the bankrupt Second International was that its words did not correspond to its deeds, that it cultivated the habit of unscrupulous revolutionary phrase-mongering (note the present attitude of Kautsky and Co. towards the Basel Manifesto).'

December 1916. The positions taken by the anti-war conferences in Zimmerwald and Kiental are addressed in the third section below. From: Lenin *Collected Works*: Volume 23, Moscow: Progress Publishers, 1964, pp. 94-104. http://www.marxists.org/archive/lenin/works/1916/oct/01. htm

I love my arms and legs – Anonymous

'I love my flag, I do, I do, which floats upon the breeze.
I also love my arms and legs, and neck and nose and knees.
One little shell might spoil them all or give them such a twist,
They would be of no use to me; I guess I won't enlist.

I love my country, yes, I do; I hope her folks do well.
Without our arms and legs and things, I think we'd look like hell.
Young men with faces half shot off are unfit to be kissed,
I've read in books it spoils their looks; I guess I won't enlist.'

14 April 1917. From *Industrial Worker*, (USA). Another IWW argued: 'Why be a soldier? Be a man join the IWW and fight on the job for yourself and your class. A policeman is a pumpkin a soldier a boil on the body politic both the — of a diseased system. A soldier is the man behind the gun, but the man behind the man behind the gun is to blame for war.'

Power in Kronstadt

'From now on power in the city of Kronstadt is located only in the hands of the Soviet of workers' and soldiers' deputies, which for affairs concerning the whole country places itself in contact with the provisional government. All administrative posts in the city of Kronstadt will be taken by members of the executive committee and therefore the latter will be proportionately augmented by new members taken from the Soviet's deputies. Administrative post will be distributed proportionally amongst the various political fractions, and the latter will be responsible for the activities of their representatives.'

26 May 1917. The sailors of this Russian naval base, some twenty miles west of St Petersburg, were at the forefront of the Russian revolution. They were the first to insist on the removal of the imperial shoulder insignia from military uniforms. Here they are asserting their solidarity, and the authority of their soviet (council). Resolution adopted by 211 members, with 41 against and one abstention. From: Ida Mett, *La Commune de Cronstadt, crépuscule sanglant des soviets*, Paris: Spartacus, 1977, pp. 23-4.

Defiance – Siegfried Sassoon, British Army Officer

'I am making this statement as an act of wilful defiance of military authority, because I believe that the war is being deliberately prolonged by those who have the power to end it. I am a soldier, convinced that I am acting on behalf of soldiers. I believe that this war, on which I entered as a war of defence and liberation, has now become a war of aggression and conquest. I believe that the purpose for which I and my fellow soldiers entered upon this war should have been so clearly stated as to have made it impossible to change them, and that, had this been done, the objects which actuated us would now be attainable by negotiation. I have seen and endured the sufferings of the troops, and I can no longer be a party to prolong these sufferings for ends which I believe to be evil and unjust. I am not protesting against the conduct of the war, but against the political errors and insincerities for which the fighting men are being sacrificed. On behalf of those who are suffering now I make this protest against the deception which is being practised on them; also I believe that I may help to destroy the callous complacency with which the majority of those at home regard the contrivance of agonies which they do not, and which they have not sufficient imagination to realize.'

Summer 1917. Sassoon was a Lieutenant in the 3rd Battalion, Royal Welsh Fusiliers; he spent some time on sick leave and later returned to the front. From *Workers' Dreadnought*.

Rebel Now – Green Corn Rebellion, Eastern Oklahoma

'Now is the time to rebel against this war with Germany, boys. Boys, get together and don't go. "Rich man's war. Poor man's fight".[39] The war is over with Germany if you don't go and J.P. Morgan & Co. is lost. Their great speculation is the only cause of the war. Rebel now.'

August 1917. The USA's draft laws had impacted heavily on poor workers, many of them were drafted whilst rich folks were given exemptions. Thousands gathered with weapons, in Sasakwa, at the farm of John Spears in opposition to the war – poor white farmers (many with mortgages) and agricultural workers – some members of the Working Class Union[40]. They hoped for support from the Industrial Workers of the World and from other anti-war groups. Later some hid in backwoods to avoid conscription. Three people were killed and hundreds were arrested. 150 persons were sentenced, some to ten years of imprisonment.[41] See also http://monthlyreview.org/2010/11/01/dreams-of-revolution-oklahoma-1917

Revolt in Turin

'Take your rifles and throw them to the ground,
We want peace, we want peace.
We want peace, and no more war.
Take your knapsacks and throw them to the ground,
We are brothers, we are brothers
We are brothers, we want no more war.'

August 1917. A mass protest erupted in Turin in. Speculators were making huge profits, wages were not keeping up with the cost of living. Women led protests and demanded bread. Anti-war songs were sung, demanding peace. The police fired on civilians. Workers came out on strike. Working-class districts were barricaded, but workers had few arms. The city centre was occupied by the army. Some soldiers had no stomach for fighting civilians. Over forty civilians and ten members of the armed forces were killed in three days of protests. To quell these troubles a thousand workers were mobilised, and 300 were sent to army punishment battalions; 822 arrests were made. News of these events was censored. The editor of the Socialist paper *L'Avanti*, Giacinto Menotti Serrati, was convicted as an 'accessory' to this revolt, and was sentenced in a military court to three years imprisonment.

Enough! – Anarchist leaflet, Turin

'Bring the rifles you make onto the streets and the barricades. Let all the forces of the proletariat rise up and arm themselves. Let's put an end, by force of arms, to the systematic destruction of the human race. Proletarians! Raise now your axes, your picks, your barricades, the social revolution! Proletarian soldiers, desert! If you must fight, let it be against those who oppress you! Your enemy is not at the so-called border, but here. Proletarian women, rise up! Stop your loved ones going off [to war]! Let it be you, worker of the factory or in the field, conscious and strong, let it be you who throws down your tools and cries: Enough! No more! We workers no longer wish to make rifles which bring death to our brothers in struggle and in suffering.'

August 1917. From: G. Cerrito, *Un trentennio di attività anarchica 1914-45*, Cesena: L'antistato, 1953, p. 18; http://www.fdca.it/fdcaen/press/pamphlets/sla-3/1.htm After December 1915 leave from the front was unobtainable; it had been found that soldiers granted leave of absence often failed to return.

Coercion – Laurence O'Neill, Lord Mayor of Dublin

'In the fourth year of a war ostensibly begun for the defence of small nations, a law conscribing the manhood of Ireland has been passed, in defiance of the wishes of our people … no recourse was had to the electorate of Britain, much less to that in Ireland. Yet the measure was forced through within a week, despite the votes of Irish representatives and under a system of closure never applied to the debates, which established conscription for Great Britain on a milder basis.'

11 June 1918. From a letter to the President of the United States, Woodrow Wilson. The extension of conscription to Ireland had been condemned at a conference at Dublin's Mansion House for failing to recognise 'Ireland's separate and distinct nationality'[42] and the principle 'that the government of nations derive their just powers from the consent of the governed'. The British government had no right 'to impose compulsory service in Ireland against the expressed will of the Irish people'… conscription should 'be regarded as a declaration of war on the Irish Nation'. The British government ordered the arrest of nationalist activists. A massive general strike broke out on 23 April 1918.

Threatening bodies and souls – *An t-Óglách*

The government of a foreign nation, occupying our country by force of arms, not content with its usual plundering and oppression now proposes to inflict upon the manhood of Ireland a fate worse than death …'

14 September 1918. *An t-Óglách* was the paper of the Irish volunteers (later the Irish Republican Army), and campaigned against conscription.[43] From: http://www.militaryarchives.ie/collections/online-collections/an-

toglach-magazine For a description of paramilitary organising in these times see: Ernie O'Malley, *On Another Man's Wound*, Dublin: Anvil, 1979, p. 79ff.

A Suggestion (to our artists) – *Firth Worker*, No. 14

'Paint two vast heaps of mildewed human skulls
In pyramidal shape, with top depressed,
Two islands in a blood-red lake where hulls
Of stately ships rust-anchored rest;
Beyond in middle distance withered trees,
And blasted cloisters of some abbey proud
Through which trails, ghost-like, in the hidden breeze,
Black sulphurous smoke in semblance of a shroud.

Upon each pyramid a monarch stand,
Garbed in imperial robes of purple hue,
Each gripping firm the other by the hand
And whispering, Cousin, we have seen it through.
In distant background let fat vultures tear
Dead flesh from bones that seem from earth to spring,
And let your masterpiece this title bear
In letters deathly black – God save the King!'

1918. Quoted in: Bill Moore, 'Sheffield Shop Stewards 1916-1918', *Our History*, London: CPGB, 1960. Such contempt led to the suppression of the paper.

Kiel Mutiny – Hopes and Demands

'The first victory is won, the first trench is taken … in the last few days the goal of old leaders in the struggle, Marx and Lasalle has come a thousand years nearer to us than in a century of effort… come, men and women, all of you to an grand mass meeting, come all, all! The people are with us. Long live liberty! …

[The mutiny had immediate demands:]

1. Release of all detainees and political prisoners.

2. Complete freedom of speech and of the press.

3. Abolition of censorship of letters and mail.

4. Superiors to have proper relations with crews.

5. Collective amnesty from punishment for comrades returning to ships and barracks.

6. Whatever the circumstances may be, the fleet is to be prevented from leaving port.

7. Defence measures causing bloodshed are to be prevented.

8. Withdrawal of all troops not belonging to the garrison.

9. The Soldiers' Council will decide immediately on all measures for the protection of private property.

10. Superiors, if not on duty, will no longer be recognized.

11. All men to have unlimited personal freedom, from the end of a watch until the start of their next period of duty.

12. Officers who make plain their agreement with the measures of the present Soldiers' Council are to be welcome amongst us. All others are to resign from service without entitlement to support.

13. All members of the Soldiers' Council are released from all duties.

14. In future, measures and regulations may be enacted only with the consent of the Soldiers' Council.'

5 November 1918. Mutinies erupted in Kiel and spread to other ports. Sailors refused to obey orders, battleships hoisted red flags. Some sailors had wider goals. For some time socialists had been organising in secret; now they greeted each other in public with 'Long live Liebknecht!' From: *Schleswig-Holsteinische Volkszeitung*, from http://www.kurkuhl.de/en/novrev/timeline.html and: http://germanhistorydocs.ghi-dc.org/sub_document.cfm?document_id=3939

Discipline in the armed forces
– Part of the Resolution of the Congress of Soldiers'
and Workers' Council, Berlin

'3. Soldiers' councils shall be responsible for the good
behaviour of troops and for the maintenance of discipline.
4. Soldiers shall appoint their own leaders.
5. If former officers have retained the confidence of the
majority of their troops they may be re-elected.
6. The abolition of the standing army and the creation of
a Civic Guard shall be accelerated.'

16 December 1918. After the fall of the Kaiser, insignia of rank was
abolished, and the supreme command of Germany's armed forces was
vested in the hands of People's Commissars – Majority Social-democrats
and Independent Social-democrats.

We want to go home – Folkestone mutineers

'On their own signal – three taps of a drum – two thousand
men, unarmed and in perfect order, demonstrated the fact
that they were fed up – absolutely fed up. Their plan of
action had been agreed upon the night before: no military
boat should be allowed to leave Folkestone for France that
day or any day until they were guaranteed their freedom.
It was sheer, flat, brazen, open and successful mutiny.
Pickets were posted at the harbour. Only Canadian and
Australian soldiers were to be allowed to sail – if they
wanted to. As a matter of no very surprising fact, they
did not want to. ... Meanwhile troop trains were arriving
in Folkestone with more men returning from leave and
on their way to France. They were met with pickets... in
a mass they joined the demonstrators. On Saturday an
armed guard of fusiliers was posted at the quays by the
army authorities. They carried fixed bayonets and ball
cartridges. The pickets approached. One rifle made a show
of going up: the foremost picket seized it, and forthwith

the rest of the guard fell back. The mutineers visited the station in a body, after having posted their own harbour guards, and tore down a large label marked "For Officers Only" … On Saturday a great procession of soldiers, swelled now to about 10,000, marched through the town. Everywhere the townspeople showed their sympathy. At mid-day a mass meeting decided to form a soldiers' union. They appointed their officials and chose their spokesmen …. *The Herald* said: "Everywhere the feeling is the same, the war is over, we won't have to fight in Russia, and we mean to go home."'

3 January 1919. From the *Daily Herald*, 11 January 1919. Anxious to avoid trouble, demands for quick demobilisation were agreed by the War Office. See: Dave Lamb, *Mutinies 1917-1920*. London: Solidarity, 1977.

To the editor – Theodore Liebknecht, German Socialist

'The "Social-democratic" government has entrusted the enquiry into the murder of my brother Karl and comrade Rosa Luxemburg to the military authorities despite our protests. I must emphatically protest against this on behalf of the family and in face of the world. The charge concerns a crime of militarism, and every military authority is an interested party! Therefore and above all else we now demand that the enquiry should be removed from the scope of military authorities.'

16 January 1919, Berlin. Hundreds of German leftists were executed by military and para-military forces in 1919.[44]

Women and Anti-Militarism
– Anna Katalina, German Anarcho-syndicalist

'We, however, embittered and long term opponents of militarism, have a responsibility to sow the seeds of anti-militarism. Women should now rebel actively against

conscription; they should speak up when men – out of
an ill-conceived sense of duty – are pulled into a war to
protect "the wife and the home". They should use all
womanly ways and means. They should be the champions
of anti-militarism …'

June(?) 1919; Why didn't more German women oppose the war? The
war had had been fought to protect capitalism, but it was also fought
because men sought to protect – with theatrical fanfares – their women
and their homes; and because women had accepted this sacrifice. From:
Der Syndikalist, No. 24, quoted in Helge Döhring, *Syndikalismus in
Deutschland 1914-1918*, Lich (Hessen), 2013, p. 144.

War on War – Nelly Roussel, French Libertarian & Feminist

'The female worker who turns out munitions (and she at
least has the excuse that she has to earn her bread!), the
bourgeois madam who knits warm clothes for soldiers, the
great lady who founds or contributes to welfare 'work',
the nurse who looks after the wounded, all women who
make war possible are accomplices of war.'

1921; 'Guerre à la Guerre', (*La Mere Educatrice*) in Nelly Roussel, *Derniers
Combats, recueil d'articles et de discours*, Paris: L'Emancipatrice, 1932, p.
132.

* * *

The complexion of militarism changed after 1918. In
Germany some sought a political renaissance, and the army
began to fund nationalist agitators, helping Hitler take his
first steps as a political agitator. Others looked forward to a
world without war, and organised to oppose militarism in the
future.[45] Pacifists founded the War Resisters' International.
This chapter opened with remarks by Voltaire on the
glamour of war. Victoria Brittain condemned the war as a
tragic and vast stupidity, its causes always falsely represented,
its honour dishonest, its glory tawdry. She also remarked

that the enemies of war had difficulties in countering the glamour, magic and fever of war, the rush of blood that came when crisis threatened, the sense of adventure. Against these more powerful emotive and lucid forces were needed.[46] The next two chapters explore the strengths and weaknesses of forces working for civilization and socialism.

LA CONSCRIPTION

C'est le triomphe du trust des armements, des fournisseurs du gouvernement, des accapareurs et des souscripteurs de la caisse électorale.

The winners! arms trusts, government contractors and monopolists – for those who subscribe electoral funds.

Notes

1   Victoria Brittain noted a British public school (elite) tradition
     that stood for 'militaristic heroism unimpaired by the dampening
     exercise of reason': *Testament of Youth*, London: Virago, 1978, p.
     100.
2   The resolution is quoted below.
3   At this time the only national trade union centre in France.
4   Guillaume Davranche, 'Mai 1913: Débuts de mutineries dans les
     casernes', *Alternative libertaire*, Paris, No. 228, Mai 2013 ; http://
     www.alternativelibertaire.org/spip.php?article5348
5   Estimate vary between 11 and 32,000 – 4 to 12% of recruits.
6   Report to the 1907 party conference, quoted in: Konni Zilliacus,
     I Choose Peace, Harmondsworth: Penguin, 1949, pp. 340-341.
     Zilliacus remarks: 'The outbreak of the First World War, which
     came as a stunning surprise to public opinion, was the price the
     people paid for leaving these matters to the ruling class.' Only a tiny
     revolutionary minority took seriously resolutions of the Second
     International.
7   Who was British in these times? Who was excluded and who
     included, and by what criteria?
8   Henry McShane, *No Mean Fighter*, London: Pluto Press, 1978, p. 69.
9   Kieran Allen, *The Politics of James Connolly*, London, Pluto Press,
     1990, p. 148.
10   Robert Graves, *Goodbye to All That*, Harmondsworth, Penguin,
     1977, p. 198, records 'official lying' in May 1915 – twenty reports of
     men shot for cowardice or desertion; whilst a Minister reported to
     the House of Commons that no sentences of death had been carried
     through in France.
11   Nicolas Offenstadt, *Les fusillés de la Grande Guerre et la mémoire
     collective, 1914-1999*, Paris: Éditions Odile Jacob, 1999, p. 24. Reports
     on the number of executions in the American expeditionary army in
     France vary, some write zero, other ten. Thirteen black soldiers were
     executed in Houston after a riot there. Executions were prohibited
     in the Australian army.
12   A government investigation in the summer of 1917 reported the
     deaths of over 200 mutinous Russian soldiers, many killed in shelling
     by French artillery.
13   An example is quoted in Robert Graves, *Goodbye to All That*,
     Harmondsworth, Penguin, 1977, p. 155.

14   Rémi Adam, '1917: The Revolt of the Russian Soldiers in France', *Revolutionary History*, Vol. 8 No. 2; http://www.marxists.org/history/etol/revhist/backiss/vol8/no2/adam.html

15   For example General Ludendorff noted that bodies of German soldiers were surrendering to isolated enemy soldiers; troops returning from the front were shouting to new-comers to go back, to refuse to feed the war. Erich Ludendorff, *My War Memories*, London: Hutchinson, 1919. http://archive.org/details/MyWarMemories19481918

16   A Canadian army camp, there were five deaths here in March 1919, three rioters and two soldiers on picket duty. Soldiers expressed dissatisfaction with delays over repatriation to Canada. Red flags were raised and according to *The Times*, 7 March 1919, the cry of 'Come on the Bolsheviks' was raised.

17   Italy, December 1918, some sixty black soldiers of the British West India regiment were arrested and charged with mutiny; 8,000 men were disarmed.

18   Two companies of French-Canadian troops of the 259th battalion mutinied in December 1918 prior to being shipped out to Siberia for intervention against the Russian revolution.

19   In January 1919 the British War office sent out a circular seeking reports: Were units fit to be used enforcing public order, would they help break strikes? Would they accept being drafted to go to Russia? Was there any trade union presence? David Lamb, *Mutinies 1917–1920*, London: Solidarity, 1979.

20   This is a reference to the Brussels 1868 resolution quoted above.

21   Karl Liebknecht criticised this approach, his views are quoted below.   http://gallica.bnf.fr/ark:/12148/bpt6k81937p/f30.image.r=Nieuwenhuis,%20Domela.langEN

22   The consultative parliament of the German Empire (Reich).

23   Five years later the right wing of the party – those who were ready to accept and support increased armaments and overseas imperialism – were accused of supporting capitalism. Charles Andler, 'Le socialisme impérialiste dans l'allemange contemporaine'; *Action Nationale*, November and December 1912; reprinted in: *Le socialisme imperialiste dans l'allemange contemporaine*, Paris, Bossard, 1918, pp. 124-5 and pp. 184-5. Jean Jaurès contested these views and defended the good faith of German socialists and its leadership.

24   An example is cited of co-operation between the armies of France, Germany and Luxemburg when the workers of the von Wendel factories of Longwy went on strike. One von Wendel son was a

captain in the German cavalry and another was a French army officer. 'But we have no country because we don't own anything.'

25   Karl Liebknecht rejected anarchist anti-militarism such as that expounded by Domela Nieuwenhuis (See above).

26   The veteran leader Social-democratic party leader, August Bebel, advised German army recruits to keep a low profile in the army, so that their politics went un-noticed. He advised recruits to hold their tongue. Writers who insulted the army could expect prosecution.

27   Gustave Hervé, *Leur Patrie*, Paris: Bibliographie sociale, 1905, p.183ff. A resolution, to call a general strike when wars was declared, was defeated.

28   Jaurès proposed that in border departments – near Germany – soldier should keep arms at home. Rosa Luxemburg criticised him, seeing his pacifist rhetoric as cover for anti-German militarist and chauvinist politics. *Leipziger Volkszeitung*, 9 June 1911.

29   They advocated rebellion and looked to recent examples: in Barcelona and Mexico (the Magonistas).

30   A reference to a Social-democratic party thesis of 1906.

31   Most of the population of Switzerland lived in dispersed small communities where small-scale production was common. In contrast, there were some parts of Germany where the weight of workers in the population as a whole was much greater and there a proletarian culture might be stronger. Grimm suggest different policies were appropriate for different situations.

32   A resolution of the 1889 Paris congress of the Second International had declared that war was a fatal consequence of actual economic conditions and would not disappear completely until the capitalist system disappeared. Another resolution, (London, 1896) looked for international arbitration of conflicts – without being very clear as to how that arbitration would come about; a further resolution (Paris, 1900) set out that socialists should refuse to vote for arms expenditures, and made its bureau responsible for managing ongoing anti-militarist activities. Foster's writing does not engage with the specifics of these resolutions.

33   'A people's army, not a standing army.'

34   (French) General Labour Confederation, the national trade union centre.

35   Ireland was at the time part of British and Irish state, sending representatives to the parliament in Westminster.

36   Adam Hochschild, *To End All Wars*, London: Pan Macmillan, 2012, p. 187.

37   Karl Kautsky, 1854-1938, was an influential theorist and editor, for the German Social-democratic party.

38   See below pages 129-30.

39   Almost identical words were used by the Australian anarchist, JW 'Chummy' Fleming in Melbourne, in and after 1915. Fleming suffered persecution and assault for his opposition to the war.

40   Estimates of its membership vary, some are as high as 35,000.

41   Jeanette Keith, *Rich Man's War, Poor Man's Fight: Race, Class, and Power in the Rural South during the First World War*, Chapel Hill: University of North Carolina Press, 2004, p. 97.

42   The British cabinet was given figures that 5% of Irishmen had joined the forces, as compared to an enlistment rate of 17% amongst adult men in England, Scotland and Wales. Conor Kostick, *Revolution in Ireland*, London: Pluto Press, p. 29.

43   This issue also noted that army officers were also often prominent in Sinn Fein and it would be prudent that such roles be separated to reduce the likelihood of arrest.

44   Years later, evidence was produced that Noske, (acting for the Social-democrat leader Friedrich Ebert), had approved these murders 'Ich ließ Rosa Luxemburg richten. Spiegel-Gespräch mit dem Putsch-Hauptmann Waldemar Pabst', in: *Der Spiegel*, 18 April 1962.

45   Rudolf Rocker and Arthur Lehning looked for weapons factories to take on responsible production. Transport workers in several countries impeded or prevented arms exports to Russian counter-revolutionary forces.

46   *Testament of Youth*, London: Virago, 1978, pp. 290-2.

CIVILIZATION?

In the decade before the outbreak of the First World War some parts of the left came together to oppose imperialism. What was imperialism? Did colonialism overseas help the progress of backward peoples or was a rhetoric of civilisation little more than camouflage for a rod of iron? Sometimes the politics of anti-imperialism was monochrome. For example, in the South African Boer war of 1899-1902 the left opposed British imperialism, seen as wanting to expand its influence and control gold and diamond mining resources and sympathised with the small Afrikaner republics.[1] Graphic illustrations of this was drawn by Walter Crane show a confrontation between British and Boer. Left out of this picture – and omitted from consideration – were the African peoples and their interests; such thinking was somewhat blinkered and racist.[2]

The First World War was fought between two alliances: one side included liberal France, the British Empire and autocratic Russia; the other the German and Austro-Hungarian Empires. Each imperial alliance embraced a God-given righteous nationalism promoting state and civilization. So long as it was seen as a holy war any recalcitrant could be punished with impunity – he, or she, was a defaulter letting the side down. Sometimes it was only when they spoke to each other that troops learnt that the other side was also fighting a holy war.

Few men, and fewer women, had the vote. Each side had

BOTH HAVE FOUGHT HARD, AND HAVE
SUFFERED MUCH   IN THE NAME OF
HUMANITY, STAY YOUR HANDS, AND
USE YOUR HEADS TO FIND A BASIS OF
AGREEMENT

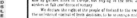

Death and destruction
in Dublin (1916)

NOTICE

THIS PLACE IS SATURATED WITH THE BLOOD OF ABOUT TWO THOUSAND INDIAN PATRIOTS WHO WERE MARTYRED IN A NON-VIOLENT STRUGGLE TO FREE INDIA FROM BRITISH DOMINATION GENERAL DYER OF THE BRITISH ARMY OPENED FIRE HERE ON UNARMED PEOPLE JALLIANWALA BAGH IS THUS AN EVERLASTING SYMBOL OF NON-VIOLENT & PEACE-FUL STRUGGLE FOR FREEDOM OF INDIAN PEOPLE AND THE TYRANNY OF THE BRITISH.

INNOCENT, PEACE-FUL AND UNARMED PEOPLE WHO WERE PROTESTING AGAINST THE ROWLATT ACT WERE FIRED UPON ON 13TH APRIL, 1919. UNDER A RESOLUTION OF THE INDIAN NATIONAL CONGRESS THIS LAND WAS PURCHASED FOR RS. 5,65,000 FOR SETTING UP A MEMORIAL TO THOSE PATRIOTS A TRUST WAS FORMED FOR THIS PURPOSE AND MONEY COLLECTED FROM ALL OVER INDIA AND FOREIGN COUNTRIES. WHEN THIS LAND WAS PURCHASED IT WAS ONLY A VACANT PLOT & THERE WAS NO GARDEN HERE.

THE TRUST REQUESTS THE PEOPLE TO OBSERVE THE RULES FRAMED BY IT AND THUS SHOW THEIR REVERENCE TO THE MEMORIAL OF THE MARTYRS.

Secretary S.K. MUKHERJI
JALLIANWALA BAGH.

Amritsar (1919)

POBLACHT NA H EIREANN.
THE PROVISIONAL GOVERNMENT
OF THE
IRISH REPUBLIC
TO THE PEOPLE OF IRELAND.

IRISHMEN AND IRISHWOMEN: In the name of God and of the dead generations from which she receives her old tradition of nationhood, Ireland, through us, summons her children to her flag and strikes for her freedom.

Having organised and trained her manhood through her secret revolutionary organisation, the Irish Republican Brotherhood, and through her open military organisations, the Irish Volunteers and the Irish Citizen Army, having patiently perfected her discipline, having resolutely waited for the right moment to reveal itself, she now seizes that moment, and, supported by her exiled children in America and by gallant allies in Europe, but relying in the first on her own strength, she strikes in full confidence of victory.

We declare the right of the people of Ireland to the ownership of Ireland, and to the unfettered control of Irish destinies, to be sovereign and indefeasible. The long usurpation of that right by a foreign people and government has not extinguished the right, nor can it ever be extinguished except by the destruction of the Irish people. In every generation the Irish people have asserted their right to national freedom and sovereignty; six times during the past three hundred years they have asserted it in arms. Standing on that fundamental right and again asserting it in arms in the face of the world, we hereby proclaim the Irish Republic as a Sovereign Independent State, and we pledge our lives and the lives of our comrades-in-arms to the cause of its freedom, of its welfare, and of its exaltation among the nations.

The Irish Republic is entitled to, and hereby claims, the allegiance of every Irishman and Irishwoman. The Republic guarantees religious and civil liberty, equal rights and equal opportunities to all its citizens, and declares its resolve to pursue the happiness and prosperity of the whole nation and of all its parts, cherishing all the children of the nation equally, and oblivious of the differences carefully fostered by an alien government, which have divided a minority from the majority in the past.

Until our arms have brought the opportune moment for the establishment of a permanent National Government, representative of the whole people of Ireland and elected by the suffrages of all her men and women, the Provisional Government, hereby constituted, will administer the civil and military affairs of the Republic in trust for the people.

We place the cause of the Irish Republic under the protection of the Most High God, Whose blessing we invoke upon our arms, and we pray that no one who serves that cause will dishonour it by cowardice, inhumanity, or rapine. In this supreme hour the Irish nation must, by its valour and discipline and by the readiness of its children to sacrifice themselves for the common good, prove itself worthy of the august destiny to which it is called.

Signed on Behalf of the Provisional Government,
THOMAS J. CLARKE,
SEAN Mac DIARMADA,   THOMAS MacDONAGH,
P. H. PEARSE,   EAMONN CEANNT,
JAMES CONNOLLY.   JOSEPH PLUNKETT.

Iraq (1920)

peoples of the state and others: minority nationalities and cultures, formal or informal colonies. China, although it retained formal independence, was subjected to unequal treaties; ports were occupied and foreign troops and administrators sequestered taxes. With 'democracy' scarce, and with much of the world ruled by colonial and imperial administrations, the defence of civilization was conjured up to make people fight.

Britain motivated war as a defence of Belgium – and of other small nations. But two years later British troops quashed the Easter rising in Dublin. Perhaps as many as 1.5 million Armenians and Greeks were killed in Ottoman Turkey. At the end of the war peoples in defeated empires found themselves placed – without any consultation – under new masters. The Japanese government presented a demand to the League of Nations (the forerunner of today's United Nations) for the recognition of the principle of racial equality. France and other small nations supported them, but not Britain or the USA.

In the non-white and colonised world there were some people who saw the war as an opportunity to rebel, but there were many more who were ready to defend 'their' states and empires. The African-American leader W E B Du Bois wrote of 'civilized nations' fighting like mad dogs over the right to own and exploit these darker peoples. But also he argued that coloured Americans fearful of race prejudice should sympathise with France and the UK because they have begun to realise the costs of race prejudice, even if they have not yet conquered it.[3] For him, this was a war for democracy,[4] coloured Americans should participate – and with eyes lifted to the hills – hoping for progress in the future. Mahatma Gandhi thought that having accepted the benefits of the British Empire he should stand by it. Very large numbers of soldiers and labourers were recruited in India for campaigns in Europe, the Middle East and Africa. There was famine in

India towards the end of the war; the war also had a terrible impact in Africa and in parts of the Ottoman Empire – through the direct impact of troops and in consequence of less direct factors disrupting societies and economies.

Sol Plaatje, one of the 'fathers' of the African National Congress of South Africa looked to Africans doing their bit for the British Empire. Marcus Garvey, the Jamaican-born inspirer of the Universal Negro Improvement Association, hoped to see progress and equality and supported the Empire. Another writer in the Caribbean motivated support declaring: 'We will be fighting to prove that we are not merely subjects, but citizens – citizens of a world empire whose watch-word should be liberty, equality and brotherhood.'[5] Africa and the Caribbean provided hundreds of thousands to the war – many of them forcibly recruited. Some served as soldiers; many more were used as porters and labourers. Black soldiers aspiring to become officers in British and Imperial forces generally had their ambitions frustrated by army regulations. One who broke the mould was Walter Daniel John Tull, formerly a professional footballer with Tottenham Hotspur and Northampton Town; he died as a Second Lieutenant in 1918.

The German army relied on local recruits to fight a long war in East Africa. The French army recruited extensively in Algeria,[6] in West Africa and elsewhere to fight in France. Some 600,000 men were mobilised in the Empire. Colonial troops were sometimes withdrawn from the line over the winter, but returned in warmer weather for offensives and attacks. Casualty rates amongst colonised peoples were high, sometimes higher than amongst Europeans.[7]

Often, rather than fighting on the front line, black peoples were segregated into labour battalions of one sort or another, and were tasked with working with munitions or various forms manual labour. African-Americans served in US forces in France.[8] American troops were well received when they first arrived, but by 1919 some French people felt they had overstayed their welcome.

In France migrants filled many factory jobs. As French women also began to work in factories to fill vacancies left by their menfolk, they were placed side by side with newcomers. French soldiers frequently expressed fears that 'their' jobs and womenfolk were being taken by 'Annamites' – peoples from Indochina – and the latter became the targets of racist abuse. Such fears were also present in Britain – male rather than female nurses were often set to care for wounded troops from India. After the war reports of race riots cited antipathy to white women consorting with black men.

Many of those who followed Gandhi, Garvey and Plaatje had looked for the recognition for the interests of colonised peoples. Non-whites, fighting with whites against other whites, expected to be treated as equals. Some ex-soldiers wore their uniforms for years, even when they became mere tatters. But when the war ended few had much to show for their effort or their trust. Non-white sailors – African, West Indian, Asian and Muslim – who had served throughout the war, often for a fraction of the rewards paid to whites, now found that they were no longer welcome in Cardiff, Glasgow, Liverpool, Newport, or South Shields. Black soldiers were not welcome in British victory parades; nor were they allowed to march in the victory parade in Paris. In the USA half a million African Americans had been drawn into northern industries but after 1918 many found that they too were not wanted, and whites feared that they would take 'their' jobs. In the naval port of Brest four persons were killed and another 38 wounded, in a riot sparked by friction between French natives and North Africans in August 1917. After the war France established an order of preference for taking in foreign workers: in the first place Italians, then Poles, Czechs, Portuguese, Spaniards, Greeks, Russians, Germans, etc. Most of the non-white workers were quickly repatriated. Black sailors in the UK faced similar experiences and complained that though they had risked life and limb serving in the war, Scandinavians and Spaniards and other whites were given preference.

In the aftermath of the war, the use of gas and bombing against civilian targets came under scrutiny, and gas at least was restricted in the civilised world. But European states continued to apply different rules of war in relation to the 'uncivilised' world – 'tribes' and 'uncivilised' peoples. Over the next twenty years various forms of irritant and toxic gasses were used in wars in Aden, Afghanistan, China, Ethiopia, Iraq, Jordan, Kurdistan, Morocco, Somalia and Syria. Aerial bombing was seen as a 'cheaper' means of keeping regions under control. In the summer of 1920 T. E. Lawrence noted that whereas the Turks had killed on average two hundred persons a year in today's Iraq, British forces had killed ten thousand Arabs.[9] So long as European commanders were ready to believe that the only thing 'they' understood was 'the heavy hand', civilisation continued to have a bitter taste for targeted peoples.

* * *

Far lower cultures – German Social-democrats

'We distinguish between an imperialism, which comes to foreign and less civilized peoples in order honourably to educate them, to teach them to take advantage of and enjoy, for themselves and for all mankind, the resources of their soil, and to introduce to them all the achievements of civilization in a manner corresponding to their lives; and on the other hand an imperialism, which aims at the oppression, the spoliation, or even the extirpation of the natives, natives in whom for all their far lower culture, we still see human beings, who must be treated as such.'

January 1907. Extract from an election address. 'Extirpation' refers to the recent war and genocide in South-West Africa (now Namibia).[10] From R.C. Ensor, Ed., *Modern Socialism as set forth by Socialists in their Speeches, Writings and Programmes*, London: Harper, 1910, pp. 373-4.

Servility – Dr. Abdullah Abdurahman, South African Civil Rights Activist

'Instead of kindly, humane treatment, we find barbarous cruelty and inhumanity. Instead of ameliorating our lot they endeavour to accentuate its bitterness. Instead of aiming at our upliftment they seek to degrade us. Instead of lending a helping hand to those struggling to improve themselves they thrust them back remorselessly and rigorously. Instead of making it possible for them to enjoy the blessings of an enlightened Christianity and a noble civilization, they refuse them the right to live, unless they are content to slave for farmers or descend into the bowels of the earth to delve the gold which enslaves the world, and before whose charms all freedom flies. In short, the object of the white man's rule to-day is not to develop the faculties of the coloured races so that they may live a full life, but to keep them for ever in a servile position.'

September 1913. A presidential address at the 10th Annual Conference of the African Political Organization. Dr Abdurahman campaigned for the human rights of African, Coloured and Indian peoples in South Africa. Quoted from: Sol Plaatje, *Native Life in South Africa*, Northlands: Picador Africa, 2007, pp. 136-7.

Civilization – Herbert Asquith, British Prime Minister

'If I am asked what we are fighting for I reply in two sentences: In the first place, to fulfil a solemn international obligation, an obligation which, if it had been entered into between private persons in the ordinary concerns of life, would have been regarded as an obligation not only of law but of honour, which no self-respecting man could possibly have repudiated. I say, secondly, we are fighting to vindicate the principle which, in these days when force, material force, sometimes seems to be the dominant influence and factor in the development of mankind, we are fighting to vindicate the principle that small nationalities are not to be crushed, in defiance of international good faith, by the arbitrary will of a strong and overmastering Power. I do not believe any nation ever entered into a great controversy – and this is one of the greatest history will ever know – with a clearer conscience and a stronger conviction that it is fighting, not for aggression, not for the maintenance even of its own selfish interest, but that it is fighting in defence of principles the maintenance of which is vital to the civilization of the world.'

6 August 1914.

The failure of male statecraft is complete

– *Votes for Women,* Suffragette newspaper

'Today, it is for men to stand down, and for the women whom they have belittled to take the seat of judgement. No picture, however overdrawn of women's ignorance, error, or folly, could exceed in fantastic yet tragic horror the spectacle with which male governments are furnishing history today. The foundations of the structure of civilization which they have erected in Europe have proved rotten. The edifice, seemingly so secure, has suddenly collapsed.'

7 August 1914. *Votes for Women,* (London), p. 682.

Imperialism, the World War and Social Democracy
– Hermann Gorter, Dutch Socialist

'The worker must therefore know that imperialism dominates all parties and must know how it does so. He must know that, by provoking wars ad infinitum, imperialism threatens the proletariat with fragmentation and ruin. He must know that, under imperialism, there can be no wars of national defence. Finally, and most importantly, he must know that imperialism (and in this respect it is so closely linked with nationalism as to be inextricably fused with it) unites all national capitals against the world proletariat, which must in turn be united against them. The worker must know, consequently, that the struggle against imperialism is the struggle for socialism. The worker must know all of this. He must know it, not in the form of hollow words and phrases, with a shallow, superficial knowledge, but with a profound and complete knowledge; this conception must be instilled into his very bones.'

September 1914. From: http://www.marxists.org/archive/gorter/1914/imperialism.htm

Africa for the Africans
– Reverend John Chilembwe,
Anti-colonialist, Nyasaland (Malawi)

'We ask the honourable government of our country, will there be any good prospects for the natives after the end of the war? Shall we be recognised as anybody in the best interests of civilization and Christianity after the great struggle is ended? ... in time of peace, the government failed to help the underdog. In time of peace, everything for Europeans only. And instead of honour, we suffer humiliation with names contemptible ...

... the poor Africans who have nothing to own in this present world ... are invited to die for a cause which is not theirs.'

November 1914. Chilembwe sent a letter to the *Nyasaland Times* asking that Africans 'who do not know the cause of your fight' should not be conscripted to fight in a British 'civilized war'. Let the rich men, bankers, titled men, storekeepers and landlords go to war and get shot, rather than Africans – leaving widows and orphans. His appeal was not published. From: G. Shepperson and T. Price, *Independent African: John Chilembwe and the origins, setting and significance of the Nyasaland native rising of 1915*, Edinburgh University Press, 1958, p. 235. Chilembwe is regarded as a national hero.

Why? – 5th Light Infantry, Indian Army

'Why should we fight for England and be killed in Europe when we are paid half a coolie's wage and our wives and children are left to starve on two or three rupees a month?'

January-February 1915, Singapore. Soldiers of the Indian army mutinied when they were told to ship out to an unknown destination. 47 were executed. From: R.W.E. Harper and H. Miller, *Singapore Mutiny*, Oxford University Press, 1985, p. 35. About the same time a suspected mutiny in Rangoon was stopped and a company of Pathans bound for East Africa were discharged, punished or executed. Some Indian Muslims refused to fight against Turkey – out of respect for the Sultan of Istanbul.

Coloured Troops and the War
– *East Rand Express* (South Africa)

'If the Indians are used against the Germans it means that they will return to India disabused of the respect they should bear for the white race. The Empire must uphold the principle that a coloured man must not raise his hand against a white man if there is to be any law or order in either India, Africa, or any part of the Empire where the white man rules over a large concourse of coloured people. In South Africa it will mean that the natives will secure pictures of whites being chased by coloured men, and who knows what harm such pictures may do?'

East Rand Express, 1915? Quoted from: Sol Plaatje, *Native Life in South Africa*, Northlands: Picador Africa, 2007, p. 273.

In the Caribbean *The Federalist*, (Grenada), looked to the black man being fairly treated in the empire and commented: 'The Boers naturally fear that if the Zulus are trained to the use of arms it will be a difficult job afterwards to control and dominate them.' (19 June 1915).[11]

Humbug – Olive Schreiner, South African Radical

'"The earth is mine and the fullness thereof" sayeth the Englishman. "Any other nation which tries to build up such an Empire as we have in India and Burma (where we depopulated whole districts) and Africa and Egypt, and to rule the sea is a vile and wicked nation on which Gods curse will surely fall. Let us pray!" Oh the cant and humbug.'

24 October 1915; Olive Schreiner to Havelock Ellis, Harry Ransom Research Center, University of Texas at Austin, Olive Schreiner Letters Project transcription, lines 18-22. © Olive Schreiner Letters Project.

Civilization? – Anarchists in London

'Civilization? So who represents that just now? Is it the German state, with its so powerful and weighty militarism, that has stifled every leaning of revolt? Is it the Russian state whose sole means of persuasion are the club, the gibbet, and Siberia? Is it the French state, with its *Biribi*, [punishment battalions] and bloody conquests in Tonkin [Indo-China], Madagascar, Morocco, and its forced recruits of black troops? The France that year on year detains in its prisons comrades whose only crime is that of having written and spoken against war? Is it Britain, which exploits, divides, starves and oppresses the peoples of its vast colonial empire? No, none of the belligerents is entitled to invoke civilization, just as none have the right to claim that they are in state of legitimate defence.'

March 1915. Alexander Berkman, Emma Goldman, Errico Malatesta, Alexander Schapiro, Bill Shatov and others. 'International Anarchist Manifesto on the War' *Freedom* (London), republished by *Volontà*, *Cultura Obrera*, *Mother Earth*, etc. (More of this is quoted below, pages 163-5.)

A destructive beast – Rosa Luxemburg, German Socialist

'The present world war is a turning point. For the first time, the destructive beasts set loose upon all quarters of the globe by capitalist Europe have broken into Europe itself. A cry of horror went through the world when Belgium, that precious jewel of European civilization, and when the most august cultural monuments of northern France fell into shards under the impact of the blind forces of destruction. This same 'civilized world' looked on passively as the same imperialism ordained the cruel destruction of ten thousand Herero tribesmen and filled the sands of the Kalahari[12] with the mad shrieks and death rattles of men dying of thirst, the 'civilized world' [looked on] as forty thousand men on the Putumayo River [Columbia] were tortured to death within ten years by a band of European captains of industry, while the rest of the people were made into cripples; as in China where an age-old culture was put to the torch by European mercenaries, practiced in all forms of cruelty, annihilation, and anarchy; as Persia was strangled, powerless to resist the tightening noose of foreign domination; as in Tripoli where fire and sword bowed the Arabs beneath the yoke of capitalism, destroyed their culture and habitations. Only today has this "civilized world" become aware that the bite of the imperialist beast brings death that its very breath is infamy. Only now has [the civilized world] recognized this, after the beast's ripping talons have clawed its own mother's lap, the bourgeois civilization of Europe itself. And even this knowledge is grappled with in the distorted form of bourgeois hypocrisy. Every people recognizes the infamy only in the national uniform of the enemy. "German barbarians!" – as though every people that marches out to do organized murder were not transformed instantly into a barbarian horde. "Cossack atrocities!" – as though war itself were not the atrocity of atrocities, as though the praising of human slaughter as heroism in a socialist youth paper were not the purest example of intellectual cossackdom!'

April 1915. From: *The Junius Pamphlet*, London: Merlin Press, 1967, pp. 80-2.

Equal Shares for Italy – The Treaty of London

'Should France and Great Britain extend their colonial possessions in Africa at the expense of Germany they will admit in principle Italy's right to demand certain compensation by way of an extension of her possessions in Eritrea, Somaliland, and Libya and the colonial areas adjoining French and British colonies. ... France, Great Britain, and Russia admit in principle the fact of Italy's interest in the maintenance of political balance of power in the Mediterranean and her rights, in case of a partition of Turkey, to a share, equal to theirs, in the basin of the Mediterranean – viz., in that part of it which adjoins the province of Adalia, in which Italy has already acquired special rights and interests ...'

Italy joined the war in May 1915, expecting to gain the German speaking Southern Tyrol, several territories east of Venice, and Adalia – i.e. parts of Turkey adjacent to the Aegean coast. The treaty was published in *Izvestia* in November 1917 and in the *Manchester Guardian* in January 1918. Between 1919 and 1922 another war was fought between Greece – supported by financial and military assistance from allied states – and Turkey.

A War for civilization
– James Connolly, Irish Socialist and Industrial Unionist

'We here in Ireland, particularly those who follow the example of the Irish Transport and General Workers' Union, have been battling to preserve those rights which others have surrendered; we have fought to keep up our standards of life, to force up our wages, to better our conditions. To that extent we have been truly engaged in a war for civilization. Every victory we have gained has gone to increase the security of life amongst our class, has gone to put bread on the tables, coals in the fires, clothes on the backs of those to whom food and warmth and clothing are things of ever pressing moment. Some of our class have fought in Flanders and the Dardanelles; the greatest achievement of them all combined will weigh but a feather in the balance for good compared with the achievements of those who stayed at home and fought to secure the rights of the working class against invasion. The carnival of murder on the continent will be remembered as a nightmare in the future, will not have the slightest effect in deciding for good the fate of our homes, our wages, our hours, our conditions. But the victories of labour in Ireland will be as footholds, secure and firm, in the upward climb of our class to the fullness and enjoyment of all that labour creates, and organised society can provide. Truly, labour alone in these days is fighting the real *war for civilization.*'

October 1915. From *Workers' Republic.*

Clichés – Alfred Rosmer, French Socialist & Syndicalist

'War of liberation, a war of civilization against barbarism, a war of races, a war for rights, a necessity to finish off enemy militarism, a war to end war, a war for the principle of nationalities, for the independence of small nations – in the conflict which broke out we see none of this. We recognise the clichés that governments bring out for each killing, which they use against one another.'

1 November 1915. Letter to subscribers of *Vie Ouvrière,* Paris.

Thoughts on Easter Week
– Sylvia Pankhurst, British Suffragette & Socialist

'Justice can make but one reply to the Irish rebellion, and that is to demand that Ireland shall be allowed to, govern herself. Differences of opinion in England, Scotland, or Wales as to what measure of self-government Ireland is to have ought not to affect the matter – by the "freedom of small nations" which the British Government has so bombastically sworn to defend, this is essentially a question for Ireland herself to decide. Let a popular vote be taken in Ireland …'

13 May 1916. From: *Women's Dreadnought* (London). *Dreadnought* reports like this were banned in the USA.

Trial Speech – Roger Casement, sometime British consul, Companion of the Order of St Michael and St George, Irish Anti-colonialist

'Gentlemen of the jury, I wish to thank you for your verdict. I hope you will not take amiss what I said, or think that I made any imputation upon your truthfulness or your integrity when I spoke and said that this was not a trial by my peers. I maintain that I have a natural right to be tried in that natural jurisdiction, Ireland, my own country, and I would put it to you, how would you feel in the converse case, or rather how would all men here feel in the converse case, if an Englishman had landed here in England and the crown or the government, for its own purposes, had conveyed him secretly from England to Ireland under a false name, committed him to prison under a false name, and brought him before a tribunal in Ireland under a statute which they knew involved a trial before an Irish jury? How would you feel yourselves as Englishmen if that man was to be submitted to trial by jury in a land inflamed against him and believing him to be a criminal, when his only crime was that he had cared for England more than for Ireland?'

29 June 1916. Roger Casement had sought arms from the German government for the Easter rising. Some five weeks later he was executed in Pentonville Prison.

An appeal to the British government
– Sol Plaatje, South African Native National Congress

'In 1913, a South African Governor signed the Natives' Land Act which made the Natives homeless in South Africa. Whereas the Government have announced their intention not to disfranchise the South African rebels,[13] judging from the present legislative tendency we fear that, unless the Imperial government can be induced to interfere, it is not improbable that should the rebels return to power after the general election, in 1916, there will be horrible enactments in store for the blacks. ...

... we are encouraged to hope that, "when peace again reigns over Europe", when white men cease warring against white men, when the warriors put away the torpedoes and the bayonets and take up less dangerous implements, you will in the interest of your flag, for the safety of your coloured subjects, the glory of your Empire, and the purity of your religion, grapple with this dark blot on the Imperial emblem, the South African anomaly that compromises the justice of British rule and seems almost to belie the beauty, the sublimity and the sincerity of Christianity. Shall we appeal to you in vain? *I hope not.*'

May 1916. From Sol Plaatje, *Native Life in South Africa*, Northlands: Picador Africa, 2007, pp. 335 and 338. Plaatje's hopes may seem somewhat naïve. The British government had chosen to conciliate Afrikaners and to subordinate or ignore Black interests.[14]

All over Whitechapel similar things were happening
– Sylvia Pankhurst

'The British people long read with horror of the Russian anti-semitic pogroms, but now, alas, we have had a pogrom of our own, and as in Russia under the Tsar's dominion, our British pogrom was carried out by the police...

... The police were catching at any men they saw and pushing them roughly into a billiard club next door to the picture palace. The girls walked on: police seemed to be everywhere, and just past New Road they saw the police dragging men out of a restaurant. A police inspector roughly pushed Miss R.C. "Oh don't push!" she protested, whereat he struck her on the face, bruising her at the side of the eye. "You swine, to hit my sister!" cried Miss A.C., whereat the Inspector struck her to the ground. "Charge them!" he called out to a constable. The girls were dragged off to Lemon Street Police Station, which was thronged with men and boys....

... In Whitechapel the number of men and boys detained is estimated to be from 1,200 to 1,500 or 2,000. Some put the number as high as three or four thousand. Yet only nine men were charged in court as absentees, and only four were handed over to the military authorities. Middle-aged men and boys under sixteen years were taken. Some of the lads were young enough to cry, and one bald-headed man who said he was a grandfather was beaten by several policemen and was bleeding at the mouth. ...

... Are we to have a recrudescence of that old disgraceful savagery in this country? The Conventions with Allied States Bill, which is passing through parliament, will give the power to force the subjects of Russia, or of any other allied power, into the British army. In the Bill as it stands they are allowed no option to go either to a neutral country or to the land of their birth. We offered free untrammelling hospitality to these fugitives: now our government holds them as prisoners, refusing them leave to go, refusing even the meagre rights of conscientious objection granted to British men.'

26 May 1917. The British government was looking to conscript aliens into the forces. Raids in the East End of London were likened to pogroms. Sylvia Pankhurst declared that 'the fight of the FJPC (Foreign Jews' Protection Committee) on behalf of their compatriots was a fight for the freedom of every section of the British people'.[15] See: Julia Bush, *Behind the Lines: East London Labour*, London: Merlin Press, 1984, p. 178; and *Women's Dreadnought*, http://www.marxists.org/archive/pankhurst-sylvia/1917/pogrom.htm

A crime against the laws of humanity, nation, nature, and God – Marcus Garvey, Jamaican, Universal Negro Improvement Association

'The East St. Louis Riot, or rather massacre, of Monday [July] 2nd, will go down in history as one of the bloodiest outrages against mankind for which any class of people could be held guilty. This is no time for fine words, but a time to lift ones voice against the savagery of a people who claim to be the dispensers of democracy. I do not know what special meaning the people who slaughtered the Negroes of East St. Louis have for democracy of which they are the custodians, but I do know that it has no literal meaning for me as used and applied by these same lawless people. America, that has been ringing the bells of the world, proclaiming to the nations and the peoples thereof that she has democracy to give to all and sundry, America that has denounced Germany for the deportations of the Belgians into Germany, America that has arraigned Turkey at the bar of public opinion and public justice against the massacres of the Armenians, has herself no satisfaction to give 12,000,000 of her own citizens except the satisfaction of a farcical inquiry that will end where it began, over the brutal murder of men, women and children for no other reason than that they are black people seeking an industrial chance in a country that they have laboured for three hundred years to make great. For three hundred years the Negroes of America have given their life blood to make the Republic the first among the nations of the world, and all along this time there has never been even one year of justice but on the contrary a continuous round of oppression.'

8 July 1917. In May and July 1917 a riot in East St. Louis caused 100 to 200 deaths, and left 6000 African-Americans homeless. Much of skilled, rooted, white labour lacked sympathy for the new black labour force. Officials of the American Federation of Labor officials were criticised.[16]

Terrible revolts – Governor-General Joost van Vollenhoven, French, Colonial Governor

'… unpopularity … has become universal from the very day when recruits were asked to serve in Europe and grim, determined, terrible revolts started against the white man, who had hitherto been tolerated, sometimes even loved, but who, transformed into a recruiting agent, had become a detested enemy, the image of a slave hunter…'

September 1917. Conscription was suspended in French West Africa. Paris was advised not to press for further recruits. From: Marc Michel, *Les Africains et la Grande Guerre: l'appel à l'Afrique (1914-1918)*, Paris: Karthala, 2003, p. 132.

We are going to offer civilization to the blacks – Georges Clémenceau, French Prime Minister

'They will have to pay for that … I would prefer that ten Blacks are killed rather than one Frenchman – although I immensely respect those brave blacks, but I think that enough Frenchmen are killed anyway and that we should sacrifice as few as possible!'

February 1918. Instructions sent to mayors in metropolitan France advised them to obstruct marriages between natives (whites) and colonials. Speech to the Senate.

Instructions to French Officers – J. A. Linard, Colonel, French Army

'We must prevent the rise of any pronounced degree of intimacy between French officers and black officers …. We must not eat with them, must not shake hands or seek to talk or meet with them outside of the requirements of military service …'

August 1918. Guidance from Colonel Linard, Chief of the French Mission at the HQ, American Expeditionary Force on relations between the French and African-Americans in the US Army: the black man was 'an inferior being' and a 'constant menace'.

Lynch Law – *The Liberator*, (New York)

'It [*The Liberator*] will assert the social and political equality of the black and white races, oppose every kind of racial discrimination, and conduct a remorseless publicity campaign against lynch law.'

March 1918. Black soldiers had rioted in Houston, Texas in August 1917, following a confrontation between a black woman and white policemen. Nineteen black soldiers were executed. American socialists denounced racism. From: *The Liberator*, Edited by Max Eastman.[17]

Not for Love of Britain – Henry Pothemont

'Prior to the great war, the coloured men who went to sea, and who made their homes in this country, were mostly British West Indians... There were also a few West

Africans, from the Sierra Leone district, who were mostly employed in ships in the African trade. These men were generally well-behaved, and loyal subjects, and there was no friction between them and the people of this country. But the outbreak of the war in 1914 brought a great change. British seamen who were reservists were called up and others volunteered for the army and navy in thousands. Several thousand of the alien seamen who were serving in our ships were removed therefrom. Thus was created a great shortage of men for the merchant service, mostly sailors and firemen, and coloured men were welcomed to fill the gap. And this is just where the trouble lies. Arabs (mostly Somalis) poured into the country, so did West Africans. These later importations were attracted by the good wages offering, and to them it was absolute wealth. They did not man our ships for love of England ...'

17 June 1919. From: *South Wales Argus*. Pothemont stressed education as a criteria for British 'citizenship'. I am indebted to Jacqueline Jenkinson, 'The 1919 Race Riots in Britain: Their Background and Consequences', PhD thesis, 1987 the University of Edinburgh, for this and other quotations.

Hunger and Revolution in India
– M N Roy, Indian Socialist

'At the present moment, India is stricken by famine such as was never known before, even in her long and tragic history of famines under British rule. The causes of this terrible epidemic are the economic exhaustion of the people and the exportation of all foodstuffs to feed the Allied armies during the four years of the war. To the mingled cries of the dying masses, the British government has responded with bombs and bayonet, and the passage of even stricter and more repressive laws to prevent the voice of an oppressed people reaching the outer world in its appeal for help.'

18 September 1919. From: *The Call.* Hundreds of demonstrators were killed in Amritsar on 13 April 1919 by forces commanded by Brigadier-General Reginald Dyer. Indian sources speak of a thousand dead. After this, and other events in Iraq and Egypt, Gandhi said serving such a government was 'sinful'.

Food and camels gone

'Excuse us, O Wingate, our country is conquered,
You took off the barley and camels and donkeys
And a lot of wheat too – now leave us alone.'

1919. The Egyptian economy suffered in the war as food and provisions were taken. General Wingate was the British High Commissioner in Egypt. Egyptian men and women saw foreign soldiers as vicious brutes.[18] The British administration was blamed and was asked to go. From a popular Egyptian poem 'Bardiun yd Wingate'. See also: a description of Australian troops in Cairo as 'locusts': Naguib Mahfouz, *Palace Walk*, London: Black Swan, 1994, pp. 11-12.

A Few Questions
– Workers Dreadnought, Socialist newspaper

'Do you wish to exclude all blacks from England? If so, do you not think that blacks might justly ask that the British should at the same time keep out of their countries? ... Do you not think that when Negroes are employed instead of British it is because it pays the employer to do it? Do not you know that if it pays to employ black men employers will get them and keep them even if the white workers kill a few of the blacks from time to time? Are you afraid that a white woman would prefer a black man to you if you met her on equal terms with him?'

June 1919. Racism was rife in several British cities. Funds were created to encourage non-whites to repatriate. The police attacked non-whites, and some of their small businesses were destroyed. Some socialists challenged race prejudice. See: 'Stabbing Negroes in the London Dock Area'. In: Jacqueline Jenkinson, 'The 1919 Race Riots in Britain: Their Background and Consequences', PhD thesis, 1987 the University of Edinburgh.

Nations proclaimed lofty concepts of humanity
– Marcus Garvey

'Now that the war is over, we find the same nations making every effort by word and deed to convince us that their blatant professions were mere meaningless platitudes never intended to apply to earth's darker millions.'

15 April 1921. Soldiers from the Caribbean protested on their return home. Some refused to join victory parades.[19] From: *Daily Gleaner*. (Some white British soldiers had attacked counterparts from the Caribbean when they heard them singing 'Rule Britannia'.)

No Love – Kamal Chunchee, Christian missionary

'My first week in the East End of London I met an English sailor lad, down and out. I took him to a magnificent building. I saw outside this building in large letters "All Seamen Welcome" ... I asked the lad to sit at one of the tables, went over to the counter, placed a shilling and asked the English girl for two cups of tea and a piece of cake. The girl stared at me and said, 'We don't serve niggers here!' What hurt me most was behind that girl on the wall, I read in large letters "God is love"! I left that place and gave the lad the shilling.'

December 1921. Chunchee was a Malay born in Ceylon (today's Sri Lanka). He fought in the British army in the war, and later he worked in Poplar (East London). From: Coloured Men's Institute Report 1945-46, (London, December 1946), p.1. Quoted in Jacqueline Jenkinson, 'The 1919 Race Riots in Britain: Their Background and Consequences', PhD thesis, 1987 the University of Edinburgh.

Not Mercenaries

We know, feel, and believe that every breast was bared in freedom's cause, every eye, heart, soul wish and imagination pointed to the same goal as the truest Englishman that ever lived.

1925. Tens of thousands of sailors in the British merchant navy were drawn from seaports around the globe, and after 1918 they were no longer welcome. From: Laura Tabili, 'The Construction of Racial Difference in Twentieth-Century Britain: The Special Restriction (Coloured Alien Seamen) Order, 1925'; in *Journal of British Studies*, No. 33, (January 1994), p. 88.

Bitterness
– Kojo Tovalou Houénou,
Anti-colonialist, from Dahomey (Benin)

'We are native Africans. Our bitterness is impossible to eradicate after discovering that, while we were fighting to deliver Douamont[20] and Verdun, certain white Frenchmen, whose lands we were freeing, have been able to use villainous laws to register our properties as vacant and ownerless. What then is this rule by decree? Feudalism in the Republic?'

From: Journal l'AOF, 1928; J. Ayo Langley, *Ideologies of Liberation in Black Africa, 1856-1970*, London: Rex Collings, 1979, p. 240. Kojo Tovalou Houénou suffered assaulted by racist Americans in a Paris night club in 1923 and died in a Dakar prison in 1936.

Notes

1   In October 1918 Labour Party candidate George Lansbury described himself as 'a convinced out and out Socialist, a pro-Boer, and a Pacifist.' Julia Bush, *Behind the Lines: East London Labour*, London: Merlin Press, 1984, p. 89.

2   Subsequently, in South Africa, there developed forms of separate development and Apartheid, consolidating violent and racist polities. Labour activists in South Africa, some with close ties to radicals in Britain and elsewhere, were sometimes blind or neglectful in confronting oppressive relations between whites and blacks. Racism was present in South Africa and in Britain. Jonathan Hyslop, *The Notorious Syndicalist J.T. Bain: A Scottish Radical in Colonial South Africa*, Johannesburg, 2004, pp. 254-5.

3   Editorial: 'World War and the Color Line,' *The Crisis*, November 1914.

4   'Close Ranks', *The Crisis*, Vol. 9, July 1918.

5   The *Federalist*, (Grenada), 27 October 1915; quoted in, Glenford Deroy Howe: *Race, War and Nationalism: A Social History of West Indians in the First World War*, Kingston (Jamaica): Ian Randle, p. 17.

6   Three Mediterranean departments of Algeria were treated as an extension of France, rather than as colonial territories. In the colonies, 'Évolués', civilized colonials were given some rights.

7   Christian Koller, 'The Recruitment of Colonial Troops in Africa and Asia and their Deployment in Europe during the First World War', *Immigrants & Minorities*, Vol. 26, Nos. 1/2, March/July 2008, p. 120.

8   Most – 80% – were non-combatants.

9   Lawrence saw so many deaths as wasteful and inefficient: 'How far will the killing of ten thousand villagers and townspeople this summer hinder the production of wheat, cotton, and oil? How long will we permit millions of pounds, thousands of Imperial troops, and tens of thousands of Arabs to be sacrificed on behalf of colonial administration which can benefit nobody but its administrators?' 22 August 1920; *The Sunday Times*. Iraqis and Kurds were bombed and gassed by the Royal Air Force.

10   Patronising and imperialist concepts of benevolent colonialism were not unique to Germany, witness concepts of a 'mission civilisatrice' or white man's burden. British Fabians views on progressive imperialism are discussed in Rhiannon Vickers, *The Labour Party*

and the World, Vol.1, 1900–51, Manchester University Press, 2004, p. 38.

11   Quoted in, Glenford Deroy Howe: *Race, War and Nationalism: A Social History of West Indians in the First World War,* Kingston (Jamaica): Ian Randle, p. 25. In December 1918 Caribbean soldiers protested when they were refused a pay rise granted to white comrades. On their return many helped form a Caribbean League. Soldiers from India complained that British officers regarded them as 'inarticulate animals'. Rozina Visram: *Asians in Britain: 400 Years of History,* Pluto Press, London: 2002, p. 194. A million Indians were recruited.

12   On this colonial history see Jürgen Zimmerer & Joachim Zeller, Eds, *Genocide in German South-West Africa: The Colonial War of 1904-1908 and its Aftermath,* Pontypool: Merlin Press, 2008.

13   This is a reference to the Afrikaners who sided with Germany and launched a short armed rebellion in South Africa. Despite their rebellion they could vote, whilst Africans could not. African veterans – e.g. Doyle Modiakgotla and S.M. Bennet Ncwana – had some influence in the Industrial and Commercial Workers' Union of Africa, one of the first large African trade unions.

14   A more strident approach was taken by J.T. Gumede and by many industrial unionists who supported the organisation of black workers and viewed many leaders of the SANNC (forerunner of the ANC) as privileged – with interests 'completely alien to the great mass of the Native proletariat'; see 'Beware of Labour Cranks' *The International,* 19 October 1917, quoted in Lucien van der Walt, in 'Revolutionary Syndicalism, Communism and the National Question In South African Socialism, 1886–1928' in Steven Hirsch, and Lucien van der Walt, Lucien, Eds, *Anarchism and Syndicalism in the Colonial and Postcolonial World,* 1870–1940, Leiden: Brill, 2010, p.72.

15   Russian radicals supported the Russian Anti-Conscription League, an organisation based at the offices of the Amalgamated Society of Tailors and Tailoresses, in Whitechapel.

16   Philip S. Foner, *History of the Labor Movement in the United States Volume 7: Labor and World War I,* New York: International Publishers, 1987, p. 226.

17   The USA had a record of atrocities greater than that of any other nation of the civilized world. Since 1885 an African-American had been lynched every four days. September 1917; *The Masses,* Vol IX, No. 11, p. 13. Mailing privileges were withdrawn from *The Masses.*

18   On 12 November 1915, a question was put in the British parliament
     to the Secretary for Foreign Affairs re riots and murders in the Haret
     el Wassa brothel district of Cairo in April and July of that year;
     could he state the number of outrages and offences committed by
     Australian forces upon Egyptians since the outbreak of war? Reports
     of an atrocity committed by the Anzac Mounted Division – the
     killing of between forty and one hundred villagers in the village of
     Surafend (Sarafand) in Palestine in December 1918, are noted in
     http://net.lib.byu.edu/~rdh7/wwi/comment/surafend.htm See also:
     Suzanne Brugger, *Australians and Egypt 1914–1919*, Melbourne
     University Press, 1980.

19   Ron Ramdin, *From Chattel Slave to Wage Earner: A History of Trade
     Unionism in Trinidad and Tobago*, London, Martin Brian & O'Keeffe,
     1982, pp. 54-5. Captain Andrew A. Cipriani and Tubal Uriah Buzz
     Butler, both former soldiers, became labour leaders in Trinidad.

20   A key fort protecting Verdun.

DUTY?
WHAT DUTY?

How did 'socialists' come to support governments in the First World War?

What swayed them away from opposition to war? The left was faced with questions as to the nature of socialism, their priorities and strategies.

Within the left three lines of thinking arose around questions of internationalism and defence: a notion of class solidarity above nationalism, a notion of defence of the progressive or modern against the reactionary, and a notion of self-defence.

The first theme asserted that workers did not owe loyalty to a nation-state. Business interests were international. To win trade disputes, workers needed solidarity, both at home and abroad. The International Working-Men's Association, or First International, founded in 1864, came together to obstruct strikebreaking and to facilitate workers from one country helping comrades in another. The International embraced all. The 'forces of order' used against workers were often drawn from far away, and authorities took care to ensure that soldiers and strikers had no opportunities to fraternise, mix and understand each other. Distance helped prevent questions being asked, and facilitated the use of the force, repression and murder. Tensions between communities fed a second theme in left thinking one that sought to defend the 'progressive' against the reactionary and the imperialist.

Deciding what was progressive was not always so clear. In France, the model of 1789 was to hand – the model of a progressive or revolutionary nation in arms. In Germany socialists had often seen Russia as a centre of despotism and reaction. But after 1905, after the first mass effervescence of workers' soviets, another Russia was struggling to emerge. Neither the German nor the Russian empire were democracies, so was there much to choose between them? Why then should Germans or Russians join imperial armies to fight each other?

Some lefts contrasted the modernity of their own nation state with less industrialised nations and states and concluded that some were more progressive than others. Modernity was one thing 'progress' another. Progress, like beauty was something best seen in the eye of the beholder. Seeing one nationalism as better than another – whether this was justified in terms of modernity, progress, culture or civilization – might elevate an 'us' against a 'them'; and led to solidarity within a state, against another state.

Socialists sometimes embraced other forms of patriotism, taking pride not in the state's official trappings – its armed forces, church, constitution, ethnicity, honours-system, law, machismo, or orderliness – but rather in a popular ethic – fair play, fair go – evolving as working peoples organised for themselves, promoting mutual respect and seeking to overcome divisions arising from varied vectors of oppression. Such patriotism was not exclusive: it might appreciate the distinctiveness and values of more than one culture. This patriotism was (and still is) an anathema to parts of the British press. An early leader of the Labour Party, Keir Hardie, was the butt of invective when, on 27 August

1914, he used the House of Commons to ask questions about
negotiations and how the war might have been avoided. He
was denounced for insulting the King; 'queer Hardie' was
pro-Zulu and pro-German.[1] Almost a century later the same
paper, the *Daily Mail*, attacked Ralph Miliband – father of
the current Labour Party leader, Ed Miliband – as 'The man
who hated Britain', an enemy who failed to fully embrace
and love their take on nationalism.[2]

A third theme in left thinking promoted self-defence.
This was something easily used and manipulated. Rosa
Luxemburg noted that wars were 'made' and pretexts
fabricated. The German declaration of war against France
in 1914 was justified as self-defence – French aircraft were
said to have bombed Germany.[3] Germany's declaration of
war against Russia was motivated as a response to the threat
posed by Russian mobilization. The justification of much of
the French labour movement supporting their state's war
effort sprang from self-defence when Germany invaded. On
all sides there were stories of atrocities, demon 'Huns' …
clichés all.

As the First World War progressed soldiers protested
against the horrors they endured and the incompetence of
generals. At home workers protested against deteriorating
conditions: the harassment of defaulters, rising costs of
food and rent, the unequal nature of food rationing, the
erosion of skill and trade-union rights, profiteering. Radical
feminists, socialists, anarchists and syndicalists wanted to do
more than protest against the symptoms of war: they wanted
to eradicate the causes of the disease. They asked questions:
Why was war not prevented? How to end it? How to uproot
the society that bred war? How to make a revolution to
overthrow warring states? How to turn a war between
nations into an insurrectionary war destroying capitalism
and the state?

Such questions were addressed at international gatherings

of socialists and syndicalists. One meeting took place in Lugano in September 1914, involving only the Italian and Swiss Socialist parties. An international peace congress met in El Ferrol in Spain in April 1915. It was mainly supported by the revolutionary syndicalists around the Spanish National Labour Confederation (CNT) and by kindred organisations in Portugal. Other delegates, from socialist, republican, co-operative, anarchist and youth organisations, came from Latin America, Italy and France. In all 47 delegates attended from 170 bodies in eight countries. It looked to promote an anti-war general strike in all countries and the initiation of a revolutionary movement. The police intervened. Some foreigners who had managed to attend – evading border controls – were arrested and deported. Organisers were accused of being in the pay of the German government. A follow-up peace congress was organised in Brazil, in Rio de Janeiro, in October, with two members of the El Ferrol congress present. The harassment of the Spanish government was also denounced in Argentina at a protest meeting in Buenos Aires on 30 May: 'The work of the border guards, of the hoisters of flags, of everything that so eloquently fashions the name of patria is no more than mierda.'⁴ Two further anti-war meetings took place in central Switzerland, at Zimmerwald in September 1915, and in the Kiental in April 1916. These meetings escaped police raids, unlike the congress in El Ferrol they were not public events. Switzerland was accessible to delegates from neighbouring countries, and invitations were sent to anti-war Socialists and to some syndicalists. The left at these two meetings, influenced by Lenin, produced some influential texts which are quoted at length below.

The war accentuated and accelerated broader social changes. Industries were expanded both in neutral and warring countries and their dependencies. Rents, prices and taxes rose. Working people had to strike, protest and struggle to obtain compensation. Many workers faced militarised conditions, the state had access to a wider range of measures to intimidate and punish: conscription into the armed forces, deportation, censorship, obstruction of meetings, etc. Often working people had to confront both the state and much of the leadership of the labour movement which, having promised social peace to the state, attempted to head-off dissent, shackle labour protest and discipline trouble-makers.

There were also times and places where labour was able to fight with some success to defend its interests. Where skilled labour was scarce, some workers were in a stronger position, better able to win concessions in conditions and pay. With so many men absent at the front, jobs were filled by women and by immigrants, including many non-Europeans. Such social changes posed new challenges: was relative privilege and the interests of entrenched skilled sectors to be defended and were such interests in conflict with the development and promotion of wider popular interests? How could new workforces and their interests advance? If the task was to incorporate new workers into unions, how was that to be done? How to react when the new workforce mobilised in the war was made redundant at the end of the war?

* * *

The Press – Peter Kropotkin, Russian Anarchist

'In general, the more that our statist bourgeois civilization advances, the more the press ceases to be an expression of what has been called public opinion, and the more it itself works, through the most despicable procedures, to fabricate opinion. The press, in all large states is comprised already [of just] two or three groups of financial and business schemers, who make whatever opinion is needed in the interest of their affairs. The large newspapers belong to them and the rest do not count.'

1912. Kropotkin suggested that army regiments should be named for sponsoring arms manufacturers: for Krupps, Putilov, or Vickers. From 'La Guerre' published in Paris by *Les Temps Nouveaux*, No. 59, 1912, pp. 15-16. http://gallica.bnf.fr/ark:/12148/bpt6k81967m

Against War
– Extraordinary International Socialist Conference

'At its congresses at Stuttgart and Copenhagen the International formulated for the proletariat of all countries these guiding principles for the struggle against war:

"If a war threatens to break out, it is the duty of the working classes and their parliamentary representatives in the countries involved supported by the coordinating activity of the International Socialist Bureau to exert every effort in order to prevent the outbreak of war by the means they consider most effective, which naturally vary according to the sharpening of the class struggle and the sharpening of the general political situation.

In case war should break out anyway it is their duty to intervene in favour of its speedy termination and with all their powers to utilize the economic and political crisis created by the war to arouse the people and thereby to hasten the overthrow of capitalist class rule."[5]

More than ever, recent events have imposed upon the proletariat the duty of devoting the utmost force and energy to planned and concerted action.'

24-25 November 1912; Basel.

Resolution of the International Socialist Bureau

'[T]he Bureau considers it an obligation for the workers of all nations concerned not only to continue but even to strengthen their demonstrations against war in favour of peace and a settlement of the Austrian-Serbian conflict by arbitration. The German and French workers will bring to bear on their governments the most vigorous pressure in order that Germany may secure in Austria a moderating action, and in order that France may obtain from Russia an undertaking that she will not engage in conflict. On their side, the workers of Great Britain and Italy shall sustain these efforts with all the power in their command.'

29 July 1914, meeting in Brussels. Socialists passed resolutions against war, but did not specify what they would do if war broke out. The resolutions above envisaged action being coordinated across countries, leaving open the question of what should be done if one or more countries started a war over the protest of labour. Social-democratic parties had no obligation to act unilaterally to obstruct war.

Against War
– French General Labour Confederation (CGT)

'To the people! To the Workers! In the current grave situation the CGT reminds everyone that it is implacably opposed to all war. Organised workers have a duty to show themselves ready to rise to these challenges and through conscious, collective action – coordinated throughout the country and internationally beyond the frontiers – to prevent the occurrence of the gravest of world-wide perils. The CGT declares that a European war must and can be prevented, if workers' protests, conjoined with that of all partisans of peace, is strong enough to silence the chants of war. ...

Recalling the declaration of the International that "all peoples are brothers" and the decisions of its national congresses: "All wars are nothing but an attack against the working class, a bloody means and a terrible diversion away from our demands",[6] it demand firmness from all workers' organisations; an attitude dictated by a concern to peacefully preserve all the rights that labour has acquired. In no way can war be a solution to the problems of the day. It is, and will remain a calamitous human disaster. Let us do everything to avoid it! Everywhere, in rural communes and in industrial towns, without orders, let popular protest grow, becoming stronger – intensifying in proportion as danger becomes more pressing. Down with war! Long live peace!'

29 July 1914. CGT Federal committee manifesto in *L'Humanité*.

Austria is provoking Serbia
– *Schleswig-Holstein Volkszeitung*
(Social-democratic newspaper)

'Austria-Hungary wants war, and is committing a crime that may drown all Europe in blood ... Austria is playing *va banque*. It dares a provocation of the Serbian state that the latter, if it is not entirely defenceless, will certainly refuse to tolerate ... Every civilized person must protest emphatically against the criminal behaviour of the Austrian rulers. It is the duty of the workers above all, and of all other human beings who honour peace and civilization, to try their utmost to prevent the consequences of the bloody insanity that has broken out in Vienna.'

24 July 1914. Quoted in Rosa Luxemburg, *The Junius Pamphlet*, London: Merlin Press, 1967, p. 14.

Say no to this frivolous provocation!
Don't allow yourselves to be used as cannon fodder!
– Appeal of the Social-democratic Party Leadership

'Not a single drop of blood from a single German soldier should be sacrificed for the benefit of war-hungry Austrian despots or for commercial interests. Comrades, we call on you to express in immediate mass demonstrations the unshakeable will for peace of the class-conscious proletariat! ... Everywhere the ears of despots must ring with: "We want no war! Down with war! Long live brotherly solidarity between peoples!"'

25 July 1914. From: *Vorwärts*. http://tintinrevolution.free.fr/fr/aufruf. html However, some German Social-democrats had made promises to defend 'civilization'. A popular crack had it that some were *Royal* Social-democrats.

To Be, or Not to Be
– Friedrich Stampfer, German Social-democrat

'When the fateful hour strikes workers will stand by the promises given ... "Unpatriotic souls" will do their duty and set an example for even the greatest patriots.'

31 July 1914. This article signalled a change of line. The party leadership began to talk of overwhelming conditions forcing their hands. They warned against ill-considered actions that might 'harm our cause'.[7] Stampfer (1874-1957) was a party journalist. *Sein oder Nichtsein*, http://www.bpb.de/geschichte/deutsche-geschichte/ersterweltkrieg/155302/ausloesung-und-beginn-des-krieges

Down with War
– *Die Einigkeit,* (Syndicalist newspaper, Berlin)

'We do not recognise the Austrian, the Serb, the Russian, the Italian, or the French, etc. We know only brother workers. To prevent this enormity we hold out our hand to the workers of all countries.'

1 August 1914. German Syndicalists rejected the Social-democrat's new pro-war line.[8] Helge Döhring: *Syndikalismus in Deutschland 1914-1918*; Lich (Hessen): Verlag Edition AV, 2013, p. 60.

Russia

Russia

Ireland

Munich

Zurich

Glasgow

Barbarism?

– *Chemnitzer Volksstimme* (Social-democratic newspaper)

'At this moment we all feel it our duty to fight first against the Russian knout. German women and children shall not become the victims of Russian bestiality, German territory must not fall into the hands of the Cossacks. For if the Entente[9] is victorious, not the French republicans, but the Russian Tsar will rule over Germany. In this moment we defend everything that we possess of German culture and German freedom against a pitiless and barbarous foe.'

2 August 1914. Quoted in Rosa Luxemburg, *The Junius Pamphlet*, London: Merlin Press, 1967, p. 32.

German Social-democrats vote for war credits

– Hugo Haase, German Social-democrat

'To avert this danger, to protect civilization and the independence of our land, we stand by what we have always maintained, and we will not desert the fatherland in this dangerous hour. We feel ourselves in harmony with the [Socialist] International which has recognised at all times the right of every nation to national independence and self-defence ...'

4 August 1914. Speech by Haase,[10] the party spokesman in the Reichstag (parliament). From: Ernst Rudolf Huber, *Dokumente zur deutschen Verfassungsgeschichte*, Stuttgart: Kohlhammer Verlag, 1961, Vol 2, pp. 456-57. http://germanhistorydocs.ghi-dc.org/sub_document.cfm?document_id=816&language=german

As on the road to Damascus, Saul had become Paul

– *Mitteilungsblatt,* (German syndicalist newspaper)

'All who yesterday were still together in harmonious friendship, with the French, Russians, British, Belgians and Japanese, all that was tied together in body and soul, pledged for all time in social and fraternal trust, all have today become bitter enemies. All international links have been dissolved. Centuries may pass before they come together again.'

August 1914. Social-democrats' conversion, to an opposite position, lampooned. From *Mitteilungsblatt, # 3*; Helge Döhring: *Syndikalismus in Deutschland 1914-1918*; Lich (Hessen): Verlag Edition AV, 2013, p. 60.

This is an old game
– Rosa Luxemburg, German Social-democrat

'Was the obvious background of the war, and the scenery that so scantily concealed it, was the whole diplomatic performance that was acted out at the outbreak of the war, with its clamour about a world of enemies, all threatening the life of Germany, all moved the one desire to weaken, to humiliate, to subjugate the German people and nation – were all these things such a complete surprise? Did these factors actually call for more judgment, more critical sagacity than they possessed? Nowhere was this less true than of our party. It had already gone through two great German wars, and in both of them had received memorable lessons.

Even a poorly informed student of history knows that the war of 1866 against Austria was systematically prepared … But not enough! In the year 1870 there came the war with France, and history has united its outbreak with an unforgettable occurrence: the Ems dispatch, a document that has become a classic byword for capitalist government art in war making, and which marks a memorable episode in our party history. Was it not old Liebknecht, was it not the German social democracy who felt in duty bound, at that time, to disclose these facts and to show to the masses 'how wars are made'?

Making war simply and solely for the protection of the

fatherland was, by the way, not Bismarck's invention. He only carried out, with characteristic unscrupulousness, an old, well-known and truly international recipe of capitalist statesmanship. When and where has there been a war since so-called public opinion has played a role in governmental calculations, in which each and every belligerent party did not, with a heavy heart, draw the sword from its sheath for the single and sole purpose of defending its fatherland and its own righteous cause from the shameful attacks of the enemy? This legend is as inextricably a part of the game of war as powder and lead. The game is old. Only that the Social-democratic party could play it is new.'

Rosa Luxemburg[11] argued that German Social-democracy should have been ready: for government tricks, for the cry of 'The fatherland is in danger!' for lies that this was a war of national defence of the German nation, or a war to defend European civilization. From: *The Junius Pamphlet*, London: Merlin Press, 1967, pp. 17-18.

Why did they support the War?
– Frank Bohn, American Socialist

'With a vast majority, it has been a matter of salary, of the commonest sort of economic determinism. They receive three thousand marks a year. Most of them have salaries from the party beside, the members of the party executive receiving from us over five thousand marks a year. This whole crowd began life as poor, hopeless lawyers or school teachers. They are now perfectly quiet, respectable middle-class persons who would no more think of losing their position in life than they would of going into the streets naked....

[*Bohn's conclusion.*] On August 1, last, the German party numbered about nine hundred thousand dues-paying members. Of these, perhaps one hundred thousand were really socialists. If these had stood alone, with a press and a leadership devoted to revolutionary ideals, there would have been no war. If ten thousand men and women had been perfectly willing to face the firing squad or had packed the jails; had they sent messages of true rebellion to their comrades in France, Belgium and England, all the king's horses and all the king's men would have stayed within the borders of Germany. One person went to jail – heroic Rosa Luxemburg.'

Looking back one year later (August 1915). Frank Bohn in conversation with Franz Mehring.[12] From: 'The Reds of Germany' *International Socialist Review* (United States), Vol. XVI, No.2, pp.79-82.

Danger – Jean Jaurès, French Socialist

'At all costs the working class should be preserved from panic and madness ... the greatest danger is ... that as disquiet is propagated, as sudden impulses are generated born of fear, of acute incertitude, in prolonged anxiety, a lack of nerve should become general. In such mad panic, crowds may give way, and one cannot be sure that governments might not give way ....'

31 July 1914. From *L'Humanité*; an editorial written by Jaurès[13] shortly before his assassination at 9.40pm. The next quotation comes from a speech made five days later by Léon Jouhaux, the general secretary of the General Labour Confederation (CGT), at Jaurès's funeral, seeking to justify support for the government.

The shade of Jaurès – Léon Jouhaux, French syndicalist

'... if peace did not triumph it was neither your fault (Jaurès), nor ours ... this war, we didn't want it. Those who began it, despots with blood on their minds, dreaming of some criminal hegemony should pay the price ... Being constrained to fight, we set out to repel the invader, to safeguard the patrimony of civilization and that generous ideology bequeathed to us by history. We do not wish those few liberties so painfully ripped from evil forces to lapse ...

Our desire has always been to expand popular rights, to widen the field of liberties. It is in harmony with this will that we reply to the order for mobilisation with "present". We will never work for a war of conquest. No comrades, our ideal of human reconciliation and working for social happiness will not lapse ...

We will be soldiers of liberty, conquering a regime of freedom on behalf of the oppressed to create harmony between peoples through a free understanding amongst the nations, through alliances between peoples. This is the ideal that will allow us to win. The shadow of the great will attest this for us.'

4 August 1914, Paris. Other trade union leaders also supported their governments.

Manifesto – International Woman Suffrage Alliance

'We women of twenty-six countries, having banded ourselves together in the International Women's Suffrage Alliance with the object of obtaining political means of sharing with men the power which shapes the fate of nations, appeal to you to leave untried no method of conciliation or arbitration for arranging international differences which may help to avert deluging half the civilised world in blood.'

August 1914.

Manifesto to the British People
– Keir Hardie & Arthur Henderson, British Labour Party

'The long-threatened European war is now upon us. For more than one hundred years no such danger has confronted civilization. It is for you to take full account of the desperate situation and to act promptly and vigorously in the interest of peace. You have never been consulted about the war. Whatever may be the rights and wrongs of the sudden, crushing attack made by the militarist Empire of Austria upon Serbia, it is certain that the workers of all countries likely to be drawn into the conflict must strain every nerve to prevent their governments from committing them to war. Everywhere socialists and the organised forces of labour are taking this course. Everywhere vehement protests are made against the greed and intrigues of militarists and armament-mongers. We call upon you to do the same here in Great Britain upon an even more impressive scale. Hold vast demonstrations against war in every industrial centre.'

1 August 1914. Statement for the British Section of the International Socialist Bureau. Keir Hardie was a former leader of the Labour Party. He was disappointed that many of his Merthyr Tydfil constituents supported the war. It is said that the war broke his heart. He died in September 1915.

At all cost, no war!
– *La difesa delle lavoratrici*, (Italian Socialist newspaper)

'We won't give a penny or soldier. The proletariat is ready with all its force to prevent this slaughter. We recorded previously that women more than men would uproot rails and throw themselves onto them to prevent soldiers departing; then it was a matter of the [war in] Africa [Libya], should it be different now? ... The proletariat has one faith and one certainty: the faith in socialism ...'

2 August 1914. Italian Socialists say: workers won't kill workers to satisfy the barbaric instincts of any government.
From: *La difesa delle lavoratrici* (Milan),[14] http://91.212.219.213/browsie/index.asp

Our Duty in this Crisis
– James Connolly, Irish Socialist and Industrial Unionist

'What ought to be the attitude of the working-class democracy of Ireland in face of the present crisis? In the first place, then, we ought to clear our minds of all the political cant which would tell us that we have either "natural enemies" or "natural allies" in any of the powers now warring. When it is said that we ought to unite to protect our shores against the "foreign enemy" I confess to be unable to follow that line of reasoning, as I know of no foreign enemy of this country except the British government and know that it is not the British government that is meant. In the second place we ought to seriously consider that the evil effects of this war upon Ireland will be simply incalculable, that it will cause untold suffering and misery amongst the people, and that as this misery and suffering have been brought upon us because of our enforced partisanship with a nation whose government never consulted us in the matter, we are therefore perfectly at liberty morally to make any bargain we may see fit, or that may present itself in the course of events. Should a German army land in Ireland tomorrow we should be perfectly justified in joining it if by doing so we could rid this country once and for all from its connection with the brigand empire that drags us unwillingly into this war. Should the working class of Europe, rather than slaughter each other for the benefit of kings and financiers, proceed tomorrow to erect barricades all over Europe, to break up bridges and destroy the transport service that war might be abolished, we should be perfectly justified in following such a glorious example and contributing our aid to the final dethronement of the vulture classes that rule and rob the world.'

9 August 1914, *Irish Worker*. (This paper was suppressed in December 1914.) James Connolly helped lead the Easter 1916 rising for Irish independence.

War! What For?
– Industrial Workers of the World (Australia)

'For the workers and their dependents: death, starvation, poverty and untold misery. For the capitalist class: gold, stained with the blood of millions, riotous luxury, banquets of jubilation over the graves of their dupes and slaves. War is hell! Send the capitalists to hell and wars are impossible.'

10 August 1914, *Direct Action*.

A Continental Revolution – James Connolly

'For a generation at least the socialist movement in all the countries now involved has progressed by leaps and bounds, and more satisfactory still, by steady and continuous increase and development. The number of votes recorded for socialist candidates has increased at a phenomenally rapid rate, the number of socialist representatives in all legislative chambers has become more and more of a disturbing factor in the calculations of governments. Newspapers, magazines, pamphlets and literature of all kinds teaching socialist ideas have been and are daily distributed by the million amongst the masses; every army and navy in Europe has seen a constantly increasing proportion of socialists amongst its soldiers and sailors, and the industrial organisations of the working class have more and more perfected their grasp over the economic machinery of society, and more and more moved responsive to the socialist conception of their duties. Along with this, hatred of militarism has spread through every rank of society, making everywhere its recruits, and raising an aversion to war even amongst those who in other things accepted the capitalist order of things. Anti-militarist societies and anti-militarist campaigns of socialist societies and parties, and anti-militarist resolutions of socialist and international trade union conferences have become part of the order of the day and are no longer phenomena to be wondered at. The whole working class movement stands committed to war upon war – stands so committed at the very height of its strength and influence. And now, like the proverbial bolt from the blue, war is upon us, and war between the most important, because the most socialist, nations of the earth. And we are helpless!

What then becomes of all our resolutions; all our protests of fraternisation; all our threats of general strikes; all our carefully-built machinery of internationalism; all our hopes for the future? Were they all as sound and fury, signifying nothing? When the German artilleryman, a socialist serving in the German army of invasion, sends a shell into the ranks of the French army, blowing off their heads; tearing out their bowels, and mangling the limbs of dozens of socialist comrades in that force, will the fact that he, before leaving for the front "demonstrated" against the war be of any value to the widows and orphans made by the shell he sent upon its mission of murder? Or, when the French rifleman pours his murderous rifle fire into the ranks of the German line of attack, will he be able to derive any comfort from the probability that his bullets are murdering or maiming comrades who last year joined in thundering "hochs" and cheers of

greeting to the eloquent Jaurès, when in Berlin he pleaded
for international solidarity? When the socialist pressed
into the army of the Austrian Kaiser, sticks a long, cruel
bayonet-knife into the stomach of the socialist conscript
in the army of the Russian Tsar, and gives it a twist so that
when pulled out it will pull the entrails out along with it,
will the terrible act lose any of its fiendish cruelty by the
fact of their common theoretical adhesion to an anti-war
propaganda in times of peace? When the socialist soldier
from the Baltic provinces of Russia is sent forward into
Prussian Poland to bombard towns and villages until a red
trail of blood and fire covers the homes of the unwilling
Polish subjects of Prussia, as he gazes upon the corpses of
those he has slaughtered and the homes he has destroyed,
will he in his turn be comforted by the thought that the
Tsar whom he serves sent other soldiers a few years ago
to carry the same devastation and murder into his own
home by the Baltic Sea?

But why go on? Is it not as clear as the fact of life itself
that no insurrection of the working class; no general strike;
no general uprising of the forces of Labour in Europe,
could possibly carry with it, or entail a greater slaughter
of socialists, than will their participation as soldiers in
the campaigns of the armies of their respective countries?
Every shell which explodes in the midst of a German
battalion will slaughter some socialists; every Austrian
cavalry charge will leave the gashed and hacked bodies
of Serbian or Russian socialists squirming and twisting
in agony upon the ground; every Russian, Austrian, or
German ship sent to the bottom or blown sky-high will
mean sorrow and mourning in the homes of some socialist
comrades of ours. If these men must die, would it not be
better to die in their own country fighting for freedom for
their class, and for the abolition of war, than to go forth to
strange countries and die slaughtering and slaughtered by

their brothers that tyrants and profiteers might live?

Civilization is being destroyed before our eyes; the results of generations of propaganda and patient heroic plodding and self-sacrifice are being blown into annihilation from a hundred cannon mouths; thousands of comrades with whose souls we have lived in fraternal communion are about to be done to death; they whose one hope it was to be spared to cooperate in building the perfect society of the future are being driven to fratricidal slaughter in shambles where that hope will be buried under a sea of blood. I am not writing in captious criticism of my continental comrades. We know too little about what is happening on the continent, and events have moved too quickly for any of us to be in a position to criticise at all. But believing as I do that any action would be justified which would put a stop to this colossal crime now being perpetrated, I feel compelled to express the hope that ere long we may read of the paralysing of the internal transport service on the continent, even should the act of paralysing necessitate the erection of socialist barricades and acts of rioting by socialist soldiers and sailors, as happened in Russia in 1905. Even an unsuccessful attempt at social revolution by force of arms, following the paralysis of the economic life of militarism, would be less disastrous to the socialist cause than the act of socialists allowing themselves to be used in the slaughter of their brothers in the cause.

A great continental uprising of the working class would stop the war; a universal protest at public meetings will not save a single life from being wantonly slaughtered. I make no war upon patriotism; never have done. But against the patriotism of capitalism – the patriotism which makes the interest of the capitalist class the supreme test of duty and right – I place the patriotism of the working class, the patriotism which judges every public act by its effect upon the fortunes of those who toil. That which is good for the working class I esteem patriotic, but that party or movement is the most perfect embodiment of patriotism which most successfully works for the conquest by the working class of the control of the destinies of the land wherein they labour. To me, therefore, the socialist of another country is a fellow-patriot, as the capitalist of my own country is a natural enemy. I regard each nation as the possessor of a definite contribution to the common stock of civilization, and I regard the capitalist class of each nation as being the logical and natural enemy of the national culture which constitutes that definite contribution. Therefore, the stronger I am in my affection for national tradition, literature, language, and sympathies, the more firmly rooted I am in my opposition to that capitalist class …'

15 August 1914. From: *Forward*. http://www.marxists.org/archive/connolly/1914/08/contrev.htm

War: What it means to you – James Connolly

'You are asked to stop and consider what this war will mean to the working class of this city and country. It already means that increased prices will be demanded for all food and household necessities. In every bite of food you eat you will be compelled to pay for the war; and as you are already poor and have at the best of times a struggle to live, the war will mean hunger and misery to thousands – less food on their tables, less clothes on their backs or beds, less coal for their fires, less boots and shoes on their children's feet and their own. War will mean more unemployment and less wages. Already the mills of Belfast are put on short time, which means starvation wages, ware-rooms are closing down, and all foundries and engineering works which make machinery for the continent, if they have not closed down already, are getting ready to do so. Thus before a shot has been fired by the British army on land, before a battle has been fought at sea, ruin and misery are entering the homes of the working people. What will be your case? Many thousands of you will die of slow starvation, or perish of cold and long-drawn-out misery before the end of the war if you suffer so much before it is begun. Some people tell you it will be over in a fortnight. They said the same about the Boer War, but it lasted three years. And the Boer War was a mere picnic compared to what this war will be. Remember that Lord Kitchener tells all joining now that they must be prepared to serve three years. And he knows.

You women! Remember that it is the children you suckled at your breast, reared at your knees, whose little steps you watched and prayed over and were proud of, it is they who will be sent to fight the battles of the Empire – an Empire that despises you and them – an Empire under whose rule three million Irish people were thrown on the roadside to starve, four million driven like wild beasts out of their own country, an Empire under which in less than fifty years a million and a half of Irish men, women and children died of hunger in the midst of smiling harvests, and under which YOU have lived a lifetime of sweated misery and badly paid toil. Women of Belfast, will you send your husbands, fathers, sons or sweethearts to be slaughtered in defence of an Empire that stood quietly by and allowed the Orangemen to arm against you and against freedom for Ireland, but sent its soldiers to shoot down the unarmed people of Dublin when they attempted to arm in defence of Irish nationality?

… But who will win and guarantee the independence of Ireland? Will the Volunteers? Will the anti-Irish aristocrats who are rushing in to become your officers allow you to take a stand for Irish nationality? Remember the words of Wolfe Tone:

"When the aristocracy come forward the people fall backward; when the people come forward the aristocracy, fearful of being left behind, insinuate themselves into our ranks, and rise to be timid leaders, or treacherous auxiliaries."[15]

We want Ireland, not for peers or the nominees of peers, but Ireland for the Irish.'

1914. Speech to Belfast Division of the Irish Citizen Army. From James Connolly, *Collected Works: Volume 1*, Dublin: New Books Publications, 1987, pp. 281ff.

The Tasks of Revolutionary Social Democracy
– V. I. Lenin, Russian Social-democrat

'The European and world war has the clearly defined character of a bourgeois, imperialist and dynastic war: a struggle for markets and for freedom to loot foreign countries, a striving to suppress the revolutionary movement of the proletariat and democracy in the individual countries, a desire to deceive, disunite, and slaughter the proletarians of all countries by setting the wage slaves of one nation against those of another, so as to benefit the bourgeoisie – the real content and the meaning of the war is only in all of this. The conduct of the leaders of the German Social-democratic party, the strongest and the most influential in the Second International, a party which has voted for war credits and repeated the bourgeois-chauvinist phrases of the Prussian Junkers and the bourgeoisie, is sheer betrayal of socialism.... The betrayal of socialism by most leaders of the Second International signifies the ideological and political bankruptcy of the International.... rejecting the fundamental truth of socialism, set out long ago in the *Communist Manifesto*, that the workers have no country;

by confining themselves, in the struggle against militarism, to a sentimental philistine point of view, instead of recognising the need for a revolutionary war ...'

August 1914. Lenin[16] was in exile in near Cracow when war broke out but thereafter took refuge in Switzerland. For some days he refused to believe that German Social-democrats had voted credits to finance the war. He wrote the above text with fellow exiles, members of the Bolshevik wing of the Russian Social-democratic party. From: http://www.marxists.org/archive/lenin/works/1914/aug/x01.htm

Workers' interests are not bound up in the struggle – Socialist Party of Great Britain

'... declaring that no interests are at stake justifying the shedding of a single drop of working-class blood, enters its emphatic protest against the brutal and bloody butchery of our brothers in this and other lands ... Having no quarrel with the working class of any country, we extend to our fellow workers of all lands the expression of our good will and socialist fraternity, and pledge ourselves to work for the overthrow of capitalism and the triumph of Socialism.'

September 1914. From: 'The war and the Socialist position', *Socialist Standard*.

Anti-War Manifesto
– The Independent Labour Party, (Britain)

'It was not the Serbian question or the Belgian question that pulled this country into the deadly struggle. Great Britain is not at war because of oppressed nationalities or Belgian neutrality. Even had Belgian neutrality not been wrongfully infringed by Germany we should still have been drawn in. If France in defiance of treaty rights had invaded Belgium to get at Germany, who believes we should have begun hostilities against France? Behind the back of parliament and people, the British Foreign Office gave secret understandings to France, denying their existence when challenged. That is why this country is now face to face with the red ruin and impoverishment of war. Treaties and agreements have dragged Republican France at the heels of despotic Russia, Britain at the heels of France. At the proper time all this will be made plain, and the men responsible called to account.

Socialism Will Yet Triumph

We are told that International Socialism is dead, that all our hopes and ideals are wrecked by the fire and pestilence of European war. It is not true. Out of the darkness and the depth we hail our working-class comrades of every land. Across the roar of guns, we send sympathy and greeting to the German Socialists. They have laboured unceasingly to promote good relations with Britain, as we with Germany. They are no enemies of ours but faithful friends. In forcing this appalling crime upon the nations, it is the rulers, the diplomats, the militarists who have sealed their doom. In tears and blood and bitterness the greater democracy will be born. With steadfast faith we greet the future; our cause is holy and imperishable, and the labor of our hands has not been in vain. Long live freedom and fraternity! Long live International Socialism!'

August 1914. National Council of the Independent Labour Party

Awake! – *Freedom*, Anarchist newspaper, London

'It is possible that the social revolution will be the last act in the present tragedy; possible that murderous militarism will be drowned in the blood of its numberless victims; that the people of the different countries will unite against the bloody regimes of modern capitalism and its institutions, and finally produce a new social culture upon the basis of free socialism.'

14 September 1914.

Our Business – John Maclean, British Socialist

'... it is our business as socialists to develop a 'class patriotism', refusing to murder one another for a sordid world capitalism. The absurdity of the present situation is surely apparent when we see British socialists going out to murder German socialists with the object of crushing Kaiserism and Prussian militarism. The only real enemy to Kaiserism and Prussian militarism, I assert against the world, was and is German Social-democracy. Let the propertied class go out, old and young alike, and defend their blessed property. When they have been disposed of, we of the working class will have something to defend, and we shall do it.'

17 September 1914, *Justice*. John Maclean was a leading Glaswegian member of the British Socialist Party.

Prepare – Italian Syndicalist Union (USI)

'The general council of the USI expresses its confidence in the proletariat of neutral and belligerent countries – that it will find within itself a spirit of class solidarity and revolutionary energy – and will take advantage of the inevitable weakening of state forces, and of the general crisis engendered by the war itself, to work through common action towards the overthrow of monarchical and bourgeois states that have been making conscious and cynical preparations for war for half a century.'

September 1914. A small pro-intervention minority was expelled by the USI general council.[17]

Reassert old principles! Fight against the extension of this war – Italian and Swiss Socialists

'The present catastrophe is the result of the imperialist policy of the great powers, which in absolute monarchies are identical with dynastic interests. The European war is not a struggle for higher culture, for the freedom of the people. It is at once a struggle of the capitalist classes for new markets in foreign lands, and a criminal attempt to break down the revolutionary movement of the proletariat and the Social-democracy at home. The German and Austrian bourgeois have no right to defend the war with reference to Tsarism and the freedom of national culture. For not only have the Prussian Junker-dom, with William II at its head, and the powerful capitalists of Germany always befriended this damnable reign of the Russian Tsar, but the governments of Germany and Austria-Hungary have also suppressed the national culture of their people, have cast into chains those who have struggled for liberty of the working class. Nor have the French and English bourgeois the right to uphold their own countries by denouncing German imperialism, by declaiming about the freedom of the nations of Europe. Their aim is not the liberation of the people from capitalist and military oppression, their alliance with the Russia of the Tsar has increased this oppression and has hindered the progress of civilisation. The real cause and the true character of this war have been purposely hidden by the ruling classes of the European nations in a frenzy of chauvinism, and parts of the working class have been swept into this chauvinistic whirlpool.'

27 September 1914. Joint declaration of Italian and Swiss Socialist parties, meeting in Lugano. From: William English Walling, *The Socialists and the War*, New York: Holt, 1915, pp. 206-7.
https://archive.org/stream/socialistswardoc00walluoft#page/225/mode/1up

The Duty of Working Women in Wartime
– Clara Zetkin, German Social-democrat

'No, a thousand times no. Let us not allow the working masses to forget that the war has been caused by world-wide economic and political complications, and not by ugly and despicable personal qualities in the peoples with which Germany is fighting. Let us have the courage, when we hear the invectives against "perfidious Albion," the "degenerate French," the "barbaric Russians", etc., to reply by pointing out the ineradicable riches contributed by these peoples to human development, and how they have assisted the fruition of German civilization. The Germans, who have themselves contributed so much towards the international treasury of civilization, ought to be able to exercise justice and veracity in judging other peoples.'

November 1914. Clara Zetkin[18] noted that the press had circulated stories of atrocities committed against German soldiers. She rejected Germany's enemies being portrayed as barbarians. Shortly after this article was published *Gleichheit* was suppressed. Other newspapers with far greater circulation, such as the *Berliner Tageblacht* were suspended until they promised to refrain from criticising the war. Some Social-democratic papers did not go along with the line taken by the party leadership. Opposition was maintained for some time in the *Bremer Bürgerzitung* (Bremen), *Volksfreund* (Brunswick); in the *Leipziger Volksblatt* and the *Schwäbische Tageblatt* (Würtemburg).[19] From: *Gleichheit*, http://www.marxists.org/archive/zetkin/1914/11/19.html.

Legitimate self-defence
– Errico Malatesta, Italian Anarchist

'[T]he oppressed are always in a state of legitimate self-defence and have always the right to attack the oppressors. I admit, therefore, that there are wars that are necessary, holy wars: and these are wars of liberation, such as are generally 'civil wars' – i.e., revolutions …

If, when foreign soldiers invade the sacred soil of the Fatherland, the privileged class were to renounce their privileges, and would act so that the 'fatherland' really became the common property of all the inhabitants, it would then be right that all should fight against the invaders. But if kings wish to remain kings, and the landlords wish to take care of *their* lands and of *their* houses, and if the merchants wish to take care of *their* goods, and even sell them at a higher price, then the workers, the socialists and anarchists, should leave them to their own devices, while being themselves on the look-out for an opportunity to get rid of the oppressors inside the country, as well as of those coming from outside. In all circumstances, it is the duty of the socialists, and especially of the anarchists, to do everything that can weaken the state and the capitalist class, and to take as the only guide to their conduct the interest of Socialism; or, if they are materially powerless to act efficaciously for their own cause, at least to refuse any voluntary help to the cause of the enemy, and stand aside to save at least their principles – which means to save the future.'

November 1914. Article by Malatesta[20] 'Anarchists have forgotten their principles' in *Freedom* and *Le Réveil*. See also: Vernon Richards, Ed., *Malatesta: Life and Ideas*, London: Freedom Press, 1965, pp. 243-7.

Summing up
– Alfred Rosmer, French Socialist & Syndicalist

'One should note that with its new attitude *Bataille Syndicaliste* incorporated revolutionary syndicalism into the French state, in a wholehearted manner, rallying to a policy of social peace; from now on it sung its part in the national choir, it barked like the worst of chauvinists, in all areas it followed government instructions strictly.'

Rosmer[21] condemned the CGT newspaper for changing sides, becoming a slavish follower of the government policy. From: *Le mouvement ouvrier pendant la première guerre mondiale: de l'union sacrée a Zimmerwald*, Paris: Librairie du Travail, 1936, p. 145.

The Downfall of the International
– Anton Pannekoek, Dutch Socialist

'While the proletarian masses, obedient to the rulers, dissolved into national armies, are slaughtering one another in the service of capital, the international Social-democracy has broken up into groups of jingo politicians who bitterly attack one another. The Second International is dead. But this ignoble death is no accident; like the downfall of the First International, the collapse of the Second is an indication of the fact that its usefulness is at an end. It represents, in fact, the downfall of the old fighting methods of the epoch. Not in the sense that they will disappear or become useless, but in the sense that the whole world now understands that these methods cannot bring the revolution. They retain their value as preparation, as auxiliary means. But the conquest of power demands new revolutionary forms of struggle. To have pointed these out, to have put before us the new problems which it itself was incapable of solving—this is the bequest to us of the Second International. These will be fully developed by the new capitalist world that will grow out of this world-war—a world of mightier capitalist development, increased oppression of the proletariat, more pronounced antagonism of the three great world powers, Germany, England and America. And out of these new conditions a new International of Labour will grow, more firmly founded, more strongly organized, more powerful and more socialistic than the one that now perished. Looking beyond the terrible world-fire, we revolutionary socialists boldly erect upon the ruins the standard of the new, the coming Internationalism:

'C'est la lutte finale, groupons-nous, et demain L'Internationale sera le genre humain.' (Let's get together, this is the final struggle and tomorrow the International will be the human race.)'

November 1914. From: *New Review*, from http://www.marxists.org/ history/usa/pubs/newreview/1914/index.htm. Pannekoek[22] also made the comments below, on the majority leadership of German Social-democratic party:

'To expect from narrow parliamentarians and bureaucrats like Scheidemann and Ebert any revolutionary initiative would have been ridiculous, and just as little could one expect that the masses, accustomed to do only what the party ordered, would now come forward independently without the leaders of the party. On Tuesday evening, the 28th of July, well attended meetings were held to protest against the war. That was all. And in these meetings there was a total lack of enthusiasm. With a feeling of depression, they realized that fate was approaching without being able to stop it. The question how the war could be resisted was never even raised, because the question whether the war ought to be resisted was not even answered with a decisive "Yes".... In wide circles, even among party members, they were for the war. In the *Vorwärts* and many other party papers the war was set forth as a "war against the blood-Tsar", a war against Russian barbarism. They cited Karl Marx, who in 1848 had urged Germany to a war against Russia; they overlooked the fact that that applied only so long as Russia dominated and threatened Europe as its most powerful military state. Thus the war was made popular among the working masses. In vain did a few newspapers of the left lift their voice against it.'

In Reply to Kropotkin
– Alexander Berkman, Russian American Anarchist

'It is a most painful shock to us to realize that even Kropotkin, clear thinker that he is, has in this instance fallen a victim to the war psychology now dominating Europe. His arguments are weak and superficial. In his letter to Gustav Steffen he has become so involved in the artificialities of "high politics" that he lost sight of the most elemental fact of the situation, namely that the war in Europe is not a war of nations, but a war of capitalist governments, for power and markets. Kropotkin argues as if the German people are at war with the French, the Russian or English people, when as a matter of fact it is only the ruling and capitalist cliques of those countries that are responsible for the war and alone stand to gain by its result. Throughout his life Kropotkin has taught us that "the reason for modern war is always the competition for markets and the right to exploit nations backward in industry." Is the proletariat of Germany, of France, or of Russia interested in new markets, in the exploitation of nations backward in industry? Have they anything to gain by this or any other capitalist war?

… Kropotkin strangely fails to mention the working classes of the contending powers. He speaks a great deal of the military ambitions of Prussia, of the menace of German invasion and similar governmental games. But where do the workers come in in all this? Are the economic interests of the working classes of Europe involved in this war, do they stand to profit in any way by whatever result there might be, and is international solidarity furthered by sending Russian and French workers to slaughter their brother workers in German uniform? Has not Kropotkin always taught us that the solidarity of labour throughout the world is the cornerstone of all true progress, and that labour has no interest whatever in the quarrels of their governmental or industrial masters?

Kropotkin dwells on the menace of Prussian militarism, and on the necessity of destroying it. But can Prussian militarism be destroyed by the militarism of the allies? Does not the militarism of a country – of any country – ultimately rest on the consent of the people of that country, and has not Kropotkin always argued that the revolutionary consciousness and economic solidarity of the workers alone can force capital and government to terms, and ultimately abolish both? Surely Kropotkin will not claim that carnage, rapine and destruction advance the civilization of one country as against that of another. He has always emphasized that real culture – in the sense of social liberty and economic well-being – rests with the people themselves, and that there is no difference in the true character of government, whatever its particular form. Indeed, he has repeatedly said that the "liberal" governments are the more subtle and therefore the more dangerous enslavers of humanity.

We regret deeply, most deeply, Kropotkin's changed attitude. But not even the great European catastrophe can alter our position on the international brotherhood of man. We unconditionally condemn all capitalist wars, with whatever sophisms it may be sought to defend the one or the other set of pirates and exploiters as more "libertarian". We unalterably hold that war is the game of the masters, always at the expense of the duped workers. The workers have nothing to gain by the victory of the one or the other of the contending sides. Prussian militarism is no greater menace to life and liberty than Tsarist autocracy. Neither can be destroyed by the other. Both must and will be destroyed only by the social revolutionary power of the united international proletariat.'

November 1914. Berkman was imprisoned in 1917, for conspiracy to oppose conscription.[23] He condemned Peter Kropotkin for his support for France's war effort and for viewing Prussian militarism as the greater danger. From: *Mother Earth*, Vol. 9, No. 9.

Not a war of Liberation
– Karl Liebknecht, German Social-democrat

'The liberation of the Russian people, as also the liberation of the German people, must be accomplished by the people themselves. Its historical basis and its course at the start make unacceptable the pretence of the capitalist government that the purpose for which it demands credits is the defence of the fatherland. A speedy peace, a peace without conquests, this is what we must demand. Every effort in this direction must be supported. Only by strengthening jointly and continuously the currents in all the belligerent countries which have such a peace as their object can this bloody slaughter be brought to an end. Only a peace based upon the international solidarity of the working class and on the liberty of all the peoples can be a lasting peace. Therefore, it is the duty of the proletariats of all countries to carry on during the war a common socialistic work in favour of peace.'

Like other Social-democratic deputies, Liebknecht had voted war credits in August, but in December 1914, he broke the unity of the parliamentary Social-democrat group and refused to support the war. He prepared this statement for the Reichstag. Published two weeks later in *Justice* (journal of the Social Democratic Federation). http://www.marxists.org/archive/liebknecht-k/works/1916/future-belongs-people/ch06.htm

French Syndicalist leaders didn't think straight
– Pierre Monatte, French Syndicalist & Socialist

'It is understandable to some extent that the popular masses – misled and excited by the press from one day to the next (by all the press) – should have accepted as an article of faith every government statement. But that syndicalist militants should be devoid of clear thinking; that they were unable to bring a critical spirit to their analysis of government assertions, that they should let themselves be swayed by a fever of national arrogance – forgetting those principles that had governed them hitherto, that is the most saddening of spectacles.'

December 1914. Monatte[24] wrote this letter to explain why he had resigned from the CGT national committee. From: Alfred Rosmer, *Le mouvement ouvrier pendant la première guerre mondiale : de l'union sacrée a Zimmerwald*, Paris: Librairie du Travail, 1936, p. 179.

Why did we fail to mobilise more workers?
– Georges Dumoulin, French Syndicalist & Socialist

'The proletariat does not have hate for things that affect it, because it does not hold it [capitalism] responsible for the war. The sacred union was possible because capitalism was not yet recognised by the exploited masses.

We had not established that responsibility and culpability clearly.'

The CGT leader, Jouhaux, had been a key decision-maker. He excused his support for the government by blaming the German union leader, Legien. Applause at anti-war meetings was well and fine – but what did it signify in practice? From: 'Les syndicalistes français et la guerre'. Published in June 1918.

http://bataillesocialiste.wordpress.com/documents-historiques/1918-06-les-syndicalistes-francais-et-la-guerre-dumoulin/

An appeal for peace – Sébastien Faure, French Anarchist

'If it was not in our power to stop this calamity – and that will be something that our generation will regret and be ashamed of, well, let us at least try to stop its disastrous consequences at once, that will be us joy our and rehabilitation. Once again, today's duty is there – it is imperious, indisputable, sacred! …. It is not for France to abase itself in front of Germany, nor for the latter to abase itself for the former. France does not need to beg for peace, neither does Germany. Rather, now already, in France as in Germany, peace has its resolute and ardent partisans. And I know perfectly well that in Russia, Britain, Austria and Belgium, as much as in France and Germany, part of the people secretly but passionately desires an end to massacres. On the one hand, what is needed in each nation, is that the partisans of peace assert themselves, come together, announce their holy crusade, multiply, and develop, bring about and create a current of opinion in favour of peace. Furthermore what is needed, is that neutral countries, those ready to offer their mediation, know that in all the countries crushed by the burden of war, alongside those who systematically decline at any price to hear talk of peace until the enemy is entirely smashed, there are many people who would be happy to see governments consent to consider the possibility of finishing with war as quickly as possible and [ready to] consider peace terms acceptable to all in the present; [terms]which would offer guarantees against the return of such a calamity. More than ever an enemy of war, more than ever committed to peace …'

January 1915. This appeal – to socialists, syndicalists, revolutionaries and anarchists – was circulated widely and reached the trenches. See: Maurice Barres, *L'Ame française et la guerre (Les Tentacules de pieuvre)*, Paris: Emile-Paul frères, 1920, pp. 254-5.

A Critique of Karl Kautsky
– William English Walling, American Radical

'… if it comes to war in spite of all the efforts of the Social-democracy, then each nation must protect its skin as well as it can. Therefore the Social-democrats of each nation have the same right or duty to take part in this defence and none of them has the right to blame the others. …

Since conscription prevails in all Continental countries and insurrection at the outbreak of the war is regarded by the overwhelming majority of continental Socialists as impracticable, there is little question that they must all go to war, without any reproach from the Socialists of hostile countries. The only question is whether they should give their governments voluntary financial and moral support by voting war loans and similar actions. And it is this that Kautsky specifically defends.

… Kautsky has ceased to be the spokesman of international Socialism and has settled down into the role of official apologist for the German Party – a position more than ever dubious after the nationalistic stand of that Party majority in the present war.'

January 1915. Kautsky was once reputed to be the 'Pope' of Social-democracy. Walling wrote that he chose new criteria, and abandoned his pre-war positions. From 'A Socialist Digest, Kautsky's New Doctrine', *New Review* (New York).

Hurrah for the Socialist Women's International!
– Clara Zetkin, International Secretary of Socialist Women

'We share your deep sympathy for the sufferings of the lands which have been laid waste by this bloody strife. We think with deep grief of the horrors of devastation in East Prussia and Galicia, and with no less pain of the disaster which stalks along the roads of France, and which in unhappy Belgium has caused a wicked breach of international law. We join with you in demanding what we claim for ourselves in every land as a matter of course: the safety and inviolability of our native lands, the integrity of national autonomy and independence. We share your conviction that no diplomatic intrigues, no militarist governments, no provocation on the part of jingo patriots should divide the working men and women of the world. We unite our wills to yours and march on together in the fight for peace. Together with you, we shall unceasingly strive against the exploitation and oppression of labour by property. Nothing can make us doubt that the struggle for the freedom of the working people is at the same time the most fruitful preparation, and the truest surety for the peace of nations the whole world round. Does not this very war remind us that the class cleavage between exploiters and exploited in the nations is the root of that enmity which is the first cause of this war between the peoples.

We socialist women of all nations recognise imperialism as the foe which is now driving on the peoples to fight each other, in order to exhaust and enslave them. There is no possibility of any compact between imperialism and socialism. Therefore it is our fixed determination to give all the strength of our wills and all the ardour of our hearts to make socialism triumph over imperialism. Such a great historical event as that, this war teaches us, is only possible with the socialist international as a foundation, only when the exploited of all lands stand together against their exploiters and masters. Socialism will triumph over imperialism, and with it also over capitalism, when men and women of the working class have resolved to bring to the defence of their own interests and the realisation of their aims as much power, passion and inspiration, and to make as great sacrifices of life and property, as imperialism now demands for its own ends.

Women comrades of Great Britain, your sisters in all countries rejoice with proud satisfaction to know that, as your message shows, we stand together unshaken and estimate the violent events of this time from a socialist standpoint. We stand together in sisterly sympathy for all those who are suffering from these events, and with an unshaken determination to fulfil faithfully our duty as socialists, and not to be led astray when the international enemies of the peoples seek to deceive us, nor to be alarmed by the threat of danger and persecution. Far over the battlefields, with their unspeakable horrors, we stretch out to you our hands with deep emotion, and send you our most heartfelt greetings. On with international socialism!'

January 1915. From: *The Labour Woman*, Vol. II No.9; https://www.marxists.org/archive/zetkin/1915/01/reply.htm

Immutable internationalism! – Italian Anarchists

'Reaffirming: our uncompromising opposition to all war – other than for our own liberation and social emancipation – and our immutable internationalist and anarchist beliefs, in opposition to all forms of compromise and collaboration with bourgeois and militarist classes of whatever nationality or race; we give a mandate to the comrades of the anarchist press present at this conference to fashion an accord with comrades from abroad to call an international meeting able to make concrete plans for activities to prevent the extension of the war, to impose its cessation and to reaffirm internationalist principles; furthermore, working to promote immediately anti-war activities; directing a manifesto towards the people and proposing rallies, organising movements against unemployment and the high cost of living, and working towards the launching of first, a general protest strike, and subsequently, insurrection.'

January 1915. Resolution of the anarchist conference held in Pisa. From Adriana Dada, *L'anarchismo in Italia fra movimento e partito: Storia e documenti dell'anarchismo italiana*, Milan: Teti Editore, 1984, p. 264.

War and revolt – James Connolly

'No, there is no such thing as humane or civilized war! War may be forced upon a subject race or subject class to put an end to subjection of race, of class, or sex. When so waged it must be waged thoroughly and relentlessly, but with no delusions as to its elevating nature, or civilizing methods.'

30 January 1915. From: *The Worker*. This paper was suppressed in February 1915. Governments sought to censor and ban the dissident press. In Ireland had an active rebel press,[25] and prepared the way for the Easter Rising.

Revolt! – International Anarchist declaration

'The truth is that the cause of wars, of that which at present stains with blood the plains of Europe, as of all wars that have preceded it, rests solely in the existence of the state, which is the political form of privilege. The state has arisen out of military force, it has developed through the use of military force, and it is still on military force that it must logically rest in order to maintain its omnipotence. Whatever the form it may assume, the state is nothing but organized oppression for the advantage of a privileged minority. The present conflict illustrates this in the most striking manner. All forms of the state are engaged in the present war; absolutism with Russia, absolutism softened by parliamentary institutions with Germany, the state ruling over peoples of quite different races with Austria, a democratic constitutional regime with England, and a democratic republican regime with France.

The misfortune of the peoples, who were deeply attached to peace, is that, in order to avoid war, they placed their confidence in the state with its intriguing diplomatists, in democracy, and in political parties (not excluding those in opposition, like parliamentary socialism). This confidence has been deliberately betrayed, and continues to be so, when governments, with the aid of the whole of their press, persuade their respective peoples that this war is a war of liberation. We are resolutely against all wars between peoples, and in neutral countries, like Italy, where the governments seek to throw fresh peoples into the fiery furnace of war, our comrades have been, are, and ever will be most energetically opposed to war.

The role of the anarchists in the present tragedy, whatever may be the place or the situation in which they find themselves, is to continue to proclaim that there is but one war of liberation: that which in all countries is waged by the oppressed against the oppressors, by the exploited against the exploiters. Our part is to summon the slaves to revolt against their masters. Anarchist action and propaganda should assiduously and perseveringly aim at weakening and dissolving the various states, at cultivating the spirit of revolt, and arousing discontent in peoples and armies. To all the soldiers of all countries who believe they are fighting for justice and liberty, we have to declare that their heroism and their valour will but serve to perpetuate hatred, tyranny, and misery.

To the workers in factory and mine it is necessary to recall that the rifles they now have in their hands have been used against them in the days of strike and of revolt and that later on they will be again used against them in order to compel them to undergo and endure capitalist exploitation. To the workers on farm and field it is necessary to show that after the war they will be obliged once more to bend beneath the yoke and to continue to cultivate the lands of their lords and to feed the rich. To all the outcasts, that they should not part with their arms until they have settled accounts with their oppressors, until they have taken land and factory and workshop for themselves. To mothers, wives, and daughters, the victims of increased misery and privation, let us show who are the ones really responsible for their sorrows and for the massacre of their fathers, sons, and husbands.

We should take advantage of every discontent and movement of revolt to ferment insurrection, to organise the revolution, from which we hope to achieve the end of all social inequality. No discouragement, not even in the face of a calamity such as this present war. It is in such troubled periods – in which men in their thousands give up life heroically, for an ideal, that we have to demonstrate to such men the beauty, grandeur and generosity of anarchist ideals; social justice achieved through the free organisation of producers; militarism and war suppressed for ever, the complete liberty, achieved through the wholesale destruction of the state and of its organs of coercion. Long live anarchy!'

March 1915. Alexander Berkman, Emma Goldman, Errico Malatesta, Alexander Schapiro, Bill Shatov and others.

'International Anarchist Manifesto on the War' *Freedom* (London), republished by *Volontà, Cultura Obrera, Mother Earth*, etc. (Paragraphs on civilization from this Manifesto are included above, page 107.)

Revolutionary Unionism and War – James Connolly

'... how could this war have been prevented, which is another way of saying how and why did the socialist movement fail to prevent it? The full answer to that question can only be grasped by those who are familiar with the propaganda that from 1905 onwards has been known as "industrialist" in the United States and, though not so accurately, has been called "syndicalist" in Europe. The essence of that propaganda lay in two principles. To take them in the order of their immediate effectiveness these were: First, that labour could only enforce its wishes by organising its strength at the point of production, i.e., the farms, factories, workshops, railways, docks, ships – where the work of the world is carried on, the effectiveness of the political vote depending primarily upon the economic power of the workers organised behind it. Secondly, that the process of organising that economic power would also build the industrial fabric of the socialist republic, build the new society within the old. It is upon the first of these two principles I wish my readers to concentrate their attention in order to find the answer to the question we are asking. In all the belligerent countries of western and central Europe the socialist vote was very large; in none of these belligerent countries was there an organised revolutionary industrial organisation directing the socialist vote nor a socialist political party directing a revolutionary industrial organisation. The socialist voters having cast their ballots were helpless, as voters, until the next election; as workers, they were indeed in control of the forces of production and distribution, and by exercising that control over the transport service could have made the war impossible. But the idea of thus co-ordinating their two spheres of activity had not gained sufficient lodgment to be effective in the emergency. No socialist party in Europe could say that rather than go to war it would call out the entire transport service of the country and thus prevent mobilisation. No socialist party could say so, because no socialist party could have the slightest reasonable prospect of having such a call obeyed. The executive committee of the socialist movement was not in control of the labour-force of the men who voted for the socialist representatives in the legislative chambers of Europe, nor were the men in control of the supply of labour-force in control of the socialist representatives. In either case there would have been an organised power immediately available against war. Lacking either, the socialist parties of Europe when they had protested against war, had also fired their last shot against militarism and were left like "children crying in the night." ... To sum up then, the failure of European socialism to avert the war is primarily due to the divorce between the industrial and political movements of labour. The socialist voter, as such, is helpless between elections. He requires to organise power to enforce the mandate of the elections and the only power he can so organise is economic power – the power to stop the wheels of commerce, to control the heart that sends the life blood pulsating through the social organism.'

March 1915, *International Socialist Review*. Mailing privileges were later withdrawn from the left press, such as *The Masses* and *International Socialist Review*.

Wading in Blood – Rosa Luxemburg

'Violated, dishonoured, wading in blood, dripping filth – there stands bourgeois society. This is it. Not all spic and span and moral, with pretence to culture, philosophy, ethics, order, peace, and the rule of law – but the ravening beast, the witches' Sabbath of anarchy, a plague to culture and humanity. Thus it reveals itself in its true, its naked form. In the midst of this witches' Sabbath a catastrophe of world-historical proportions has happened: International Social-democracy has capitulated.'

April 1915. From: *The Junius Pamphlet*, http://www.marxists.org/archive/luxemburg/1915/junius and Merlin Press edition, 1968. In: *International Socialist Review*, November 1915, Vol. XVI, No. 15; pp. 274-6. Leftists were condemned by the majority Social-democrats.[26]

Women judge war differently
– Dr. Aletta H. Jacobs, Dutch Radical

'We women judge war differently from men. Men consider in the first place its economic results. What it costs in money, its loss or its gain to national commerce and industries, the extension of power and so forth. But what is material loss to us women, in comparison to the number of fathers, brothers, husbands and sons who march out to war never to return. We women consider above all the damage to the race resulting from war, and the grief, the pain and misery it entails. We know only too well that whatever may be gained by a war, it is not worth the bloodshed and the tears, the cruel sufferings, the wasted lives, the agony and despair it has caused.'

28 April 28 – 1 May 1915 at The Hague. Despite obstruction from several governments 1136 women from twelve countries attended an International Congress of Women for Peace held in The Hague. The above text was the welcoming address. Those able to attend – despite travel difficulties and government restrictions – came from Austria-Hungary, Belgium, Canada, Denmark, Germany, Great Britain, Italy, the Netherlands, Norway, Sweden and the United States.

Censored – Alphonse Merrheim,
French Socialist & Syndicalist

'Nine months! Of the press inventing all sorts of lies and slanders... cultivating fratricidal hatred between peoples; appealing to the most base passions, the most vile instincts, the most miserable feelings, the most ferocious reprisals – all this we define as a crime against dignity, thought, humanity ...'

May 1915. Declaration of the Metalworkers' Federation. Merrheim attended the Zimmerwald anti-war congress and helped galvanise anti-war activities. From: Alfred Rosmer, *Le mouvement ouvrier pendant la première guerre mondiale : de l'union sacrée a Zimmerwald*, Paris: Librairie du Travail, 1936, p. 238

Peace Congress, El Ferrol: resolutions

'To create a permanent international peace congress committee,

That this committee of five persons should be responsible for looking after the archives and documentation of the congress,

That the committee should prepare in the languages of the warring nations – every fortnight – a revolutionary address and work for is dissemination to trenches and battlefields.'

April 1915. It was agreed that this committee should be based in Portugal. The congress also facilitated an organisation of Portuguese and Spanish syndicalists, as a part of a future anti-war labour international. See: M. J. de Sousa, *O sindicalismo em Portugal: esboço histórico,* Comisão Escola e Propaganda do Sindicato do Pessoal de Câmaras da Marinha Mercante Portuguesa, Lisboa, 1931, pp. 107-9; Abad de Santillán: *Contribuciones a la historia del movimiento obrero español: De 1905 a la proclamación de la Segunda República,* (Vol. 2), Puebla (Mexico): Editorial Cajica, 1965, pp. 121-3.

Coercion – James Connolly

'Now when the miners threaten a stoppage to enforce their claims the government declare a strike illegal, and proclaim the whole South Wales mining area.[27] Surely a more flagrant case of partiality and class bias was never before exhibited. It means that the employing class have been systematically using the pretext of the war in order to increase their profits; that while the working class was sending their best blood and flesh to the trenches the employers were quietly robbing the helpless ones left behind; it means that this most awful of all wars has been used by a heartless gang of bloodsuckers to enable them to plunder with impunity, and that whilst they rioted in the plunder of the poor, the government looked smilingly on, but as soon as the poor commenced to call a halt to the plunder, the same government ordered out its soldiers, and denounced as "treason" the attempts of the workers to protect their interests. Good luck to the Welsh miners! Good luck to all who attempt to stem the tide of tyranny and robbery which, under cover of military safety, is allowed to run unchecked throughout the length and breadth of the land. Such revolts will serve to unmask the real enemy, serve to show how they who are loudest in denouncing militarism are the quickest to use it to keep their poorer fellow-citizens in the chains the master class are forging for the nation!'

17 July 1915. The British Munitions of War Act of July 1915 had placed fetters on workers and trade unions in war industries. Amongst its provisions was a clause setting out that workers could not change jobs without the permission of employers. Miners were not munitions workers, but when a strike threatened in South Wales the strike was declared illegal. The Miners' federation disregarded this and went ahead with it. In the light of this the government stepped in, sanctioned a wage increase and prevented legal action being taken against the miners and their union. From *The Workers' Republic*, 'Coercion in England'; http://www.marxists.org/archive/connolly/1915/07/coerceng.htm

To all Clyde Workers – Clyde Workers' Committee

'The support given to the Munitions Act by the officials was an act of treachery to the working class. Those of us who refused to be *sold* have organised the above committee, representative of *All Trades* in the Clyde area, determined to retain what liberties we have, and to take the first opportunity of forcing the repeal of all the pernicious legislation that has recently been imposed upon us. In the words of a manifesto issued by the Trade Union Rights Committee, recently formed in London:

"Let us preserve what rights still remain and refuse steadfastly to surrender another inch to our allied foes –

the capitalists and politicians. The liberty and freedom of the organized worker is the one thing; our fight is the fight that matters, and now is the time to act.'"

Summer 1915.

Munitions Act, Slavery Act
– *Forward*, (Glasgow Socialist newspaper)

'When the Munitions of War Act 1915 was placed on the stature book of the country we stated that it was meant to 'Prussianise' the trade unionists. We stick to that opinion, and before long the trade unionists will come round to that way of thinking. The Munitions of War Act does not restrict the liberty of the employers; it gives them more liberty by making it a criminal offence to go on strike even when there is provocation. The main fact of the Act is: that it is illegal for workers to withhold their labour.'

14 August 1915; after it carrying reports of lively popular opposition to Lloyd George, *Forward* was banned.

Letter to Christian Rakovsky
– Dušan Popovič, Serbian Social-democrat

'However, for us, the decisive fact was that the war between Serbia and Austria was only a small part of a totality, merely the prologue to universal European war and this latter, we were profoundly convinced, could not fail to have a clearly pronounced imperialist character. As a result, we – being part of the great socialist, proletarian International – considered that it was our bounden duty to oppose the war resolutely.'

September 1915. From: 'The Balkan Socialist Tradition', *Revolutionary History*, Volume 8, No. 3, London, 2003, p. 238.

Socialism and War
– G. Zinoviev & V.I. Lenin, Russian Social-democrats

'Social-chauvinism is adherence to the idea of "defending the fatherland" in the present war. From this idea follows repudiation of the class struggle in war time, voting for military appropriations, etc. In practice the social-chauvinists conduct an anti-proletarian bourgeois policy, because in practice they insist not on the "defence of the fatherland" in the sense of fighting against the oppression of a foreign nation, but upon the "right" of one or the other of the "great" nations to rob the colonies and oppress other peoples.

The social-chauvinists follow the bourgeoisie in deceiving the people by saying that the war is conducted for the defence of the freedom; and the existence of the nations; thus they put themselves on the side of the bourgeoisie against the proletariat.'

September 1915. Some forty socialists and syndicalists met in neutral Switzerland in September 1915 in the small village of Zimmerwald. The left at the event looked to set an uncompromising line.

Draft resolution of the delegates of the Left
– International Socialist Conference at Zimmerwald

'The World War, which has been devastating Europe for the last year, is an imperialist war waged for the political and economic exploitation of the world, export markets, sources of raw material, spheres of capital investment, etc. It is a product of capitalist development which connects the entire world in a world economy, but at the same time permits the existence of national state capitalist groups with opposing interests. If the bourgeoisie and the governments seek to conceal this character of the world war by asserting that it is a question of a forced struggle for national independence, it is only to mislead the proletariat, since the war is being waged for the oppression of foreign peoples and countries. Equally untruthful are the legends concerning the defence of democracy in this war, since imperialism signifies the most unscrupulous domination of big capital and political reaction. Imperialism can only be overcome by overcoming the contradictions which produce it, that is, by the socialist organization of the advanced capitalist countries for which the objective conditions are already ripe. At the outbreak of the war, the majority of the labour leaders had not raised this only possible slogan in opposition to imperialism. Prejudiced by nationalism, rotten with opportunism, at the beginning of the World War they betrayed the proletariat to imperialism and gave up the principles of socialism and thereby the real struggle for the everyday interests of the proletariat.'

September 1915.

Appeal to the Clyde Munitions' Workers
– James D. MacDougall, British Socialist

'… in connection with any action against the Munitions Act the workers need expect nothing but opposition from their paid organisers and secretaries. That will not matter much. At the moment, in the Clyde area, the officials are discredited and count for little, the real leaders of the men are to be found in the workshops. Over and above that, the exceptional circumstances at present existing are producing something very like the beginnings of a real industrial union movement. The need for solidarity is breaking down the old craft jealousies, the spread of socialism is showing to workers their essential unity as a class, in spite of all superficial differences of occupation. In many shops on the Clyde vigilance committees, composed of delegates from each of the trades in the shop, have been formed, and have already many times demonstrated their usefulness. It should be the duty of militant socialists and unionists in shops where such committees do not exist, or where they have been only partially formed, as in Beardmore's, Clydebank, to see that a complete organisation is set up. Then the vigilance committees are linked together in a central committee, which contains the most trusted men of the labour movement in Glasgow. The business of the men meantime should be to practise "thrift", so that when the strike comes, they will be able to hold out for a day or two or a week or two, as the case may be, without depending on any strike benefits. For a strike of this kind, it is unlikely that pusillanimous officials and reactionary executives will find any money.

When the Government sees the temper of the men and learns of their preparations, it is quite possible that, in order to prevent the threatened strike, they will grant the repeal of this obnoxious measure. If they do, all will be better than well, the claws of tyrannical managers and foremen and greedy bosses will, once again, be clipped. If they refuse, then a dispute may arise the magnitude of which will surprise them. The Clyde workers are conscious of the strong position they hold, the excessive overtime many are working has given them, in spite of rising prices, a reserve fund to fall back upon, and last but not least, at the same time as the Government is irritating them with restrictions on personal liberty, the influence of revolutionary socialism among the Clyde workers has reached a higher point than ever before.'

October 1915. From: *Vanguard*, (Glasgow) http://www.marxists.org/history/international/social-democracy/vanguard/1915/clyde-munitions.htm *Vanguard* was the paper of the Glasgow area British Socialist Party until it was banned early in 1916.

Our Freedom is Going – John Maclean

'The Munitions Act, better known as the Industrial Slavery Act, since it was meant to tighten the chains of economic slavery on the workers, was the outcome of the suggestions of Mr. William Weir of Cathcart, whose upstart arrogance forced his men to stop work and precipitate the Clyde Engineers' strike, the first great workers revolt after the Great Slaughter Match commenced. He demanded that the government ought to prevent the workers' unions from being used to force up wages or improve conditions during the war. The government has not only practically adopted his ideas, but it has appointed him supreme controller of munition supplies in Scotland. The men, and even the women, inside his big workshop, ate, bubbling over with discontent, as are those employed from end to end of the Clyde smelting, engineering, and ship building area. The Munitions Act has been applied cunningly in petty cases with fines starting at 2/6[28] each. Now a number of shipwrights have been fined £10 each. These men will be fools to pay the fine, or let the union pay it. That would make them criminals, and acknowledged criminals at that. As other workers see the drift of the Act now, all are afraid that they will sooner or later be trapped and likewise made criminals at the request of the masters who rob them. Every worker who recognises the infamy of the Act must be ready to down tools and follow the example of the Welsh miners if these shipwrights are sent to prison. The Clyde is ripe for a blow at the infamous audacity of the masters. Let them have it, comrades. Remember that you shall have the backing of many of our Lanarkshire comrades of the mining villages. These men have assured us that they are prepared to do their bit in the great conflict, if one is needed.

Then, again, the railwaymen are demanding more money, and are being met by threats from the press. In a leading article in the *Glasgow Herald* on Tuesday, 14 September, the railwaymen are threatened with what happened in France about five years ago. You remember that, when the railwaymen struck, the government called the men up as reservists of the French Army and made them do the work. (France is fighting for liberty). We challenge the government and the *Glasgow Herald*, and the whole propertied class, to try militarising the railway system of this country. Let them shoot railwaymen. That is exactly what the filthy threat means. We throw down the gauntlet to them in return. We swear that for every worker killed we shall have one of the killing class. Two can play at the game of compulsion.

Workers, do you realise fully the meaning of this hell-born *Glasgow Herald*, or is it government suggestion? "Do as we tell you or we shall shoot you!" That is just the position of 1911-1912. Are you going to lie down to the fellows who dish out such insults and degradation? Is this the freedom your mates are fighting for on the continent?

It is quite apparent that the workers will have to send all their leaders to the front and keep them there … and then settle down unitedly to sweep the slave measures and methods aside.

The root of the unrest is that the plundering class, at home and abroad, has added almost three hundred million pounds to the workers' cost of living since the war started, and has only doled out increases to a fifth of the workers to the insignificant extent of twenty million pounds inside the same period. Prices are still rising, and pounds are being put on to rents. The limit is not in sight. When the workers ask more to meet the increased difficulty to live, they are insulted as traitors who ought to be shot. These insults and threats come from the very men who ask us to throw away our lives for freedom! If the workers strike to get more money they are denounced as drunkards and shirkers, and are held responsible for a war failure absolutely due to the incompetence of the men who blackguardise them …'

October 1915. From: *Vanguard*. http://www.marxists.org/archive/maclean/1915/10/freedom-going.htm

Truth and Lies

'I cannot tell how passionate my interest was when I found out about them. Such a long time has passed since we heard reason and truth, that we were somewhat surprised when a voice was raised to denounce bluffs and lies of every sort. I can tell you that I ended up despairing, when I saw that those we ought to be able to count on most, were sounding the trumpets of war. So, this is to say how well your initiative appeared, how much it cheered us up …'

Autumn 1915. News of Zimmerwald was received with enthusiasm in France. From: Alfred Rosmer, *Le mouvement ouvrier pendant la première guerre mondiale : de l'union sacrée a Zimmerwald*, Paris: Librairie du Travail, 1936, p. 405.

French Metalworkers denounce

'For women and children exploitation is worse than ever, beyond anything that can be imagined. It is monstrous. Never have our organisations seen so many ill and injured, and above all maimed, as amongst these women and children, who moreover, are victimised by insurance companies. Let us repeat: the officials are no way ignorant of this painful situation. To every complaint they say "there's a war on". But that doesn't impede the toleration of scandalous profiteering by industrialists and their various intermediaries; whilst there is still talk of the duty of workers working for the war, and the need for a reduction of wages.'

October 1915. From: Alfred Rosmer, *Le mouvement ouvrier pendant la première guerre mondiale : de l'union sacrée a Zimmerwald*, Paris: Librairie du Travail, 1936, p. 449. As the war went on, unions began to demand equal pay for equal work.

Workers in control of industry
– Industrial Workers of the World, USA

'With the workers in control of industry, wars cannot take place against their will. On the other hand, without that control on the side of the workers, no proclamations, resolutions, or pledges, no matter how strongly worded, will avail to prevent them from shouldering arms, if their masters order them to do so.'

October 1915, *Solidarity*. The United States would come into the war in 1917. The IWW saw things coming. How to prevent the war?

Glasgow Rent Strike – William Gallacher, British Socialist

'In Govan, Mrs. Barbour, a typical working-class housewife, became the leader of a movement such as had never been seen before, or since for that matter. Street meetings, back-court meetings, drums, bells, trumpets – every method was used to bring the women out and organize them for the struggle. Notices were printed by the thousand and put up in the windows: wherever you went you could see them. In street after street, hardly a window without one: *We Are Not Paying Increased Rent.*

These notices represented a spirit amongst the women that could not be overcome. The factors (agents for the property owners) could not collect the rents. They applied to the courts for eviction warrants. Having obtained these, sheriff's officers were sent to serve them and evict the tenants. But Mrs. Barbour had a team of women who were wonderful. They could smell a sheriff's officer a mile away. At their summons women left their cooking, washing or whatever they were doing. Before they got anywhere near their destination, the officer and his men would be met by an army of furious women who drove them back in a hurried scramble for safety.

Attempt after attempt was made to secure eviction, all of which ended in futility. The increased rent could not be collected, the tenants could not be evicted.'

November 1915. Threatened by a rent strike[29] and an industrial strike the courts requested instructions from Lloyd George, the Minister of Munitions. 'The workers have left the factories. They are threatening to pull down Glasgow. What am I to do?' 'Stop the case,' they were told, 'a Rent Restriction Act will be introduced immediately.' William Gallacher, *Revolt on the Clyde: An Autobiography,* London: Lawrence and Wishart, 1990, pp. 52ff.

The Conscription Menace – *Vanguard,*
(Glasgow newspaper of the British Socialist Party)

'This war was declared to be a war for freedom. We socialists considered that a deliberate lie, because the promoters of the statement know quite well that the workers of the world are their slaves, and will continue to be their slaves no matter the issue of the war. It certainly is a war of freedom for one national section or other of the robbing propertied class to corner for itself the whole, or the greater part, of the surplus wrung from the wage-slave class. Obviously, that is no concern of the workers one way or the other.

We have repeatedly expressed our perfect willingness to let those who benefit by capitalism enter the war, and slaughter one another to their heart's content. That is their affair, not ours. Their mutual extermination might, in fact, smooth the path leading to socialism, so that even many socialists might be excused if they departed from the policy of indifference and became active recruiting agents amongst the propertied class, urging them with fiery eloquence to defend their King and their country. We have furthermore refrained from the attempt to prevent workers enlisting if they sincerely believed that Britain was entitled to enter the war. In fact, we usually insisted on them enlisting as the only logical outcome of their beliefs.

It is an entirely different matter when an attempt to force conscription on us is threatened. We socialists, who believe that the only war worth fighting is the class war against robbery and slavery for the workers, do not mean to lay down our lives for British or any other capitalism. If we die, we shall die here defending the few rights our forefathers died for. To us it is nobler to die for our own class than for the class which has robbed, ruled, despised, and imprisoned us.

They dare not murder us, for that would lift the veil of cant they have blinded the eyes of neutrals with…. They also had better not enlist us, for we will prove more dangerous with arms than without them. A reign of terror would certainly ensue. History backs us up in that assertion, for the mass of the men who refuse now to enlist do so on principle and not through fear.'

December 1915. *Vanguard*: attributed in the paper to the initials of James D. MacDougall; attributed also to John Maclean. http://www.marxists.org/archive/maclean/1915/12/conscription-menace.htm

Johannesburg Socialist Conference resolution
– International Socialist League, South Africa

'That we encourage the organization of the workers on industrial or class lines, irrespective of race, colour or creed, as the most effective means of providing the necessary force for the emancipation of the workers.'

January 1916; conference notes, *The International*. This journal had noted: '… an internationalism which does not concede the fullest rights which the native working-class is capable of claiming will be a sham… Not until we free the native can we hope to free the white.' October 1915; *The International*, 'The Parting of the Ways'. It was not only in South Africa that the Labour movement was divided on racial lines. At about the same time similar steps were made in Western Canada by anti-war radicals to build bridges with Asian workers.

Strike against War – Helen Keller, American Socialist

'Strike against all ordinances and laws and institutions that continue the slaughter of peace and the butcheries of war. Strike against war, for without you no battles can be fought. Strike against manufacturing shrapnel and gas bombs and all other tools of murder. Strike against preparedness that means death and misery to millions of human being. Be not dumb, obedient slaves in an army of destruction. Be heroes in an army of construction.'

5 January 1916. Americans could see war looming; concluding remarks from a speech for the Women's Peace Party and the Labor Forum, Carnegie Hall, New York.

Why did the German Social-democratic party fail to fight? – Anton Pannekoek

'This weakness was much worse, essentially a lack of readiness to fight – a lack of intellectual strength – an absence of class struggle will and resolution. If, in elections, the party won only one third of the vote, if it had, in a population of 70 million only one million persons – of which the immense majority paid dues only – anyone could have predicted that such a party could not overthrow and defeat the bourgeoisie. But given this numerical force the party appeared to have enough strength to set off a strong protest movement against the war and become the centre of a mighty protest movement. That no such attempts were made, that weapons were cast aside without a fight, shows that the party was rotten on the inside and incapable of fulfilling its new agenda.

The Social-democratic parties originated out of the conditions and relations of an earlier pre-imperialist period, they were materially and by instinct adapted to the agenda of proletarian struggle of earlier times. Their agenda was, in the period of capitalism's growth, to struggle for reforms, inasmuch as these were possible under capitalism, and by these means and to this end to bring together and organise the proletarian masses. Thus also were created mass trade-unions and parties; but meanwhile the struggle for improvement degenerated more into a striving for reforms at any price, into begging and compromise with the bourgeoisie, to a limited politics, into demands for small immediate gains which no longer took into consideration the general interests of the class as a whole, and gave up on class struggle itself. Under the influence of substantial prosperity, which greatly reduced the worst miseries of unemployment, there was brought to a part of the proletariat some measure (Geist) of contentment and of indifference as to general class interests. Reformism dominated Social-democracy more and more, and showed up the degeneration and decadence of old methods precisely at a time when a new agenda began to open up for the proletariat.

This new agenda consisted of the struggle against imperialism. Against imperialism one could not rely on old methods. In parliament one could criticise its symptoms (armaments, taxes, reaction, inaction in respect of social legislation) but one could not influence its policy, given that this was made not by parliaments, but rather by small groups of people (in Germany by the Kaiser and some nobles, generals, ministers and financier; in England by three or four aristocrats and politicians; in France by a few bankers and ministers). Trade unions had difficulty defending their skin against trade combines; all the skill of their officials broke on the hard rocks of lords of industry. Reactionary electoral laws could not be changed through elections alone; new means of struggle were needed. The proletarian masses themselves needed to show up, with active methods of struggle. [...]

A small group of left radicals attempted to draw the party towards this course of mass struggle and particular persons attempted to promote awareness of imperialism. But the leading layers of the party, its leadership, its party-bureaucracy, Kautsky and his friends barred the way to this tendency. For them imperialism and rearmament was just one of the of the bourgeoisie's follies, a folly fed by big capitalists a folly from which they might be turned away by sound argument. They sought their salvation in the "return to the old and proven tactics" with which they had vainly attempted to repress revisionism. They opposed new revolutionary tactics. The bureaucracy of officials and leaders, which naturally identified their own particular group interests – for a calm and peaceful development of the party – with the interests of the proletariat, resisted with all their strength the "anarcho-syndicalist adventures" into which the [partisans of] mass activity wished to hurry along the party. With its press, structures and reputation the bureaucracy reigned over the party both in material and in intellectual terms. Thus it came about that the party's structure, as it was formed in an earlier period was not up to the job of taking on new responsibilities. It had to be submerged. The outbreak of the war was a catastrophe for it. Surprised by events, stunned and confused, unprepared for resistance of any sort, carried away by nationalist slogans, gutless – the proudest organisation of social democracy foundered as an organ of revolutionary socialism. And with it went, in the same way, almost all the Social-democratic parties of Europe, which for the most part had long since been corroded from within by reformism. In what way a new Socialist combative force may latter arise out of this wreckage is something that has to be left for the future.'

Janaury 1916, *Der Vorbote*, No. 1, 'Imperialism and the tasks of proletarian revolution'.

Pro-Government Anarchists (Response to the 'Sixteen') – Errico Malatesta

'It will be said that these things will come to an end when the German people have rid themselves of their tyrants and ceased to be a menace to Europe by destroying militarism in their own country. But, if that is the case, the Germans who think, and rightfully so, that English and French domination (to say nothing of Tsarist Russia) would be so more delightful to the Germans than German domination to the French and English, will desire first to wait for the Russians and the others to destroy their own militarism, and will meanwhile continue to increase their own country's army. And then, how long will the revolution be delayed? How long anarchy? Must we always wait for the others to begin?

The line of conduct for anarchists is clearly marked out by the very logic of their aspirations. The war ought to have been prevented by bringing about the revolution, or at least by making the Government afraid of the revolution. Either the strength or the skill necessary for this has been lacking. Peace ought to be imposed by bringing about the revolution, or at least by threatening to do so.[30] To the present time, the strength or the skill is wanting. Well! There is only one remedy: to do better in future. More than ever we must avoid compromise; deepen the chasm between capitalists and wage slaves, between rulers and ruled; preach expropriation of private property and the destruction of states as the only means of guaranteeing fraternity between the peoples and justice and liberty for all; and we must prepare to accomplish these things. Meanwhile it seems to me that it is criminal to do anything that tends to prolong the war that slaughters men, destroys wealth, and hinders all resumption of the struggle for emancipation. It appears to me that preaching "war to the end"[31] is really playing the game of the German rulers, who are deceiving their subjects and inflaming their ardour for fighting by persuading them that their opponents desire to crush and enslave the German people. To-day, as ever, let this be our slogan: Down with capitalists and governments, all capitalists and governments! Long live the peoples, all the peoples!'

April 1916. In March 1916 fifteen anarchists – Kropotkin included – had declared that German imperialism was the 'greater threat' and until that threat was removed it was not the right time to stop the war. Other anarchists repudiated this position and wrote that Kropotkin and friends did not speak for the international anarchist movement. They rejected the line that sought to delay action until the other side disarmed. They noted that states were in a position to manipulate information and could present aggressive wars as defensive. Given secret diplomacy and the absence of a critical press, people could easily be misled. From: *Freedom.* Vernon Richards, Ed., *Malatesta: Life and Ideas,* London: Freedom Press, 1965, pp. 248-251. Censors prevented the printing of this text in *Ce qu'il faut dire.* In Italy it circulated under an innocuous title to avoid censorship.

After the war ends – Anton Pannekoek

'The experiences gained from the organization of industry and trade under national control, have impressed the idea of state socialism favourably upon many bourgeois minds. The advantage of uniform, controlled production, over chaotic private production has become too apparent.

The most important of the large industrial branches could be brought, easily, into national ownership. This could be done without difficulty with the direct war industry. The question of employment for the returning soldiers, too, would be solved for the bourgeoisie. The danger that threatens, when great rebellious masses call for work, bread, assistance, could thus be averted, by drafting them immediately into the war industries, and then, gradually, as conditions in private industry become more settled, dismiss them from military service. Other advantages, too, might arise from such a plan. In the first place production would be greatly cheapened by the exclusion of all middlemen. Everyone realizes how much could be saved by government organization of production. All technical and organizational improvements of the war period would be applied. It would do away with the problem of unemployment insurance. Wages could be regulated; for against this powerful employer labour unions would be powerless, even if they were permitted to exist. It would mean for the workers increased dependence; would mean greater curtailment of their personal freedom than was possible under private ownership. National ownership of large branches of industry is synonymous with their militarization. Unquestionably, the ruling class fears the day after the war, when military dictatorship, war-laws, press censorship and the state of siege have become things of the past. The militarization of the national industrial forces will present itself as the most effective means of keeping great masses in harness, and curbing their desire for political opposition. To the proletariat this state socialism can mean only an aggravation of its sufferings and increased pressure upon the burden of life. Notwithstanding this, it is to be expected that a large part of our Social-democracy will not oppose this plan but will lend it its heartiest support. Their old ideals make them the prisoners of this new system of national exploitation.

Even before the war every proposal to pluck the consumers by new monopolies was heralded as a "beginning of socialism, which deserved our heartiest support!" Socialism is not based upon national ownership, but upon the strength, the might of the proletariat. In the past the conceptions of socialism and state industries have been hopelessly confused in the minds of our Social-democracy; in the future, this party will face the state socialist plans for the increased enslavement of the working class, with neither mental weapons nor a clearly defined attitude.

To the revolutionary wing of the socialist movement belongs the duty to strike the first blow at these new and dangerous shackles upon the proletarians. The fight against state socialism will bring in its wake a radical clarification of ideas concerning the relations between the proletariat and the new imperialism. It will usher in a period of new, practical conflict. As the new, imperialistic state more and more unmistakably assumes the guise of oppressor and exploiter, the proletariat will see in the nation its great enemy, against whom it must fight, before all others, by means of mass action. And the Kautsky tradition, that we must preserve the state in order to use it for our own purposes, will be practically shattered.'

April 1916. Anton Pannekoek was looked towards a post-war future and reflecting on state regulation. The shape of the economy had been changed in the course of the war. The state was directing industries, organising transport and production; the market economy had been made to serve the interest of nations at war. Could the economy be directed to serve the interests of working people too? If so, who would manage things? From: *Vorbote* No. 2; *The Class Struggle,* Volume I, No. 1, May-June, 1917; http:// www.marxists.org/archive/pannekoe/1917/after-war-ends.htm

May Day – Sébastien Faure

'It is said that the International is dead. And moreover the First of May is the day of the International. Since it no longer exists there is no longer any reason for this day to exist. Let us be frank and admit it. There is truth in this opinion, but only a partial accuracy. If by International one means the organisation that existed before the war, disseminating its statements a little everywhere and having as its aim the creation amongst all members of the working class, whatever their nationality, ongoing relations and close and permanent cohesion – having in mind common action given identical interests – it is correct to say that this International is dead. It could not be otherwise, the war killed it. The International was dead from that day onwards when the proletariat made common cause with respective governments working for national defence and gave and shed its blood in the service of its country …'

April 1916. Sébastien Faure was seeking to revive socialist morale after twenty months of war, reaffirming the need to celebrate May Day. He drew support from anarchists, socialists and workplace unionists. His paper, *Ce qu'il faut dire* (What needs to be said), had a print run of 20,000 in November 1916. Censorship cut the last quarter of this article and often mangled it. From: http://gallica.bnf.fr/ark:/12148/bpt6k55815614

The Provisional Government
of the Irish Republic to the people of Ireland

'… We declare the right of the people of Ireland to the ownership of Ireland, and to the unfettered control of Irish destinies, to be sovereign and indefeasible. The long usurpation of that right by a foreign people and government has not extinguished the right, nor can it ever be extinguished except by the destruction of the Irish people.'

Easter Monday 1916; proclamation read by Patrick Pearse at the General Post Office in Dublin. Pearse and other leaders were executed by the British army.

Time to Protest
– French Building Workers Union and others

'In that time militants – dispersed in the army, or isolated and reduced to silence by the rigour of the state of siege – could not help being disorientated by the magnitude and the suddenness of events. Earlier weaknesses and failures might therefore be excusable, given an initial disarray of an immense disaster, but after two year of horrible killing, to no end, it is about time that workers' consciousness should revive, and should clearly face up to its duties and responsibilities. This is what the undersigned seek to do: to denounce the lie of a "sacred union"; we condemn those who help consolidate this new regime; their actions and attitude makes it a duty for us to denounce them and draw to the attention of French workers' organisations that seek to keep intact their syndicalist and internationalist ideals.'

May-June 1916. Text signed by representatives of ten unions and others. See: Alfred Rosmer, *Le mouvement ouvrier pendant la première guerre mondiale: de Zimmerwald à la révolution russe*, Paris: Mouton, 1950, p. 196

Peace and the proletariat – Kiental Anti-War conference

1. The present war is the consequence of antagonisms between imperialists and results from the development of the capitalist regime. Imperialist forces work to exploit in their interest unsolved problems of nationality, dynastic aspirations and survivals from a feudal past. War aims in reality consist of decisions as to how backward countries will develop economically and how a new division of colonial possessions will be made.

2. Being unable to do away with either capitalist regimes or forms of imperialism this war is also unable to eliminate the causes of future wars. It is strengthening financial oligarchy, it is unable to resolve old problems of nationality, and it has no capacity to end the struggle for worldwide hegemony. Rather, it makes all these problems more complicated, and creates new antagonisms, which further accentuate political and economic reaction, and it strengthens germs of war for the future.

3. Thus governments – and their bourgeois socio-nationalist agents – when they assert that the war should produce lasting peace, are consciously falsifying the truth or failing to take into account the conditions needed to achieve these aims. Annexations, political and economic alliances amongst imperialist states, cannot assure a lasting peace within a capitalist regime, any more than can compulsory arbitration tribunals, restrictions on armaments or what is called the democratisation of foreign policy.

4. Annexations, achieved by violent force, excite hatred between peoples and produce new causes of complaint and conflict. Coalitions of imperialist powers and political alliances are means fit to spread and lengthen economic wars, provoking ever more vicious conflagrations throughout the world.

5. Projects aiming at eliminating the risk of war, through overall disarmament, through compulsory arbitration presume the existence of effective and generally recognised sanctions and the existence of a material force capable of bringing equilibrium to antagonistic state interests imposing on these its authority. But such sanctions and such an authority do not exist and capitalist development – which further aggravates antagonisms between the bourgeoisie of respective coalitions or of various nations – offers no hope or prospect of such a mediating power.

True democratic control over foreign policy supposes the wholesale democratisation of the modern state; the proletariat might find in this a weapon, useful in its struggle against imperialism, but never the decisive means which would help transform diplomacy into an instrument of peace.

6. For these reasons the working class should reject the fantastic proposals made by bourgeois pacifists and by nationalistic socialists; these would replace old illusions with new ones, they would thus trap the masses, turning them away from class struggle and making them the object of a policy of "seeing things through to the end".

7. Given that a lasting peace cannot be assured by a capitalist regime, only socialism can create the necessary conditions to accomplish it. Indeed, in abolishing private property in the means of production, socialism simultaneously eliminates the exploitation of the masses by the classes owning wealth, the oppression of peoples, and thereby the causes of war. That is why the struggle for a lasting peace is, all in all, nothing other than the struggle to accomplish socialism.

8. Whenever the working class renounces class struggle, and sides with exploiters, whenever it subordinates its wishes to those of governments and of the ruling classes, it distances itself further from its goal – the achievement of a lasting peace. In acting this way the working class entrusts to bourgeois governments and capitalist classes a task which it alone can fully accomplish, worse still it delivers up its best forces to the butchery of war and it allows the destruction of its most able and healthy elements, which in wartime as in peacetime, should be called on to fight above all for socialism.

9. The proletariat's attitude towards war should not be determined by the strategic or military situation of belligerent countries. In conformity with decisions of

international congresses of Stuttgart, Copenhagen and Basel the vital duty of the proletariat is therefore one of demanding peace now, and an immediate armistice to start peace talks.

10. The working class will succeed in hastening the end of this war and in influencing the terms of peace if this appeal find an echo in the ranks of the proletariat, promoting vigorous activity, the aim of which will be to overthrow capitalist domination. If the working class does not respond to this appeal, peace-terms will be determined by the ruling classes, governments and diplomats, totally disregarding peoples' hopes and interests.

11. In its mass revolutionary struggles for socialism and for human liberation from the disaster of capitalist militarism the proletariat should simultaneously oppose all annexionist tendencies. The proletariat does not consider the world political set up, such as it was before the war, as being something which answered popular interests. But it opposes all arbitrary changes of frontiers, even in cases where mutilated states are constituted on the pretext of liberating peoples, where these have only artificial independence and are in truth subject to domination [by others]. Socialism itself, through an economic and political unity of peoples on a foundation of democracy tends to suppress all national oppression. Such unity is unobtainable with the confines of a capitalist society. But it is annexation in particular – whatever its form – which renders this task more difficult and make the conditions of proletarian struggle more painful, whenever it dismembers peoples, divides them up, or incorporates them in large capitalist states.

12. Until socialism brings freedom and the equality and rights of all peoples, it is the proletariat's constant duty to fight resolutely against all national oppressions, against all violence directed towards weaker peoples, to obtain

their autonomy through class struggle on an entirely democratic basis, as well as the protection of national minorities.

13. War indemnities as demanded by imperialist powers cannot accord with proletarian interests. Just as each countries' dominant classes seek to place the weight of war expenditures on the shoulders of their own working class, they will also attempt to place the weight of war indemnities on the proletariat of vanquished countries. Such a situation will also harm the workers of winning nations, as the aggravation of social and economic burdens on any given country will have inevitable repercussions on that of others and will render more difficult conditions for international class struggle. The action of any one nation's proletariat should not consist of throwing the war's financial and economic burdens onto the workers of another nation but of placing that burden on the wealthy of all countries through the elimination of public debt.

14. There will be further intensification of the struggle against war and imperialism as a consequence of the ruination and sufferings brought on by the calamities of this imperialist age. Socialism will develop and direct mass movements against the rising costs of life, in favour of the demands of agricultural workers; against unemployment, new taxes and against political reaction until it culminates in an international struggle for the final triumph of the proletariat.'

24-30 April 1916. This international conference was held in Switzerland in April 1916, and was attended by 44 socialists and syndicalists. Final resolution. Translated from the text in French, Archives Lenine /Archives Trotsky.

All our strength for revolution
– Bruno Misèfari, Italian Anarchist

'… The era of the old criminal world, the era of capitalism, the state and religion has had its day, and from all the ends of the earth the social revolution is rising and criticising looking to a new age. The triumph of statist-capitalist reaction would be death both to workers and for society as a whole; the triumph of anarchism will allow your life to flourish, benefitting and giving liberty to all. So, take up your place in the struggle on our side. Do not let yourselves be deceived by the siren calls of "gradual advances" deliberately made by a false socialism … All our passion, all our courage, all our strength should be for revolution, that is for a life with bread, freedom and love. The capitalist regime can only make things worse. Don't betray yourselves! Don't be unworthy of the bright heroic age we are going to encounter! One and all, together on this wartime First of May, let us demand our rights – all of them!'

1 May 1916. From: Furio Sbarnemi & Bruno Misefari, *Diario di un disertore*, Florence: La nuova Italia, 1973, pp. 69-9. Misefari escaped and spent the next two years in Switzerland in the company of other Italian anarchists. Paul Schreyer of the Hamburg Anarchist Federation, editor of its weekly paper *Kampf* also entered Switzerland to avoid conscription. Swiss law gave no protection to deserters who were often returned to their countries of origin. In Schreyer's case this led to his death in a military prison.

Assemby Call – Karl Liebknecht

'Workers, comrades, women and all: do not let this second First of May of world war go by without a demonstration of international socialism, an act of protest against imperialist butchery! On this First of May we hold out our fraternal hand over barriers and frontiers, to the people of France, Belgium, Russia, England, Serbia – to the whole world. On this first of May in thousands and millions our voices cry: Stop this infamous crime, this murder of peoples! Down with those responsible – the decision makers, the provocateurs, the profiteers! Our enemies are not peoples – the French, the Russians or the English – but the German gentry, German capitalists, and their executive committee the German government! Let us fight these – deadly enemies of all freedom – let us fight for everything that goes with the future and the well-being of the cause of labour, humanity and culture! Stop the War! We want peace! Long live socialism! Long live the International of labour! Workers of the world, Unite!'

1 May 1916.

Duty – J. O. Bentall, American Socialist

'The duty of socialists at this time is clear. First to create an anti-war psychology in press, in speech, in campaigns. Secondly, to organise and crystallise the anti-war sentiment into militant, fearless working class organisation that can and will take charge. Thirdly, to acquire power by acquiring actual industries one after another, beginning with the food industry and continuing along the lines of greatest needs. The organisation to do this must be wholly made up of socialists, socialists who stand together one the rock foundation of class struggle. Half-baked socialist politicians should be tabooed. Don't let them in.'

May 1916. From: 'The Crisis in the Movement', in: *International Socialist Review,* November 1915, Vol. XVI, No. 11; p. 678. The author was a candidate in the Minnesota gubernatorial election of 1916, and won 23,000 votes,

Court Martial defence – Karl Liebknecht

'The present war is not a war for the protection of national
integrity, nor for the freeing of oppressed people, nor for
the welfare of the masses. From the standpoint of the
proletariat it signifies the most extreme concentration and
extension of political oppression, economic exploitation,
militaristic slaughtering of the working classes, body and
soul – for the sake of capitalism and despotism.'

3 May 1916.

Appeal by Women to Women
– Vida Goldstein (Australian Feminist & Pacifist), et al

'When British men believed that they were going out
to protect a "Little Nation," and to do their part in the
"War to end war and Prussian militarism," they came
forth in their thousands as free men. But as time went
on, they found that "Little Belgium" was forgotten, that
the rights of "Little Ireland," "Little Finland" and "Little
Greece" seemed to be set aside by other "Big Nations."
They found that, while they were destroying a European
menace, they were setting up what they believed was
another and nearer menace. They found that, instead of
Prussian militarism being destroyed, it was being hailed as
the saviour of the British Empire. They found that instead
of England being the "Land where girt by friends or foes,
a man may speak the thing he will." she had become the
land of military and industrial slaves, of shackled speech
and shackled conscience. They found that, instead of this
being the "war to end all war", all nations, neutral as well
as belligerent, are preparing for future wars, and arming
more and more feverishly. Under these circumstances,
do you wonder that free Australian men have come to
see that the war is not being fought for the great ideals of

freedom that were held before them at the beginning, and that, therefore, the few men who might still volunteer in the cause of freedom refuse to volunteer in a cause that aims at riveting the chains of European militarism on Australia? They begin to see that the belief in might throws the nations into a bottomless pit of hate, and oppression, and debt. They begin to see that conscription entrenches militarism still more deeply and breeds endless war, to which every conception of right and freedom must be ruthlessly sacrificed. Therefore, they say, "To vote *no*" means the beginning of the end of militarism in Australia, and of every other nation; the beginning of the reign of right as the only might there is or can be.'

5 October 1916. Over 300,000 Australians had volunteered to fight abroad. A plebiscite was held on to introduce compulsion for overseas military service. The Australian Labor party divided into opposing factions. A small majority of men and women voted 'No'. Over 60,000 Australians died in the war. Vida Goldstein was a pacifist and chaired a Peace Alliance. Adela Pankhurst, the sister of Sylvia Pankhurst, supported her. Two months later the Unlawful Associations Act targeted the IWW, over a hundred members were sentenced to terms of six months imprisonment.

Feminist address
– Hélène Brion, French Feminist & Pacifist

'Having no political or civil rights we were unable to do anything to prevent this war and all our heart is with you in wishing an end to it. All our heart is one with you in wishing, the moment it ends, or later, that attempts be made to establish a more equitable and just social system in Europe which on the one hand, would render war less frequent through some sort of federation of nations, and moreover would assure within each federation a broader and less precarious life for the immense majority of workers. We women are side by side with the mass of workers because where they are, we are; wherever the oppressed are found, we are there. We women are oppressed everywhere, and to a much greater extent than any other class of workers. Workers, like you, and more than you, we suffer from wars, and therefore we want to work to prevent their return. But before joining with you in a more decisive phase of activity we wish to highlight the motives which make us act, and to work on you so that you consider the facts which impel us. Workers, you have not been just vis-à-vis the women who have helped your struggles. Workers, vanguard feminists await your response and leave you to meditate on these words of Considérant:[32] "When women are initiated into social questions revolutions will no longer be made with rifle fire".'

23 October 1916. This note was handed over to Alphonse Merrheim, the metal workers leader, a key figure in the post-Zimmerwald Committee for the Resumption of International Relations. Hélène Brion[33] argued that the war was engendered by a society in which the 'Rights of Man' did not obtain for both sexes. http://www.marievictoirelouis.net/document.php?id=182&auteurid=183

We'll fight against you! – *Industrial Worker,* (USA)

'Capitalists of America, we will fight against you, not for you! There is not a power in the world that can make the working class fight if they refuse.'

10 February 1917, *Industrial Worker.* After the USA's declaration of war in April, raids were made on IWW halls. 165 IWW leaders were charged under the Espionage Act for hindering conscription. It is still part of the legal code of the USA. Religious bodies and film distributors have featured amongst those sanctioned.

Appeal to the Peoples of the World
– Petrograd Soviet of Workers' and Soldiers' Deputies

'Comrade-proletarians, and toilers of all countries: we, Russian workers and soldiers, united in the Petrograd Soviet of Workers' and Soldiers' Deputies, send you warmest greetings and announce the great event. The age-old despotism of the Tsar has been shattered in the dust by Russian democracy, which [now] enters your family of nations as an equal, and as a mighty force in the struggle for our common liberation. Our victory is a great victory for the freedom and democracy of the world. ...

We appeal to our brother-proletarians of the Austro-German coalition, and, first of all, to the German proletariat. On the first day of the war, you were told that by taking arms against autocratic Russia, you were defending the European civilization against Asiatic despotism. Many of you saw in this a justification of that support which you were giving to the war. Now even this justification is gone: democratic Russia cannot be a threat to liberty and civilization.... [We appeal to you]: Throw off the yoke of your autocratic rulers, as the Russian people have shaken off the Tsar's autocracy; refuse to serve as tools of violence and conquest ...'

Izvestia, No. 15, 28 March 1917. Women protestors drawn from munitions factories of St Petersburg (Petrograd) demonstrated in tens of thousands on International Women's day. Revolt escalated, the Tsar abdicated and the Russian Revolution began.

Workers have common interests
– Big Bill Haywood, American Socialist

'All class conscious members of the Industrial Workers of the World are conscientiously opposed to spilling the blood of human beings, not for religious reasons... but because we believe that the interests and welfare of the working class of all countries are identical.'

April 1917; From: Philip S. Foner, *History of the Labor Movement in the United States Volume 7: Labor and World War I*, New York: International Publishers, 1987, p. 109. The IWW did not take an official position opposing conscription. Despite this its offices were raided and some four hundred members were jailed. Frank Little took the view that it was better to go out in a 'blaze of glory' – war would mean the end of free speech, free press, free assembly. Little was murdered by vigilantes in Arizona, in August, whilst helping organising a miners' strike. See: William D. Haywood, *The Autobiography of Big Bill Haywood*, New York: International Publishers, 1929; Joyce L. Kornbluh, *Rebel Voices An IWW Anthology*, London: Merlin Press, 2011, chapter 11.

Monopolistic, oppressive and unjust
– George Huddleston, American Democrat

'The interests behind conscription are largely big business and big finance. Its champions are dreamers, but they dream vicious dreams of world conquest and exploitation. Their dreams are of the American flag sent into the remote corners of the world to protect their operations and to guard the extension of the systems whereby they have brought America under their feet.'

25 April 1917; Speech in the US congress, Huddleston was a democrat party congressman for Alabama. He later voted for the US declaration of war. Quoted in: Jeanette Keith, *Rich Man's War, Poor Man's Fight: Race, Class, and Power in the Rural South during the First World War*, Chapel Hill: University of North Carolina Press, 2004, p. 12

Abandon Illusions – The Socialists of Naples

'Socialists of every country should direct their energy towards ending the war inciting the proletariat to become conscious of its own strength and through its intransigent class activity should provoke the immediate cessation of hostilities working to transform the crisis into a struggle to achieve the revolutionary aims of socialism. The Socialist Party should, in the period following an eventual peace between bourgeois governments, continue its unceasing propaganda work amongst the working masses to prepare them and to push them to prepare the party's maximum programme, finally abandoning illusion as to the benefit of reforms which may be agreed by a bourgeois regime ...'

8 May 1917; From Amadeo Bordiga, *Histoire de la gauche communiste*, Volume 1 - 1912 – 1919, Saguenay, Québec: 2005, Chapter 27. www. matierevolution.org/IMG/doc/hist_gc_1.doc Bordiga looked to guard the frontiers of the Socialist party at a time when others sought co-operation between all who shared in common opposition to the war – socialists and syndicalists.

Not our business – Albert 'Ginger' Goodwin, British/Canadian Socialist & Trade Unionist

'[T]o do all in his power to prove to the workers that the war was none of their business ... *[Earlier he had written:]*

To accept the teachings of nationalism is to segregate the workers of the world and make out of them enemies ready and willing to fly at each other's throats when the exploiters want them. The boundary lines of the various countries do not cover the cloak of exploitation ... The slaves of England, Germany, Austria, France, Russia, USA and other countries under the yoke of capitalism, live under the same general condition of wage slavery... We are international in kind, and our enemy is the class that live from the produce of our toil.'

June and September 1917. An anti-war left made gains in Western Canada. A special Labour convention met in Vancouver over Labour Day to explore ways of opposing conscription and heard this pledge from a miner. From: *The Western Clarion*. In November 1917 Goodwin[34] wrote to the *BC Federationist:* 'It is the hope of the writer that capitalism will fang itself to death, and out of its carcass spring the life of the new age with its blossoms of economic freedom, happiness and joy for the world's workers'. Quoted in: Benjamin Isitt, *From Victoria to Vladivostok: Canada's Siberian Expedition, 1917-19*, Vancouver: UBC Press, 2000, pp. 30-31.

Only the people
– Emma Goldman, Russian-American Anarchist

'… only the people must decide whether they want war or not, and as long as the people have not given their consent I deny that the President of the United States has any right to declare it; I deny that the President, or those who back the President, have any right to tell the people that they shall take their sons and husbands, and brothers and lovers, and shall conscript them in order to ship them across the seas, for the conquest of militarism and the support of wealth and power in the United States.'

14 June 1917, speech in Forward Hall, New York.

Making the world safe for democracy – Emma Goldman

'[M]ay there not be different kinds of patriotism as there are different kinds of liberty? I for one cannot believe that love of one's country must needs consist in blindness to its social faults, to deafness to its social discords, of inarticulation of its social wrongs. Neither can I believe that the mere accident of birth in a certain country or the mere scrap of a citizen's paper constitutes the love of country. I know many people – I am one of them – who were not born here, nor have they applied for citizenship, and who yet love America with deeper passion and greater intensity than many natives whose patriotism manifests itself by pulling, kicking, and insulting those who do not rise when the national anthem is played. Our patriotism is that of the man who loves a woman with open eyes. He is enchanted by her beauty, yet he sees her faults. So we, too, who know America, love her beauty, her richness, her great possibilities; we love her mountains, her canyons, her forests, her Niagara, and her deserts – above all do we love the people that have produced her wealth, her artists who have created beauty, her great apostles who dream and work for liberty – but with the same passionate emotion we hate her superficiality, her cant, her corruption, her mad unscrupulous worship at the altar of the Golden Calf. We say that if America has entered the war to make the world safe for democracy, she must first make democracy safe in America. How else is the world to take America seriously, when democracy at home is daily being outraged, free speech suppressed, peaceable assemblies broken up by overbearing and brutal gangsters in uniform; when free press is curtailed and every independent opinion gagged. Verily, poor as we are in democracy, how can we give of it to the world?'

June 1917; trial speech, on charges of conspiracy to prevent conscription.

The Battle to maintain Liberty in the United States is fast and furious – American Legal Defence League

'Meetings are being broken up, men and women searched without warrants, men and women arrested for reading or wearing a button "Our Rights but No War", for asking congress to repeal conscription, for talking on behalf of conscientious objectors, or for no reason at all.'

Autumn 1917; advertisement in *The Masses,* Vol. 9.

Leeds Conference, Talk Reason – Robert Smillie, Labour Party & Miners' Trade Union leader

'We in this country had reached the stage at which we were not in a position to call our souls our own. The right to call our bodies our own had gone a considerable time before. If it is a right thing that the Russian people are to be congratulated on securing their freedom, surely it cannot be a wrong thing for Britain to desire freedom also. Now, we have not come here to talk treason. We have come here to talk reason. (Cheers.) I am glad to know that practically all opposition has been removed so far as the first three resolutions are concerned. Surely no person in this meeting or in this city or in Great Britain can now afford to refuse to send congratulations to our comrades in Russia. I don't see how there can be any reasonable objection to the demand for a restatement of foreign policy and war aims. As for the third resolution, civil liberty to me is one of the most important things in the world. Without civil liberty life is not worth living. We haven't civil liberty in this country now. ("Hear, hear.") I come to the last resolution. Our soldiers are inarticulate. They have no organisation to advocate their claims and to call attention to their grievances. Does anyone say there is no need for such an organisation to be set up? Has the treatment of the relatives and dependents of those at the front been so good up to the present time that nothing further need be done? Has the treatment of the soldiers themselves at the front, or when they were wounded, or when they were retired from the army – has it been all that could be desired? There must be a closer link between the civil population and the military population.'

June 1917, Chairman's speech. 1150 delegates from unions, labour and socialist political organisations and women's organisations all over Britain met in a conference in Leeds. Four resolutions were agreed: (1) hailing the Russian Revolution; (2) pledging work for a general peace without domination, annexations or indemnities; based on the rights of nations to decide their own affairs; (3) calling for a charter of liberties, complete political rights for all men and women, unrestricted freedom of the press, freedom of speech, a general amnesty for all political and religious prisoners, full rights of industrial and political association, and the release of labour from all forms of compulsion and restraint; and (4) calling for the creation of Councils of Workmen and Soldier's Delegates. Smillie was active in the Miners' Federation of Great Britain, in the National Council against Conscription, and in the No-Conscription Fellowship; he was later elected an MP.

A soldier of the 548th Division – reported by John Reed

'Comrades, he cried, and there was real anguish in his drawn face and despairing gestures. The people at the top are always calling upon us to sacrifice more, sacrifice more, while those who have everything are left unmolested. We are at war with Germany. Would we invite German generals to serve on our staff? Well we're at war with the capitalists too, and yet we invite them into our government. Show me what I am fighting for. Is it Constantinople, or is it free Russia? Is it the democracy, or is it the capitalist plunderers? If you can prove to me that I am defending the revolution then I'll go out and fight without capital punishment to force me. When the land belongs to the peasants, and the factories to the workers, and the power to the soviets, then we'll know we have something to fight for, and we'll fight for it!'

September 1917. The revolution of March 1917 had unleashed new forces in Russia. Workers armed themselves in the cities. Soldiers abandoned the front. In Kronstadt sailors arrested their officers.[35] In September General Kornilov marched on Petrograd to make himself military dictator of Russia; in reaction moderate and revolutionary Socialists came together in self-defence. From, *Ten Days that shook the World*, Chapter 2.

General Kornilov threatened St Petersburg
– Nestor Makhno, Ukrainian Anarchist

'When the session was opened I read the despatches and presented my report on what our priorities for action should be and on the means at our disposal. In its message the central committee soviet executive suggested the formation of local committees of public safety. One was immediately elected from amongst the members of the assembled: it took the name of Committee for the Defence of the Revolution, and I was given the job of directing its work. It was at once resolved to begin disarming the bourgeoisie of the region in its entirety, to abolish its rights over the people's wealth: lands, workshops, factories, print-shops, meeting rooms, and other public works. To stop Kornilov's army we had first of all to put an end to the domination of the bourgeoisie.'

29 August 1917; Gulyai-Polye, Ukraine. Russiuan peasants were taking possession of the land. The text above report how a small town in the Ukraine responded to the news from Petrograd.[36] From Nestor Makhno, *Mémoires et ecrits*, Paris: Editions Ivrea, 2009, pp. 114-5. Makhno died from tuberculosis in Paris in 1934.

Stop the war – Leon Trotsky, Russian Social-democrat

'"Immediate cessation of the war" is the watchword under which the Social-democracy can reassemble its scattered ranks, both within the national parties, and in the whole International. The proletariat cannot make its will to peace dependent upon the strategic considerations of the general staffs. On the contrary, it must oppose its desire for peace to these military considerations. What the warring governments call a struggle for national self-preservation is in reality a mutual national annihilation. Real national self-defence now consists in the struggle for peace. Such a struggle for peace means for us not only a fight to save humanity's material and cultural possessions from further insane destruction. It is for us primarily a fight to preserve the revolutionary energy of the proletariat. To assemble the ranks of the proletariat in a fight for peace means again to place the forces of revolutionary socialism against raging tearing imperialism on the whole front. The conditions upon which peace should be concluded – the peace of the people themselves, and not the reconciliation of the diplomats – must be the same for the whole International. *No Reparations – The Right of every nation to Self-Determination – The United States*

of Europe: without monarchies, without standing armies,
without ruling feudal castes, without secret diplomacy.'

1917. From: *The Bolsheviki and World Peace,* New York: Boni & Liveright,
1918, pp. 229-231.

The League of Nations
– Theodore Rothstein, Russian Social-democrat

The war is an imperialist war. It arose, not out of the
"irreconcilable" opposition of two "ideals", of autocracy
and democracy, of despotism and liberty, of Kaiserdom
and Lloyd Georgeism. It arose from the long rivalry and
clashing interests of various "national" financial groups
for places in Chinese, Persian, Moroccan, Turkish, Central
African and other similar "suns" which bring forth
and mature railway and mining concessions and other
interesting things yielding dividends on capital and quick
"earnings" on the stock exchange. Yet we know that had it
not been for certain "accidentals" – history is apparently
full of them – we might have avoided the war. We might
have avoided it by way of internationalisation of finance,
which already began to strike roots in international politics.
It was the same process which was, and still is, observable
among trusts. Trusts arise and fight one another; then
the moment comes when the mutual squabbles begin
to be too expensive. The idea of fusion, of alliance, of
pooling dawns upon the minds of the trust magnates,
and eventually the trusts bury the battle-axe and combine
into one concern. The beginnings of the same process
were observable in the domain of imperialist rivalries
shortly before the war. In 1909, after much fruitless and
expensive bickerings over and in Morocco, Germany and
France, after much squabbling between their respective
diplomats, acting on behalf of their respective "national"
finance, the powers came to an agreement to cease all

quarrels and to work henceforth hand in hand by means of joint enterprise in all concessions and in the execution of orders. Schneider combined with Krupp, Syndicat des Mines Marocaines combined with Thyssen and Kirdoff, and the Banque de Paris et des Pays-Bas worked hand in glove with the Deutsche Bank. The eve of the war somewhat similar arrangement arrived at between our own and the German diplomacy for the joint construction of the Baghdad Railway and the joint exploitation of the mines of the Katanga. But the most classical example was the internationalisation of the financial business in China by means of a Four, then Six, and then, again, Five Powers' Syndicate, which had for its object to do away with all rivalry between the "Great" Powers (England, France, Germany, Belgium, Russia, Japan, and America) in the discharge of the high mission of providing China with loans, and obtaining from her various concessions. This process, as we say, was in fair way of being extended throughout the domain of international finance as the natural result of competition. There was, in addition, the special influence of America, a new capitalist country without colonies or spheres of influence of her own, who was naturally interested in gaining access to all financial markets, and therefore, championed the principle of the open door and internationalisation. At one time America went so far as to propose even the internationalisation of the railways in China and to suggest a complete and all-embracing international scheme for the exploitation of Turkey.

But the process was not consummated, and the war broke out. Indeed, the war itself will be regarded by the future historian as an incident in that process which could not overcome the resistance offered to it by the human factor (the imbecility and greed and prejudice of the individual financiers and diplomats) except by force.

The result, however, will be that taught by experience of this terrible conflict, the personae dramatis will take up the broken thread and, freed from their imbecility and greed and prejudice, hasten to conclude consciously and according to plan what they had been groping after experimentally and with so much friction before the war. That is precisely the sense of the Wilson-Asquith-Michaelis[37]-Pope scheme for a League of "Nations." Of course, the word "nations" is not meant for the "peoples", but for the financial cliques which everywhere constitute the prime moving and organising force of modern capitalism and which, as such, dominate the state and the world. Down with the international financial rivalries! Down with the constant quarrels, responsible for the never-ending armaments, never-ending diplomatic crises. Down with quarrels that brought about the war which has shown the equal strength of the two main contesting groups! Finance must become internationalised, and then the quarrels will disappear; the need for armaments will be gone, and a court of arbitration will be able to dispose of all minor disputes which may arise on purely technical and legal points. The world will be one, the armies will be abolished (with the exception of an international armed force to put down rebel Negroes or Chinamen, as well as rebel workers), and the old dream of eternal peace come true.

Utopia? Not a bit of it. National syndication in every country, international syndication among the "Great" Powers – such seems to be the irresistible trend of economic development, for which the first suitable forms will be found at the next peace conference. Imperialism and capitalism will attain a higher level – with what results to the "backward" and small countries as well as the working class, may well be imagined.'

4 October 1917. The views, published in the newspaper of the British

Socialist Party, provide a critical perspective on proposals for a League of Nations. They may be compared with the fourteen points[38] of American President, Woodrow Wilson. See also comments by Chicherin one year later, below. From: *The Call*, Theodore Rothstein, using alias John Bryan. http://www.marxists.org./archive/rothstein/1917/10/league.htm

To all, announcing the October Revolution
– The Military Revolutionary Committee

'The Petrograd garrison has overturned the government of Kerensky,[39] which had risen against the revolution and the people…. In sending this news to the front and the country, the Military Revolutionary Committee requests all soldiers to keep vigilant watch on the conduct of officers. Officers who do not frankly and openly declare for the revolution should be immediately arrested as enemies. The Petrograd Soviet interprets the programme of the new government as: immediate proposals of a general democratic peace, the immediate transfer of great landed estates to the peasants, and the honest convocation of the constituent assembly. The people's revolutionary army must not permit troops of doubtful morale to be sent to Petrograd. Act by means of arguments, by means of moral suasion – but if that fails, halt the movement of troops by implacable force. The present order must be immediately read to all military units of every branch of the service. Whoever keeps the knowledge of this order from the soldier-masses…. commits a serious crime against the revolution, and will be punished with all the rigour of revolutionary law. Soldiers! For peace, bread, land, and popular government!'

8 November 1917; from, *Ten Days that shook the World*, Chapter 5.

Patriotism – John Maclean

'It was not the workers who instigated the war. The workers have no economic interest to serve as a consequence of the war, and because of that, it is my appeal to my class that makes me a patriot so far as my class is concerned, and when I stand true to my class, the working class, in which I was born, it is because my people were swept out of the Highlands, and it was only because of my own ability that I remained. I have remained true to my class, the working class, and whatever I do I think I am doing in the interest of my class and my country. I am no traitor to my country. I stand loyal to my country because I stand loyal to the class which creates the wealth throughout the whole of the world.'

May 1918; speech from the dock, Edinburgh High Court. http://www.marxists.org/archive/maclean/works/1918-dock.htm

An Appeal to the German Workers

'Workers, Comrades, Citizens, denounce lithe reactionary policy of the Government and the bourgeois parties! Protest whenever you find the opportunity in public meetings, against being deprived of your political rights! Arouse the indifferent and the apathetic! Awaken the public political conscience and increase the energies of your organisations! Present a bold front against the aggravation of the conditions of life! In your meetings and intimate circles, spread the light about the reasons for the reduction of the bread ration and the real cause of misery of the people during the war! Support with all your power the struggle which the groups of the Independent Social-democratic Party are carrying on in the Parliaments for Peace, for liberty and for bread. Workers, Comrades, Citizens – away with all discouragement, all pusillanimity, all disaffection! Arm the proletariat for the inevitable struggles for a better future! Be faithful to the principles of International Social-democracy!'

27 May 1918. German Social-democrats had split over support for the war; an anti-war grouping came together, in 1917, as the Independent Social-democratic Party (USPD). http://www.marxists.org/history/international/social-democracy/justice/1918/07/german-manifesto.htm

The Canton, Ohio Speech
– Eugene Debs, American Socialist

'These are the gentry who are today wrapped up in the American flag, who shout their claim from the housetops that they are the only patriots, and who have their magnifying glasses in hand, scanning the country for evidence of disloyalty, eager to apply the brand of treason to the men who dare to even whisper their opposition to Junker rule in the United Sates. No wonder Sam Johnson declared that "patriotism is the last refuge of the scoundrel." He must have had this Wall Street gentry in mind, or at least their prototypes, for in every age it has been the tyrant, the oppressor and the exploiter who has wrapped himself in the cloak of patriotism, or religion, or both to deceive and overawe the people.'

June 1918. American patriots had called for the Kaiser to be boiled in oil. Eugene Debs[40] tried to defend sanity. From: *The Call* (USA).

Mobsters in the USA
– Elizabeth Gurley Flynn, American Socialist

'Mob violence and legal terror mounted in the country. It did not stem from the masses of the people, but from the big employers and the loud-mouthed professional patriots and witch-hunters of that period, most of whom are long since forgotten. It was directed against labour and all who opposed war in general or this war in particular, or profiteering on war. The list of victims grew, especially among those who were indiscriminately classified as "Reds" – anarchists, socialists, IWWs and progressive trade unionists. After the revolution in Russia in 1917, the details of which we knew very little here but which was greeted with great enthusiasm by Americans generally, a drive began against anyone who could be called "Bolshevik". "Fear of revolution" swept the reactionaries of this land. A wholesale attack was directed against the IWW. The Chicago indictment was followed by similar ones on Omaha, Sacramento, Wichita and Spokane. Several hundreds of IWW men were sent to prison, with sentences up to twenty years. The leaders of the Socialist Party were also singled out for attack.'

1918; From: Elizabeth Gurley Flynn, *The Rebel Girl: An Autobiography*, New York: International Publishers, 1973, p. 239.

Resolution to the Trades Council, Poplar, East London – Commandeer empty houses
– Workers' Suffrage Federation[41]

'[that] the Russian example be followed and that families made homeless by air raids and [currently] lodged in the workhouse, should have empty houses commandeered for them.'

June 1918. Proposed by Norah Smyth and agreed.

Equal Pay Strike – *Daily Mirror,* (London)

'The speakers pointed out that it was essential that women should be paid equal terms with the men, especially in view of the position of discharged soldiers later on... Between two and three hundred women in the Paddington [Great Western Railway] and Old Oak Common cleaning departments struck yesterday, demanding equal pay with the men for equal work. The strikers are demanding an additional 12/6 [62.5p] per week to bring their wages up to those of male employees.'

24 August 1918. When men and women on the London Underground Railway went out on strike for equal pay James H Thomas, a rail workers' trade union leader, advised a return to work.[42] He said: 'We are supporting, as we always have done, the claim for the same war wage for women as men …' From http://www.unionhistory.info/britainatwork/emuweb/objects/nofdigi/tuc/imagedisplay.php?irn=1121

Hands off Russia! – British Socialist Party

'This meeting believes that the overthrow of the Soviet administration would be a disaster to the organised labour movement throughout the world, and could only be construed as evidence of the intention of governments to make war on the working class. It calls upon the British government to abandon its present policy with regard to Russia and instead to offer Russia the technical and economic aid required for her reconstruction.'

29 August 1918. In the summer of 1918 the American, British, French and other allied troops were sent to Northern Russia and occupied Archangel; one of a series of interventions around the periphery of Russia. Various radical organisations called for strikes to obstruct intervention in Russia. In Britain the government ordered the seizure of radical left newspapers which opposed this intervention. From: *The Call*, statement of the BSP executive committee.

Russian thoughts on a League of Nations, proposals to President Wilson
– Georgi Chicherin, Russian Social-democrat[43]

'While agreeing to participate in the negotiations even with governments which do not as yet express the will of the people, we on our part should like to ascertain in detail from you, Mr President, your conception of the League of

Nations with which you propose to crown the work of peace. You demand the independence of Poland, Serbia, Belgium, and liberty for the peoples of Austria-Hungary. You probably mean to say that the popular masses everywhere must first take the determination of their fate into their own hands in order afterwards to associate in a free League of Nations. But, strangely enough, we have not seen among your demands the liberation of either Ireland, Egypt, India or even the liberation of the Philippines, and we greatly desire that these peoples, through their freely-elected representatives, should have an opportunity, jointly with us, to take part in the organisation of the League of Nations.'

October 1918; text of the Russian Soviet Government's Peace Proposals, issued as a pamphlet by the People's Russian Information Bureau, London; from marxists.org/archive/chicherin/1918/league-of-nations.htm

Resolution – Rhondda Miners

'…this meeting strongly protests against the armed intervention in Russia in opposition to the declared wishes of the Soviet government, and in direct contradiction to the allies' pronouncement in favour of the self-determination of all nations. This meeting believes that the overthrow of the Soviet administration would be a disaster to the organised labour movement throughout the world, and could only be construed as evidence of the intention of the government to make war on the working classes.'

October 1918, passed at a meeting of 32 South Wales branch delegates. In January 1919 a conference of 350 delegates launched a British Hands off Russia Campaign. Similar campaigns were launched in Canada, the USA and elsewhere. There were mutinies in the British, Canadian and French forces earmarked for or sent to Russia.

Now is the time for Revolution – Karl Liebknecht

'Front-line soldiers, abandon your weapons; homeland workers lay down your tools! Don't let yourselves be deceived any longer... [Act!] Stop the war yourselves and use your weapons against your rulers.'

1 November 1918.

The League of Nations is good business
– *The Liberator,* (New York)

'It is but an expression in the political sphere of something that has already happened in the business sphere. Business has become international. Capital is internationally owned. It is inevitable that an international state should be formed, to express and defend its interests. At the same time war has become destructive beyond the bounds of safe speculation even for nationalistic capital, and so the chief opposition to a guaranteed peace is removed. Only the dull and the unprogressive in the business and political community are opposed to the League of Nations. I think we can say that it is the next natural step in the development of capitalism.'

December 1918. Editorial, Volume 1, No. 10.

Starving, and with allies collapsing, rebellions broke out in Kiel, Berlin, Munich ...

To the population of Munich
– Kurt Eisner, German Social-democrat

'A provisional council of workers, soldiers and peasants has been constituted in the night of 8 November. Bavaria is now a Free State. A popular government supported by the confidence of the masses is being immediately established. All responsible men and women will have the right to vote for the constituent national assembly which will be summoned as quickly as possible. A new era has begun! Bavaria will start equipping Germany for a League of Peoples (Völkerbund). The social and democratic republic of Bavaria has the moral strength to work for peace for Germany, saving it from much worse ...

A council of workers, soldiers and peasants will assure the strictest order. Any infractions will be punished piteously. The security of persons and property is guaranteed. Soldiers based in barracks will govern themselves and maintain discipline through soldiers' councils. Officers not opposed to these changed times can perform their duties untouched. We count on the active aid of the entire population. We welcome all who will contribute to the construction of this new freedom. All officials should remain at their post. Fundamental social and political reforms will be implemented without delay. Peasants will look after the ensuring food supplies for urban areas. Old oppositions between town and country will disappear. The distribution of supplies will be rationally organised ...'

8 November 1918; *Münchener Neueste Nachrichten.* On the following day it was announced that the Kaiser had abdicated. Eisner wanted unity between socialists, a unity based on a common commitment to revolution; but he hoped in vain. He was assassinated in February 1919. Like Toller (quoted in first section) Eisner had started as a supporter of the war, but changed his mind and joined the Independent Social-democrats.

General Strike Demands
– The Committee of Olten, (Switzerland)

1. Immediate renovation of the National Council [parliament] through proportional representation.
2. Women to have the right to vote and to be elected.
3. All to have the right and duty to work.

4. Introduction of a 48 hour week into all workplaces, private and public.

5. The organisation of an entirely popular army.

6. Measures to be taken to ensure food supply.

7. Insurance (pensions) for the widowed and the aged.

8. A state monopoly of imports and exports.

9. Owners to pay public debts.

11-14 November 1918. Neutral Switzerland suffered in the war with a disrupted economy, with rising prices and unemployment, and with food shortages. 250,000 workers supported a general strike. The government took fright and threatened force. Cavalry patrolled Zurich and 100,000 soldiers were alerted. The strike was called off. Proportional representation and the 48 hour week were conceded. Swiss military courts issued accusations against 3,500 persons; 147 were condemned, some to short terms of imprisonment.

For a Forty Hour Week
– Manifesto of the Joint Strike Committee, Glasgow

'Fellow Workers, ever since the armistice was signed it has been evident that a big unemployment crisis was imminent unless steps were taken to absorb into industry the demobilised men of the army and navy. Thousands of these are being demobilised every day. Over a hundred thousand workers in Scotland have been dismissed from civil employment. They are out of a job. There are no jobs for them. There is only one remedy: reduce the hours of labour. … On the 29th a huge demonstration was held: ….There was no disorder. The demonstrations were, however, met by a vicious bludgeoning attack by the police. The authorities had evidently determined to break the strike by force, and had made their plans accordingly. With such ferocity did the police make their attack that even the members of our deputation, who were there by arrangement with the Lord Provost, were attacked, and one of them – D. Kirkwood – was brutally bludgeoned from behind as he was leaving the Council Chambers. Remember this was a peaceful and orderly demonstration of workers from all districts of the Clyde area. It was met by police batons, which were used indiscriminately upon men, women and children. ...

The organised workers of Scotland put forward an orderly and legitimate demand for the forty hours. The government's reply is bludgeons, machine-guns, bayonets and tanks. In one word, the institution of a reign of terror.

Fellow-Workers! Railwaymen, miners and all workers of Scotland, England and Wales, rally to the support of all your comrades on the Clyde!'

Response to events of 'Bloody Friday', 31 January 1919; published in February. Jobs had become scarce, strife erupted between black and white sailors, there were strikes and protests and the Riot Act was read. Tanks and troops patrolled the city. Strikers returned to work on 10 February, the forty hour week was not conceded, but the working day was reduced to 47 hours. For documents on Red Clydeside see: http://gdl.cdlr.strath. ac.uk/redclyde/redcly029.htm The confrontations between sailors in Glasgow had begun a week earlier. Similar events occurred later in seaports elsewhere in Britain. In the summer of 1919, *Workers' Dreadnought* wrote: 'Do you not know that if it pays to employ black men employers will get them and keep them even if the white workers kill a few of the blacks from time to time?' (7 June 1919); and two weeks later: 'The Seamen's and Firemen's Union has placed its ban upon the employment of Negro seamen, so they are ashore and cannot get away. They are attacked and if they retaliate they are arrested! Is this fair play? The fight for work is a product of capitalism: under socialism race rivalry disappears.' (21 June 1919). *The Socialist* – paper of the Socialist Labour Party published in Glasgow – wrote: 'The Trades Unions have prided themselves on having ousted coloured labourers from certain occupations... The very existence of capitalism depends upon driving all the elements of present day pugnacity, a trait always in prominence after a great war, into racial or national avenues. By forcing the workers to ease off their pugnacity over lines of colour, this blinds them to the class line which forms the focus of the struggle of the modern international proletariat. (10 July 1919). See: Jacqueline Jenkinson: 'Black Sailors on Red Clydeside: rioting, reactionary trade unionism and conflicting notions of 'Britishness' following the First

World War'. *Twentieth Century British History*, Volume 19, Issue 1, pp. 29 – 60.

Peoples – Nelly Roussel, French Feminist & Anarchist

'A "people" is composed of diverse elements of contradictory tendencies. Whilst among our compatriots there are many who always are strange to us, there is not a single people amongst whom each of us might be unable to find soul-sisters. Whatever may have been said, hatred between peoples is in no way a natural sentiment, or something instinctive; it is a monstrous creation by those who have, or believe that they have, some interest in armed conflict.'

Nelly Roussel, *Paroles de combat et d'espoir,* Épone, Édition de L'Avenir social, 1919, pp. 60-61.

Soldiers of Democracy
– W. E. B. Du Bois, American Civil Rights Campaigner

'… by the God of heaven, we are cowards and jackasses if now that that war is over, we do not marshal every ounce of our brain and brawn to fight a sterner, longer, more unbending battle against the forces of hell in our own land. We return. We return from fighting. We return fighting. Make way for democracy! We saved it in France, and by the Great Jehovah, we will save it in the United States of America, or know the reasons why.'

May 1919, *Crisis*; W. E. B. Du Bois was the foremost leader of African-Americans in the first decades of the 20th Century.

* * *

Some final thoughts

The left that opposed the war drew on several traditions: radical syndicalists, – such as those who had participated in the international conference held in London in 1913; anarchists, not including several important figures; and Socialists, mostly Italians, Russians and Serbians together with minorities from other European parties. In North America and Australasia there was a similar pattern with an anti-war opposition drawing on industrial unionists and socialists. In Africa and Asia some of the subjects of Empire refused to see this war as anything to do with them.

How was it that many 'lefts' supported a war between contending imperialist coalitions? Ralph Miliband wrote about circumstances in these times in 1964, as the fiftieth anniversary of the outbreak of the First World War approached. He noted that the intelligentsia, most of the lower middle class and many workers supported anti-socialist political parties:

> … it was in this period that there occurred a fundamental division within the labour movement between those who mainly saw it as an interest, and those who believed it embodied a cause, between those whose almost exclusive concern was the immediate needs, demands and grievances of Labour, and those for whom this was only part of the movement's purpose. The two perspectives are not necessarily incompatible; but in practice, the gulf between them was very deep, long before the split between social-democracy and communism tore the labour movements apart. Everywhere too, except for Britain, there were other splits, on ethnic and religious grounds, which a common allegiance to the workers' cause was quite insufficient to breach.

> Moreover, the new mass organizations, industrial as well as political had, almost from their inception, fallen

victim to the bureaucratic curse: Robert Michels was a
disillusioned socialist and the main frame of reference for
his 'iron law of oligarchy' was the experience of the West
European socialist and labour organizations. Not only
were these organizations top-heavy; they were also riddled
with energetic climbers, more concerned with place than
with purpose. The labour movements were now well
implanted in their societies, and room was found for many
of their leaders – at a price – in the conventional scheme
of politics. By 1914, they had, everywhere, become agents
of piecemeal pressure and reform, fulfilling a crucial
role as brokers and intermediaries between the rulers of
their countries and their own followers and members,
advancing the workers' claims, but also discharging a
function essential to capitalist society – that of disciplining
and moderating those claims. By then, most labour
leaders had acquired a large stake in moderate reform
within capitalism, and a deep fear of militant action.

As for the internationalism of the period, it is worth
noting that it was almost wholly concerned with the
developed capitalist white world, to whom the rest of the
world served as a coloured backcloth; and that, outside the
socialist ranks, this was a period of strong popular support
for imperialist ventures and conquests – indeed, support
for imperialism is also to be found, with suitable white-
man-burden connotations, within the socialist ranks as
well. What later came to be known as anti-colonialism
was certainly not one of the prominent features of the
labour movements of the time. The more recent record
on colonialism of the Western labour movement is
not particularly creditable. But let there at least be no
illusion about the intensity of anti-colonialism and anti-
imperialism in earlier days – save for a small minority
which certainly did not grow smaller with the years.

The leaders of the International, in the years before

1914, certainly denounced war with vehement sincerity, and equally sincere was their determination to prevent its occurrence. But the final reckoning of the character of the period, from a socialist point of view, is bound to take note of the rapidity with which socialist internationalism faded when submitted to the test of war, not least among those who had been most loud in their proclamations of that internationalism; and perhaps even more noteworthy is the support which leaders and led alike, save for small minorities, continued to give to their respective military and political elites through four years of mass slaughter.[44]

German Social-democracy was the leading party in the pre-war Socialist International. It had a million members and was allied with a trade-union movement with millions more. In recent national elections it had won almost 38 per cent of the vote. It said it was opposed to war. But for all its organisational strength German Social-democracy lacked a unified, resolute, autonomous political will opposed to capitalism and the state. Its action, or inaction in 1914 may be contrasted with more determined policies adopted before and after. For example, some seven year on from 1914, the British labour movement set up Councils of Action to prevent a new war with Russia. In 1936 Spanish workers reacted to news of an army coup by popular revolt. Working people acted en masse, for themselves. Such *active* politics contrasted with '*resolutionary*' Social-democratic politics – a politics characterised by 'orderliness and formalism',[45] a politics that delegated action to parliamentarians.

It was not just the spirit of mass revolt that was lacking in 1914. Present also was its opposite – a spirit that discipline, order and subseviance. The German Social-democratic party's trade union allies suspended all benefits for strikers and did not reinstate them until the end of the war. Officials in the apparatus of the trade-unions were determined to preserve 'their' organisational strength and their decision was followed by the officials and leaders in the Social-democratic parties. Together these forces moved from a position of opposition to the war, to one of voting to support it – albeit with some public reluctance and dragging of feet – arguing that they could do nothing else, and that events had overcome them – talking left but walking right.

Socialists, if they had insufficient strength to stage a revolution to prevent war, nevertheless were not compelled to ally themselves with the state or to vote for war credits. If unprepared for overt and active resistance to the state, parties and unions might have chosen some form of inaction or passive resistance. German Social-democracy however chose not inaction, nor waiting for better times to come, but rather to support the war, to suspend strikes, to promote labour discipline and to denounce dissidents to the authorities. By the end of the war many labour officials were viewed as little better than cops. Whilst they had some grassroots support, labour leaders and officials also had particular interests of their own. Organisation had a momentum of its own; it became a way of life. Secure employment for employees of the organisation would be placed in danger were 'their' organisation banned. Rewards were to be had if an organisation, hitherto seen as an enemy of the state, co-operated with it. So who owned labour organisations?

The apparatus resisted going beyond mere words, risking jobs and disturbing a comfortable lifestyle by opposing the state in deeds, even if such deeds were small and symbolic ones. These 'lefts' – parliamentary representatives, full-time officials of parties and unions, newspaper editors and people working in peripheral labour movement enterprises – sided with their government, expressed regrets and invoked a fight against despotism in self-defence of their nation and its civilization. In Germany and France such 'socialists' voted finances to support the war. In France and in Britain they joined the government. As working people were advised by labour movement leaders to fight each other, and as 'socialists' endorsed war, the socialism of the Second Socialist International was lost. Such 'socialists' may have hated war, but not enough to break with their governments. Tears were shed – no doubt it was said that they could not have acted otherwise, or they had no room to manoeuvre – but at base there was a lack of will to act independently for another agenda against their state. They were at heart 'parliamentary socialists'. They hoped for some international arbitrator to appear and sort out their problems. Their priority was to play a parliamentary game, with the influence and power delegated to them. They were not rooted within activist communities promoting struggle.

At root, many official 'lefts' lived conflicted lives, they were perhaps Jacobin tribunes, but often, in speaking for people in struggle they obstructed communities finding their own voice; mediators within social struggles, they had a middle-class position and interests of their own.[46] 'Socialist' strategies that empowered this layer could also disempower grassroots labour rebels. As the war dragged on and in reaction to the course taken by such 'lefts' new unofficial organisations emerged: shop stewards in Britain, Obleute in Germany, factory councils in Italy and factory committees in Russia. To some extent these acted as alternatives to official union structures and in some cases helped to engender new forms of workplace organisation. What was distinctive about these new forms was their responsibility to the grass-roots; often elections involved everyone in a workplace. While trade-union officials went along with no-strike agreements these new structures helped facilitate protest.

The priorities and expectations of Social-democracy impeded the will and determination of those who sought to organise actively to build international solidarity. Insofar as a socialist will was largely absent within much of the leadership of the left, it was not so much a case of betrayal by these leaders, but rather that this absence of will, hitherto obscured by nice words, had now become plain and explicit to a wider world.[47] The anger of many dissidents, both before and after 1914, fed the development of a range of alternatives in the labour movement, breaking with Second International 'socialism'.

Beyond the class divide there were other vectors of oppression; factors of ethnicity and gender drove some to rebel whilst others hoped that, through their support for the war, they would make some progress for themselves. Disappointment – realisation that Empires would not dissolve and grant citizenship to colonised peoples – also fed the anti-imperialist revolt. The split within the famous suffragette Pankhurst family illustrates a conflict similar to the one that divided the labour movement: two members hoped to profit from the war, allied themselves with ruling classes and supported the British Imperial state, and two members rejected it and found allies amongst rebels and down-and-outs. Many organisations promoting women's suffrage sought representation within existing political systems. American, Canadian, German, Russian and some British women were given the vote after the war ended. Experience in the war years – and the loss of jobs thereafter – combined together in an unexpected fashion: on the one hand women were thrown out of work, on the other women's membership of trade-unions increased.[48] Gender equality did not emerge through the war years, but gender relations did change. With so many men having been killed, or incapacitated, the balance between the sexes was greatly changed.

The war that came in 1914 was not a short, sharp conflict such as most socialists might have expected. It was not a brief interlude in which normal politics was suspended for a few weeks or months, but a period of years, in which militarism, nationalism, nationally-planned economics and authoritarianism gained ground and initiated or developed new forms of social organisation. As the war went on, year after year, it became ever clearer that the discourse of defending of civilization was just talk; civilised national self-defence had morphed into barbarism. The influence of commercial interests came to bear: goods were sucked out from the imperial periphery and into home countries, Germany looked to acquire Belgium; Britain stamped on rebellion in Ireland. 'Civilized' imperial powers paid lip service to respecting colonial peoples only so long as it suited imperial interest. Peoples in defeated enemy territory found themselves under new administrations not of their choosing, sometimes divided by arbitrary frontiers from their kith and kin.

The task of understanding what was happening in any war crisis was made more difficult by the absence of discussion forums in which issues could be considered. In times of crisis the lack of independent media was experienced most acutely. In 1914 public radio broadcasting was something for the future. Newspapers formed the key means of spreading news and opinion. In larger countries industrialists could buy up the national press, and use, (or buy) ambitious radicals. Some former socialists and syndicalists – among them Hervé,[49] De Ambris[50] and Mussolini[51] – supported the war and spread nationalist opinions. They had an influence through newspapers they helped edit.

Much of the liberal and left press followed the line of Liberal and Social-democratic party leaderships and supported the war effort. In all countries there were calls for civil peace and for the suspension of strikes. Isolation demoralised dissidents, people were disconnected one from another, bereft of resources, lacking the means to broadcast their views and encourage solidarity; conversely awareness that they were not alone helped encourage protestors and dissidents. Censorship also obstructed discussion of aspects of war deemed improper, notably venereal diseases. When a New Zealand nurse, Ettie Rout, developed prophylactic kits for soldiers and advocated measures to provide condoms and regulated brothels, there was a prohibition against her name appearing in print. Condoms became available but their use was not made known back in New Zealand. British and imperial armies had half a million hospital admissions for venereal diseases.

Another press developed, but not quickly; within it there was a period of debate before a settled anti-war policy was elaborated. It took time to build and rebuild networks and agree what should be done. In many countries dissident editors were imprisoned and the critical press was banned – sometimes intermittently, sometimes permanently. Censorship impeded the dissemination of critical opinion. Lurid stories of massacres and atrocities (barbarous Huns!) were spread by a patriotic press; such stories were unchallenged, unscrutinised, exaggerated, self-serving, and largely – if not wholly – mendacious.

Some lefts fled to avoid conscription. In the USA several anti-war campaigners were murdered and thousands were imprisoned. Anti-war meetings might take place in neutral countries but passports were restricted and denied to critics; geography and governmental action rather than the strength of grassroots organisation determined attendance. The war let loose a fury of rabid, racist propaganda and this had the effect of weakening the left and ultimately in preparing the way for fascism.

In 1916 a member of the British war cabinet, Lord Milner, concerned with the formation of an opposition undermining the war effort, wrote: 'All the disintegrating and reactionary elements in the state such as the pacifists, the SLP,[52] the Syndicalists, the IWW,[53] the No Conscription Fellowship, the Sinn Feiners,[54] the Union of Democratic Control and the militant section of the ILP,[55] flock to serve under the same banner.'[56] Such fears lay behind the employment of agents provocateurs, and lead to the arrest of unwary rebels such as Alice Wheeldon.[57] By 1919 British Prime Minister Lloyd George was afraid that: 'The whole of Europe is filled with the spirit of revolution. There is a deep sense not only of discontent, but of anger and revolt amongst the workers against pre-war conditions.'[58]

Although the government feared the coming together of dissident fragments, and although there were times of co-operation between them, these fragments seldom came together. Various radical fragments each had their reasons for saying 'this is not our war', all looked forward to a society in which authority was shared more equitably in one way or another – between men and women, rich and poor, bosses and operatives, and perhaps amongst all races; few looked to a radical organisation that consolidated a revolt against all these vectors of oppression.[59] J. T. Murphy[60] wrote that although strikes were often led by activists like himself, men who wanted to stop the war, yet: 'Had the question of stopping the war been put to any strikers' meeting it would have been overwhelmingly defeated.' Militant workers campaigned as custodians of labour interests, and, as they protested they created space for anti-war movements.[61]

The revolution in Russia was greeted with enthusiasm – a common enthusiasm spurred by the overthrow of despotism. Elsewhere symptoms of discontent spread in the warring states – protests, riots, local and general strikes, mutinies, desertions and mass surrenders. In Europe empires were dissolved and new states emerged. All over the world the war brought with it fundamental social changes and new state formations. After 1918 the states of Western Europe each had some claim to encompass their own nationality drawing on a common language or culture, but beyond the Rhine and the Po new states took in many more national minorities. The war fashioned a new set of relations between diverse ethnic communities, some welcomed into wider communities, others unwelcome. The conflict in Ireland escalated. There was ongoing fighting between Greece and Turkey. Elsewhere, much of the rest of the world continued to answer to overlords (American, Belgian, British, Dutch, French, Italian, South African or Spanish). In the USA whatever the state branded as dissent was met with repression: unofficial action – including brutal assault, tar and feathering, and lynching unchecked by the law – and official legal action, for example the US Sedition Act of 1918, which set out that the state might criminalise 'thought-crime', i.e. to:

> utter, print, write, or publish any disloyal, profane, scurrilous, or abusive language about the form of government of the United States, or the Constitution of the United States, or the military or naval forces of the United States, or the flag of the United States, or the uniform of the Army or Navy of the United States, or any language intended to bring the form of government of the United States into contempt, scorn, contumely, or disrepute.[62]

Where capitalist order was threatened official and unofficial action, sanctioned by various forms of state, shaded into the fascism that would emerge most virulently in Nazi Germany in 1933. When such threats were less distinct attempts were made to co-opt interest groups; whilst other, usually weaker interests, were ignored. Any hope that the First World War might be a 'war to end war' was soon dissipated. The war had encouraged hopes for 'democracy', 'revolution', 'independence' – and more. Such hopes were seldom fully realised – but that is another story.

Notes

1   *Daily Mail,* 28 August 1914; see Cohn John Lovelace, 'Control and Censorship of the Press during the First World War' (Thesis), Kings College London, 1982.

2   *Daily Mail,* 27 September 2013; Geoffrey Levy, http://www.dailymail. co.uk/news/article-2435751/Red-Eds-pledge-bring-socialism-homage-Marxist-father-Ralph-Miliband-says-GEOFFREY-LEVY. html

3   Wars are still fabricated, for example, the 2002 war against Iraq. Prime Minister Tony Blair sponsored misinformation that there might be only a 45 minute warning before weapons of mass destruction fell on Britain. No such weapons were found.

4   Leonardo Schenin in *La Protesta,* June 1915; From: Wayne Thorpe, 'El Ferrol, Rio de Janeiro, Zimmerwald, and Beyond: Syndicalist Internationalism, 1914-1918', *Revue belge de philologie et d'histoire.* Vol. 84 fasc. 4, 2006, p. 1014. (Histoire médiévale, moderne et contemporaine - Middeleeuwse. moderne en hedendaagse geschiedenis. pp. 1005-1023).

5   This is a quotation drawn from the resolution of the Second International congress at Stuttgart in 1907. Carl Schorske, *German Social Democracy: 1905-1917,* London: John Wiley, 1955, pp. 80ff discusses the political background to this resolution. Paul Frölich wrote that this formulation was created to avoid the possibility of the persecution of the Social-democratic party by the German state. The resolution was drawn up by Bebel, Lenin, Luxemburg and Martov. British and French delegates had sought a commitment to work for a general strike, but this was opposed, 'since it involved a promise which it would be hardly be possible to keep...' and because circumstances could not be foreseen. Paul Frölich, *Rosa Luxemburg: Her Life and Thought,* London: Victor Gollancz, 1940, p. 196. Gustave Hervé, at this point a socialist, argued that the idea of defensive war be rejected; and that everywhere war should be replied to with insurrections and mutinies, and strikes. The rejection of this line gave some comfort to socialists who, in 1914, voted to support the war: they believed that they had no obligation to do more than oppose war in words.

6   A reference to a CGT conference resolution of 1908.

7   Carl Schorske, *German Social Democracy: 1905-1917,* London: John Wiley, 1955, p. 287.

8   *Die Einigkeit* (Unity) was the newspaper of the German Union of Free Trade Unions (FVdG, 'localists'). It was banned on 8 August. It was replaced by *Mitteilungsblatt* and by *Rundschreiben* both of which were also proscribed. Activists were arrested or mobilised into the armed forces – troublemakers were identified by officials of the trade union movement allied with the Social-democrats. Twenty FVdG labour organisers were imprisoned in the first week of the war alone.

9   The Entente refers to Britain, France and Russia – the three major powers allied against Germany and Austria-Hungary.

10   Haase (1863-1919) would later side with rebel Independent Social-Democrats.

11   Luxemburg (1871 – 1919), was a Polish Marxist; she acquired naturalized German citizenship.

12   Mehring (1846 – 1919), was a veteran SPD activist; Bohn (1878 – 1975) an American left journalist.

13   Jaurès (1859 – 1914) was a leader of the French Socialist Party.

14   This Milan paper drew on contributions from Anna Kuliscioff, Argentina Altobelli, Maria Goia and Angelica Balabanoff. Italian women were given the vote in 1946.

15   From a United Irishmen manifesto, 1791.

16   Vladimir Ilyich Lenin (1870 – 1924) communist and leader of the Russian Soviet state after 1917.

17   The minority was led by De Ambris, it kept control of the USI journal *Internazionale*. Armando Borghi was nominated as USI secretary and edited of its new journal *Guerra di classe*. When Italy joined the war, in May 1915, he was arrested and incarcerated. Adriana Dada, *L'anarchismo in Italia fra movimento e partito: Storia e documenti dell'anarchismo italiana*, Milan: Teti Editore, 1984, p. 66.

18   Zetkin (1857–1933) stood on the left of the German Social-democratic party, she was arrested on several occasion in these war years and thereafter became part of the leadership of the Communist Party.

19   Pierre Broué, *The German Revolution, 1917-1923*, London: Merlin, 2006, p. 49.

20   Malatesta (1853–1932) was a veteran anarchist activist, and spent the war years in exile in England; he returned to Italy in 1919. His last years were spent under house arrest after Mussolini's fascists came to power.

21   Rosmer, (1877–1964) was a French syndicalist and later a communist.

22   Pannekoek (1873-1960) was a Dutch astronomer and had taught in

the SPD party school in Berlin. He became a council communist.

23 Berkman, (1870 –1936) was deported from the USA after his release, in 1919, from a spell of imprisonment.

24 Pierre Monatte (1881–1960) was a radical leftist: anarchist, syndicalist, communist, Trotskyist and revolutionary-syndicalist.

25 The weekly circulation of the Irish socialist and republican press was 20,000 copies; a high number for a small population. Kieran Allen, *The Politics of James Connolly*, London, Pluto Press, 1990, p. 142.

26 Luxemburg, Liebknecht and other co-thinkers worked to publish an opposition journal *Die Internationale*. As with a similar group producing *Lichstrahlen*, they were accused by majority Social-democrats of being a 'small group of persons [who] are busily attempting to destroy the unity of the German labour movement.' … 'Internal differences must be so managed that the unity of the [Social-democratic] movement will survive the war. Anyone who breaks this rule deals worse by the German working class than the worst enemy.' Rejecting this, they wrote that they were merely trying to preserve the principles that had been abandoned on 4 August 1914; which the party had previously promoted for some fifty year.

27 Apply legal sanctions to the area.

28 Two shillings and sixpence equals 12 ½ pence.

29 William Gallacher became a leader of the Communist Party and was elected as a member of parliament.

30 The French and German governments had few fears of such a threat in 1914. They were informed on the likely direction that events would take. The French government had lists of anti-war activists to arrest, but chose not to act. Likewise, the German chancellor Bethmann Hollweg held discussions with a member of the Social-democratic party, Südeküm and these reassured him that the SPD could be largely drawn in to support the war, and collaborate with the state. Conversely, in 1919, governments' will to intervene in Russia was constrained somewhat by the knowledge that much of their armed forces were opposed to intervention.

31 This is a quotation from 'Manifesto of the Sixteen' – http://libertarian-labyrinth.blogspot.co.uk/2011/05/manifesto-of-sixteen-1916.html

32 Victor Considérant, (1808-1893), an early French democratic socialist.

33 Hélène Brion (1882-1962) was a feminist teacher and CGT activist; she was arrested in November 1917, and in her ensuing trial declared: I am an enemy of war because I am a feminist. War is the

triumph of brute force, feminism can triumph only by moral force and by intellectual substance.' She was given a three year suspended sentence and lost her job as a teacher. French women were given the right to vote in 1945.

34   Goodwin had been given a medical status exempting him from conscription, but was called up, most likely as a reprisal for his opposition to the war. He went on the run and was shot dead in the following year whilst 'resisting arrest'.

35   Morgan Philips-Price, *Dispatches From the Revolution: Russia 1916-18*, London: Pluto Press, 1997, pp. 48ff

36   St Petersburg had been renamed Petrograd.

37   Georg Michaelis was Chancellor of Germany in 1917.

38   War aims: chiefly free trade, a League of Nations and, in Europe, national self-determination.

39   Alexander Kerensky was prime minister in the Russian provisional government that was overthrown by the November revolution.

40   Debs was imprisoned for ten years. In 1920 he ran for the presidency from prison and received over 900,000 votes. He was released in 1921.

41   The Workers' Suffrage Federation, (later Workers' Socialist Federation), was the successor to Sylvia Pankhurst's East London Federation of Suffragettes.

42   Sheila Rowbotham has written that ideas of gender equality, previously seen as utopia, became more credible after 1914. Sheila Rowbotham: *Dreamers of a New Day*, London: Verso, 2010, p. 187. In France parts of the labour movement opposed the employment of women workers in new areas such as in the postal and transport industries.

43   Chicherin, (1872-1936) was in charge of the foreign affairs in the new Soviet state from 1918 to 1930; a homosexual, his place at the heart of the new state testified to new possibilities, and the overthrow of the Tsarist legal code.

44   Ralph Miliband, 'Socialism and the Myth of the Golden Past', in Ralph Miliband & John Saville, Eds, *Socialist Register: 1964*, London: Merlin Press, 1964, pp. 94-6.

45   An epithet applied to protest as described by Adelheid von Saldern in 'Latent Reformism and Socialist Utopia: The SPD in Goettingen, 1890 to 1920' in David E. Barclay, & Eric. D. Weitz, *Between Reform and Revolution: German Socialism and Communism from 1840 to 1990*, Oxford: Berghahn, 2005, p. 205.

46   See editorial in *International Socialist Review*, November 1915, Vol.
      XVI, No. 15; p. 305.

47   The policy of most social democrats was not a surprise to radical
      libertarians, syndicalists and Marxists; these networks had
      anticipated that most Social-democrats would fall for compromised
      chauvinistic politics.

48   Barbara Drake, *Women in Trade Unions*, London: Virago 1984, pp.
      107-8 notes both a decline of three-quarters of a million women
      workers by the autumn of 1919, as compared to November 1918;
      and an increase of women's union membership later in 1919.

49   Earlier a leading anti-war campaigner in the French CGT.

50   A leader of the Italian Syndicalist Union, he was expelled for his pro-
      intervention line.

51   A socialist hitherto, the future fascist Duce.

52   The Socialist Labour Party was established in 1903, splitting from the
      Social Democratic Federation. It drew inspiration from Daniel De
      Leon. SLP members were resolutely opposed to the war. (Raymond
      Challinor, *The Origins of British Bolshevism*, London: Croom Helm,
      1977.)

53   Industrial Workers of the World.

54   The radical Irish nationalists, who, with parts of the labour
      movement, led by James Connolly, had revolted and called for Irish
      independence in Easter 1916.

55   Independent Labour Party.

56   Quoted in Sheila Rowbotham, 'Alice Wheeldon Revisited' in Mary
      Davis, Ed, *Class and Gender in British Labour History, Renewing the
      Debate (or starting it?)*, Pontypool: Merlin Press, 2011, pp. 195-6.

57   Sheila Rowbotham, *Friends of Alice Wheeldon*, London: Pluto Press,
      1986. See also http://www.derbytelegraph.co.uk/sham-trial-PM-
      murder-plot-left-family-languishing/story-19929859-detail/story.
      html#axzz2hdm7PGl2

58   Quoted in: Konni Zilliacus, *I Choose Peace*, Harmondsworth:
      Penguin, 1949, p. 24.

59   The Socialist Labour Party was working on developing its socialist
      internationalism when it argued: 'that no worker should be debarred
      from working at any job. It does not matter what the colour, sex or
      skill of the worker may be. Real industrial organisation must aim at
      protecting the international working class against the capitalist class.'
      10 July 1919, *The Socialist*, Glasgow. I am indebted to Jacqueline
      Jenkinson, 'The 1919 Race Riots in Britain: Their Background and

Consequences', PhD thesis, 1987 the University of Edinburgh for
this quotation.

60   A radical Sheffield shop stewards' leader, later a member of the
     British Communist Party. (1888-1965).

61   J. T. Murphy, *New Horizons*, London: The Bodley Head, 1941, p. 44;
     see also from the same author: *Preparing for Power*, London: Pluto
     Press, 1972, p. 120 and 132: 'much anti-war was fearlessly conducted
     at the meetings …'

62   The British Defence of the Realm Act had a similar potential, and
     criminalised dissent: 'No person shall by word of mouth or in writing
     spread reports likely to cause disaffection or alarm among any of His
     Majesty's forces or among the civilian population …' (1914).

D'yer remember all that talk about 'eroes an a 'oly war mate?

INDEX

(of persons, journals and organisations)

Also available from The Merlin Press

Jürgen Zimmerer & Joachim Zeller Eds.
GENOCIDE IN GERMAN SOUTH-WEST AFRICA:
The Colonial War of 1904-1908 and its aftermath
337 pages, Illustrated with contemporary black & white photos.
978 0 85036 573 3 Hbk £50.00; 978 0 85036 574 0 Pbk £18.95

John Newsinger
REBEL CITY:
Larkin, Connolly and the Dublin Labour Movement
A study of the great labour revolt in Ireland and of the
development of Irish trade unionism and syndicalism. 192 pages
978 0 85036 518 4 Pbk £14.95

Julia Bush
BEHIND THE LINES: *East London Labour 1914-19*
How Labour won influence in London's East End in the midst
of WW1, 'a very fine piece of work, thoroughly researched and
written in a clear and compelling style … it displays an unusual
mix of deep sympathy and critical judgement … Bush has
produced an excellent study on an important topic.' *Journal of
Canadian Labour Studies.* 254 pages
978 0 85036 306 7 Pbk £12.95

Mary Davis, Ed.
CLASS AND GENDER IN BRITISH LABOUR HISTORY:
Renewing the Debate (or starting it?)
231 pages, 978 0 85036 668 6 Pbk £16.95

Charlie Mcguire
SEAN MCLOUGHLIN: *Ireland's Forgotten Revolutionary*
Sean McLoughlin was only 21 when he became Commandant-
General of the army of the Irish Republic in the 1916 Easter
Rebellion. 186 pages, 9780850367058 Pbk £15.95

Joyce L. Kornbluh, Editor
REBEL VOICES: *An IWW Anthology*
With an introduction by Fred Thompson
The biggest and best source on IWW history, fiction, songs, art
and lore. Third Edition. 467 pages, about 50 illustrations
978 0 85036 651 8 Pbk £22.50

Cathy Porter
ALEXANDRA KOLLONTAI
Revised Edition
Alexandra Kollontai is one of the most famous women in Russian
history. She was the only woman in Lenin's government in 1917.
530 pages, 978 0 85036 640 2 Pbk £20.00

Janine Booth
GUILTY AND PROUD OF IT: *Poplar's Rebel Councillors and*
Guardians 1919-25
In the aftermath of the First World War, thirty Labour
councillors went to prison rather than accepting to inequitable
taxes. 213 pages, 978 0 85036 694 5 Pbk £12.95

www.merlinpress.co.uk